Ethical Economy. Studies in Economic Ethics and Philosophy

Volume 56

Ethical Economy describes the theory of the ethical preconditions of the economy and of business as well as the theory of the ethical foundations of economic systems. It analyzes the impact of rules, virtues, and goods or values on economic action and management. *Ethical Economy* understands ethics as a means to increase trust and to reduce transaction costs. It forms a foundational theory for business ethics and business culture.

The Series *Ethical Economy. Studies in Economic Ethics and Philosophy* is devoted to the investigation of interdisciplinary issues concerning economics, management, ethics, and philosophy. These issues fall in the categories of economic ethics, business ethics, management theory, economic culture, and economic philosophy, the latter including the epistemology and ontology of economics. Economic culture comprises cultural and hermeneutic studies of the economy.

One goal of the series is to extend the discussion of the philosophical, ethical, and cultural foundations of economics and economic systems. The series is intended to serve as an international forum for scholarly publications, such as monographs, conference proceedings, and collections of essays. Primary emphasis is placed on originality, clarity, and interdisciplinary synthesis of elements from economics, management theory, ethics, and philosophy.

More information about this series at http://www.springer.com/series/2881

Christoph Lütge • Christoph Strosetzki
Editors

The Honorable Merchant – Between Modesty and Risk-Taking

Intercultural and Literary Aspects

Springer

Editors
Christoph Lütge
Chair of Business Ethics
Technical University of Munich
München, Bayern, Germany

Christoph Strosetzki
Romanisches Seminar
Universität Münster
Münster, Germany

ISSN 2211-2707 ISSN 2211-2723 (electronic)
Ethical Economy
ISBN 978-3-030-04350-6 ISBN 978-3-030-04351-3 (eBook)
https://doi.org/10.1007/978-3-030-04351-3

Library of Congress Control Number: 2018966706

This Springer imprint is published by the registered company Springer Nature Switzerland AG
The registered company address is: Gewerbestrasse 11, 6330 Cham, Switzerland

Introduction

Merchants have had to contend with reputational problems throughout history. From antiquity to the present, they have repeatedly been confronted with moral reservations and disdain. At the same time, it seemed advisable again and again to develop alternative concepts that equated the merchant ideal with certain values, norms, and standards. Such conceptualization existed within a particular area of tension: On the one hand, the merchant was to take risks; on the other, he had demonstrated moral values such as modesty. The discussion about the honorable merchant and related models persists to this today. For instance, attempts have been made (especially in the USA) to develop and implement an oath for business school graduates.

There is already a wealth of literature on the honorable merchant and the merchant's standing in history and literature. For the most part, however, it has been limited to Europe. This volume extends this focus by systematically examining for the first time the social position, ideals, and values of the merchant in non-European and especially Asian countries.

The contributions are also distinguished by their distinct interdisciplinary character. The represented disciplines range from philosophy, literature, history, law, and political science.

The volume is divided into four parts. The first part deals with the general set of problems surrounding the merchant on the basis of a series of epoch-spanning questions. Christoph Strosetzki opens this volume by tracing the changes in the merchant's image from antiquity to the seventeenth century. Christoph Lütge then examines the role that the honorable merchant can still play in the globalized economy, concluding that structural elements such as corporate social responsibility are more important than individual virtues. Adela Cortina focuses on the "legend of excellent businessman" and argues that successful companies not only need to be able to maximize their profits but also tell good stories. Jacob Rendtorff addresses the role and perception of the honorable merchant in the theoretical and cultural context of Scandinavia. Finally, László Fekete discusses voluntary business regulation to build public trust in managers.

The second part examines the various images of the merchant in late medieval to early modern Europe. Laurenz Volkmann embarks on a journey through the world of British thought on the merchant from the Middle Ages through Elizabethan drama to Adam Smith and Bernard Mandeville.

The third part continues along this historical path up through the nineteenth century with particular emphasis on Spain. To begin with, Manfred Tietz traces the transformations of the merchant's image from "deceiver and con man" to honorable merchant in Spanish literature from the sixteenth to eighteenth centuries. Beatrice Schuchardt next examines the relationship between honor and economy in the Spanish theater of the eighteenth century, while Jan-Henrik Witthaus analyzes economic interdependencies and ethical aspects such as the common good and the merchant's honor in Spain. Christian von Tschilschke, finally, focuses on nineteenth-century Russia, devoting himself to the economic critique in Nikolai Gogol's novel *Dead Souls*.

The last part leaves the European context. Dominique de Courcelles discusses the ethics of the merchant in the Islamic world from the fourteenth century to today's Islamic financial economy. And Itaru Shimazu demonstrates that the ethics of the honorable merchant also developed in Japan with his contribution on the Confucian ethics of the influential Japanese merchant Shibusawa Eiichi.

The contributions in this volume originated from a conference of the same name at the Akademie für Politische Bildung Tutzing.

München, Bayern, Germany — Christoph Lütge
Münster, Germany — Christoph Strosetzki

Contents

Contributors

Adela Cortina University of Valencia, Valencia, Spain

Dominique de Courcelles Centre Jean Pépin -Théorie et Histoire de l'Esthétique, de la Technique et des Arts, Paris Sciences Lettres Université de la Recherche-Ecole normale supérieure Paris/CNRS, Paris, France

László Fekete Business Ethics Center, Corvinus University of Budapest, Budapest, Hungary

Christoph Lütge Technical University of Munich, Munich, Germany

Jacob Dahl Rendtorff Department of Social Sciences and Business, University of Roskilde, Roskilde, Denmark

Beatrice Schuchardt University of Siegen, Siegen, Germany

Itaru Shimazu Dokkyo University, Soka, Japan

Christoph Strosetzki University of Münster, Münster, Germany

Manfred Tietz University of Bochum, Bochum, Germany

Christian von Tschilschke University of Siegen, Siegen, Germany

Laurenz Volkmann University of Jena, Jena, Germany

Jan-Henrik Witthaus University of Kassel, Kassel, Germany

Part I
The Image of the Merchant Contemplated Across Times

Chapter 1
The Merchant from Patristics to the Honnête Homme in the Writings of Savary

Christoph Strosetzki

Abstract The first purpose is the attempt to expose the origins of the negative image of the merchant. Secondly, it searches for possible reasons for the change into a positive image, before, finally, two texts from the French seventeenth century are presented, which exemplify the good reputation of the merchant and his profession. Savary underlines the usefulness of trade, pointing out the necessity of redistributing unevenly distributed goods and approving of trade, capable of increasing joy of life and avoiding abundance that could lead to harmful idleness. Further, trade promotes friendship and provides the king with information about foreign countries. The parfait négociant described by Savary appears to be not primarily morally perfect, but perfectly efficient. That the merchant can behave morally as well as immorally has been undisputed since Aristotle, Thomas Aquinas and Neo-Scholasticism.

1.1 The Negative Image of the Merchant

The first purpose of the following article is the attempt to expose the origins of the negative image of the merchant. Secondly, it searches for possible reasons for the change into a positive image, before, finally, two texts from the French seventeenth century are presented, which exemplify the good reputation of the merchant and his profession. The acclaim of the merchant is always based on the tradition of his being criticised, which is therefore taken as the starting point.

The Church Fathers, the patrists, were the ones to form the negative image of the merchant in the first centuries after Christ until the eighth century. As moral philosophers with theological thinking, they had constructed a fixed, but unrealistic line of argumentation.

While the materialistic doctrine focuses on material things and investigates their necessity, distribution and increase, the Gospel demands, according to the patrists,

C. Strosetzki (✉)
University of Münster, Münster, Germany
e-mail: stroset@uni-muenster.de

C. Lütge, C. Strosetzki (eds.), *The Honorable Merchant – Between Modesty and Risk-Taking*, Ethical Economy 56, https://doi.org/10.1007/978-3-030-04351-3_1

escape from the world, the renunciation of the material, the repression of the sensory and the spirit's concentration on its own self. As St. Ambrose of Milan states:

> We state nothing to be useful but what will help us to the blessing of eternal life; certainly not that which will help us enjoy merely the present time. Nor do we recognize any advantages in opportunities and in the wealth of earthly goods, but consider them as disadvantages if not put aside, and to be looked on as a burden, when we have them, rather than as a loss when expended.[1]

Wealth, enjoyment and happiness are from this perspective harmful to salvation.[2] In the view of St. Ambrose, one should not focus on transient vanity.[3] And in the opinion of St. Clement of Alexandria the best wealth lies in the poverty of wishes and real pride lies in the depreciation of wealth, because wisdom cannot be bought in the market place, but will be sold in heaven "for true coin, the immortal Word, the regal gold."[4] One should not adorn the outward appearance of a person, but rather the soul, with honesty. The flesh should be provided with temperance and abundance.[5] According to St. Ambrose, it is not the external or corporal goods that lead to eternal life, but only virtue.[6]

To this can be added the interpretation of the first of the Ten Commandments "Thou shalt have no other Gods before me", which considers it impossible to serve two masters. One cannot serve God and Mammon at the same time, because while one is served, the other is hated.[7] One should not burden oneself with the acquisition of material things or emulate the lilies in the field, which simply grow there. The warning of the dangers of wealth can be found in various passages of the New Testament.[8] Particularly well known is the story of the rich young man, who asks, what good deeds he could still do, in order to get eternal life, as he already follows the Ten Commandments. Jesus commands him: "If you want to be perfect, go, sell your possessions and give to the poor, and you will have treasure in heaven. Then come, follow me."[9] It therefore follows that it is easier for a camel to pass through the eye of a needle, than it is for a rich man to enter into the kingdom of God. This is why the patrists hold the believe that possessions are not a natural right, but have become a necessary evil as a result of the fall of man.

If one possesses more than he really needs, he should give the abundance to the poor, says St. Augustine. He recommends being satisfied with nothing more than

---

[1] St. Ambrose (1890), Book I, Chapter IX, 28, p. 48; cp. Brentano (1923), p. 81, pp. 34–76 and pp. 77–143.

[2] "But those things which seem to be good, as riches, abundance, joy without pain, are a hindrance to the fruits of blessedness" St. Ambrose (1890), Book II, Chapter V, 16, p. 150.

[3] St. Ambrose (1890), Book I, Chapter XLIX, 251, p. 136.

[4] St. Clement (1885), Paedagogos (The instructor), Second Book, Chapter III, p. 248.

[5] St. Clement (1885), Paedagogos (The instructor), Third Book, Chapter II, p. 272.

[6] St. Ambrose (1890), Book II, Chapter V, 18, p. 150.

[7] Matthew 6: 24–34.

[8] Cp. Matthew 6: 19, 20, 24–34; Luke 12: 33, 34, 22–30; Mark 4: 19; Matthew 19: 21; Luke 18: 22; Luke 6: 20, 21, 24, 25.

[9] Matthew 19: 21.

food and clothing. Anything which goes beyond this, leads one to temptation, harmful wishes and avarice. Furthermore, it leads a person away from faith and causes much pain.[10] According to St. Ambrose of Milan, the accumulation of riches is as fragile as a spider web.[11] He explains this on the example of the merchant:

> Is it not vain for a merchant to journey by night and by day, that he may be able to heap up treasures? Is it not vain for him to gather merchandise, and to be much perturbed about its price, for fear he might sell it for less than he gave? that he should strive everywhere for high prices, and thus unexpectedly call up robbers against himself through their envy at his much-vaunted business; or that, without waiting for calmer winds, impatient of delays, he should meet with shipwreck whilst seeking for gain?[12]

Trade is, where aspiration for the greatest profit possible, i.e. wealth, takes place. This aspiration is already referred to as *cupiditas* in the Bible. According to the Apostle Paul, avarice is the root of all evil

> For we have brought nothing into this world and so we cannot take a single thing out either. But if we have food and shelter, we will be satisfied with that. Those who long to be rich, however, stumble into temptation and a trap and many senseless and harmful desires that plunge people into ruin and destruction. For the love of money is the root of all evils.[13]

Basil refers back to Isaiah, warning:

> Woe unto them that join house to house, that lay field to field, [...] but the covetous man has no respect for time, acknowledges no boundaries, yields not to order and succession, but mimics the force of fire: he catches hold of everything, he feeds on everything.[14]

Consequently, avarice causes immorality. According to St. Ambrose, avarice leads to chasing after personal benefit, instead of bringing about what could be beneficial to others and it even leads to wishing ill on others, for instance in order to sell one's own corn supply for a high price in case of famine.[15]

> For as long as we want to add to our possessions and to heap up money, to take into our possession fresh lands, and to be the richest of all, we have cast aside the form of justice and have lost the blessing of kindness towards all.[16]

Elsewhere, St. Ambrose points out that Joshua was capable of making the sun stand still, but not of eradicating profit-seeking.[17] Basil compares the avaricious with the visitor to a playhouse who, after having taken his seat, urges away everyone who comes after him, believing that it is all his own, when actually it is free for anyone to

---

[10] St. Augustine (1950), Book I, Chapter XX, p. 13.

[11] St. Ambrose (1890), Book I, Chapter XLIX, 254, p. 137.

[12] St. Ambrose (1890), Book I, Chapter XLIX, 252, pp. 136-137.

[13] 1 Timothy 6: 7–10.

[14] St. Basil the Great (Homilia in divites, Sermon to the Rich). In: J.-P. Migne *Patrologia Graeca* 31: 293; cp. Brentano (1923), p. 84.

[15] St. Ambrose (1890), Book III, Chapter VI, 39, p. 218.

[16] St. Ambrose (1890), Book I, Chapter XXVIII, 137, pp. 93–94.

[17] St. Ambrose (1890), Book II, Chapter XXVI, 130, p. 193.

use.[18] Cyprian proposes the contrary counter model, when he praises the owner who shares his income and fruits with the brotherhood, according to the model of equality. Whoever voluntarily donates in this way and does justice 'imitates God the Father'.[19]

The renunciation of the material and the concentration on the hereafter consequently lead to the refusal of wealth in the patristics. This makes the profession of the merchant appear senseless, especially as it is generally related to avarice and self-interest, and neglects the common good as well as discouraging generous donation.

1.2 The Change in the Evaluation of the Merchant

How did the change in the evaluation of the merchant and his profession in the long period between the patristics and the seventeenth century come about?

One possible explanation for this could be that the economy has become more differentiated during this time. Therefore, Lujo Brentano puts the scepticism against the merchant down to the fact that trade is in direct contrast to the natural economy, which characterised tribes of a lower cultural level. The merchant travelling from outside clashes with a closed economic community to which he does not belong.

In order to keep him in check as a potential enemy, markets were protected in the interest of peaceful exchange of goods. Deceiving and tricking the merchant was not reprehensible. He was allowed to charge interest, whereas the tribespeople were not.[20] When the Church forbade Christians from charging usury in the year 1179, the Jews took over monetary trade, because they were not affected by the prohibition, being foreigners of a different faith.[21]

The fact that the merchant found a fixed place in the differentiated society of early modern times has certainly contributed to his positive image.

In addition, religious factors might have played a role, such as the emergence of Protestantism and Calvinism, whose high importance in this context was stressed by Max Weber and Charles Taylor, as is commonly known.[22] Furthermore, the differentiation between morality and efficiency, as Machiavelli had proposed concerning politics in the Italian Renaissance, led to trade and ethics being considered as two systems which also needed to be separated.

For example, the *Ricordi* of Giovanni de Pagolo Morelli (1371–1444), who worked his way up as a mid-sized merchant in Florence, have Machiavellian characteristics. For him, morality is efficiency. What is good and what is useful is as one; virtue is an advantage and evil is a loss.[23]

---

[18] Cp. Brentano (1923), p. 91.

[19] Quote from ibid.

[20] Cp. Brentano (1923), p. 214–217.

[21] Cp. Gurjewitsch (2004), p. 274 f.

[22] Cp. Taylor (2012); cp. Weber (2010).

[23] Cp. Gurjewitsch, (2004), p. 297.

If one wishes to explain the change in the evaluation of the merchant, one could also consider philosophical schools of thought, such as Stoicism. It had recommended living according to the laws of nature, and considered it reasonable to aspire to riches insofar as wealth facilitates a virtuous life in contrast to poverty. All these factors have certainly made their own contribution to all this.

In what follows, however, the focus should be on a different influential school of thought. The intention is to show the role of Aristotelianism replacing patristic Platonism in the context of Scholasticism. The question is, therefore, as to how far Platonism and Aristotelianism give rise to the attitudes towards the merchant and his profession.

1.2.1 Plato and the Patristics

In view of the obvious agreement of the Bible and Plato, the idea arose that Plato might have heard or read Jeremiah while he was in Egypt. St. Augustine was of the same mind at first,[24] but then found that Plato had lived at a later time and had got acquainted with the biblical contents through interpreters.[25] The depreciation of the sensible world and of the physical, as well as their belief in the priority of the soul, link Plato and Christ, according to St. Augustine. One should despise avarice and material things in order to make the soul sound and the mind's eye strong. St. Augustine quotes from the Bible:

> Lay not up for yourselves treasures upon earth, where moths and rust destroy, and where thieves break through and steal. But lay up for yourselves treasures in heaven, where neither moths nor rust destroy, and where thieves do not break through nor steal. For where your treasure is, there your heart will be also.[26]

This and the following quote illustrate the Platonic disdain of the material reality in contrast to the spiritual. "Love not the world nor the things which are in the world. For everything that is in the world is the lust of the flesh, the lust of the eyes and the ambition of this world".[27]

The physical is transient and therefore less valuable than reason, which is the highest good and which is spoiled when occupying itself with inferior matters. St. Augustine advises searching for tranquillity in order to defeat inhibition in the corporal, freeing oneself from the love for changeable things and finding the one and simple, which is the highest idea according to Plato, and God according to St. Augustine. Plato's followers only had to modify a few ideas to become Christians,

---

[24] St. Augustine (2007b), Book II, Chapter 28, 43, p. 549.

[25] Geyer (1951), p. 103.

[26] Matthew 6: 19-21; St. Augustine (1959), p. 6.

[27] 1 John 2: 15-16; St. Augustine (1959), p. 7.

St. Augustine claims.[28] He finds Platonic foundations in the words of St. Paul.[29] The Platonist who influenced him most was Plotinus.[30] Clement of Alexandria expressly refers to Plato, when advising against aspiring to abundance of silver and gold.[31] The image he has built of Plato is also the fruit of many years of work done by several generations who interpreted his philosophy.[32] In this context, the fusion of the Platonic idea of the Good with the One, which is the universal cause of everything, i.e. the Christian concept of God, is particularly important.[33]

1.2.2 Thomas Aquinas and Aristotle

To what extent is the turn to Aristotelianism important to understand the change in the image of the merchant? According to Plato, there were two worlds, the one of Forms and the one of reality, the first one being more important, because the latter depended on it.

As has been shown, the Platonic idea of the two worlds was transferred to the Christian differentiation between this life and the hereafter. For this, the Christian concept of God claims the Platonic highest idea for itself, from which all the other ideas depend, and the world of Forms has priority over material reality. Aristotle then takes a closer look at the Platonic theory of Forms and shows its contradictions. In his view, there cannot exist ideas of works of art, of something non-material or attributive. Moreover, ideas cannot be the causes of being or becoming, motion or change.[34] Since Aristotle understands the general as being inherently inside individual objects (*universalia in re*), the world of ideas disappears. What remains is the reality and its objects, which are characterised by the four causes, namely the end, agent, material and form, as well as by change and motion. Because also Thomas Aquinas, and with him the Scholasticism and the Late Spanish Scholasticism of the Siglo de Oro, are influenced by the Aristotelian concept of reality, the stress on the hereafter diminishes in favour of this life. Therefore, Thomas Aquinas refutes Plato's belief that "man is not a being composed of body and soul, but [...] the soul itself using the body is man".[35] Following Aristotle, Thomas Aquinas holds that perceiving is not the body being moved by the soul, but being moved by external manifest objects. The soul, however, is in the body, according to Thomas Aquinas. "It is, therefore, in the whole body, and not merely in one part, according to its

[28] Cp. St. Augustine (1959), pp. 2–107.

[29] Cp. St. Augustine (2007a), pp. 107–114.

[30] Cp. Drecoll (2012), p. 192.

[31] St. Clement (1885), Second Book, Chapter III, p. 247.

[32] Cp. Wyrwa (1983), p. 317, p. 320.

[33] Cp. Beierwaltes (2014), p. 91.

[34] Aristotle (1962), Book XIII, 1097b – 1080b, pp. 205–211.

[35] Thomas Aquinas (1955), Book II, Chapter 57 [4], p. 169.

essence whereby it is the body's form."[36] Turning away from the dualistic model is linked with reevaluating this life, which becomes manifest in the use of the Biblical quotes. In contrast to the patristics, the objects of earthly life are focused on. The creatures bear witness to the Creator and, as Thomas Aquinas remarks "[f]or this reason Scripture threatens punishment to those who err about creatures, as to unbelievers, in the words of the Psalm 27:5: 'Because they have not understood the works of the Lord and the operations of His hands, Thou shalt destroy them, and shalt not build them up'".[37]

Elsewhere, he refers to the Creator as the highest Good and cause of being, with reference to John 1:3: "All things were made by Him, and without Him was made nothing".[38] The dignity of creation can therefore be derived from the Creator, as Thomas Aquinas claims referring to Genesis 1:31: "God saw all the things that He had made, and they were very good".[39] Further, with regard to the first cause and the distinction of things, Thomas Aquinas argues: "Now, God is the most perfect agent. It was His prerogative, therefore, to induce His likeness into created things most perfectly, to a degree consonant with the nature of created being."[40] The Creator did not have the intention of giving "such perfection as it is possible"[41] to his creation.

While Plato and the patristics despised the sensible world and the material, gave priority to the soul and the spiritual and aspired to the liberation from changeable things, Aristotle and Thomas Aquinas reject the division of the world into a world of Forms and the material world. They take the perceptible as a starting point, consider the soul and spirit as a form of the body and admire material objects which exist in reality as being perfect works of the Lord.

1.2.3 The Merchant and Trade in the Works of Aristotle

This change in the general attitude also has consequences for the evaluation of the merchant and his occupation which, against this backdrop, appear in a more positive light. The merchant's profession becomes useful and virtuous when practised appropriately. Aristotle differentiates between the acquisition of property and its upkeep, i.e. household management. This difference is comparable to the one between the art of making shuttles and the art of weaving. A rich supply of goods is necessary for the community of a city or household, so the activity required for this purpose is natural. In contrast, there is another art of acquisition which is not natural, because it supposes there is no limit to riches and property. If, for instance, shoes are not used as items of clothing, but as articles of exchange, this is only natural as long as useful things are

[36] Thomas Aquinas (1955), Book II, Chapter 72 [2], p. 213; cp. also Chapter 57 [5], p. 169.

[37] Thomas Aquinas (1955), Book II, Chapter 3 [7], p. 34.

[38] Thomas Aquinas (1955), Book II, Chapter 15 [9], p. 49.

[39] Thomas Aquinas (1955), Book II, Chapter 39 [8], p. 117.

[40] Thomas Aquinas (1955), Book II, Chapter 45 [2], p. 136.

[41] Thomas Aquinas (1955), Book II, Chapter 45 [9], p. 139.

exchanged for other useful ones, for example for wine or cereal. On the contrary, economising military or medical art should be viewed critically, for their real purpose of bringing victory or restoring health becomes a means of accruing wealth.

The main purpose of the profit-seeking art of accruing wealth, supported by the invention of money and by the knowledge as to where to achieve the highest profit possible by handling, is gathering riches and accumulating money. "And these riches, that are derived from this art of wealth-getting, are truly unlimited".[42] This is the reason why everyone who has a profitable profession intends to increase their money without limit. Aristotle criticizes the absence of limits here, as well as the excess of enjoyment. On balance, the art of acquisition is only to be rejected when aspiring to unlimited profit.

What are the virtues of a merchant?

Virtue is defined as a habit by Aristotle. In his view, one should avoid, as in the case of artists in well-executed works, both excess and deficiency, and seek the middle way, because the bad belongs to the unlimited and the good to the limited.[43] Applied to money matters, this means:

> In regard to giving and getting money, the observance of the mean is Liberality; the excess and deficiency are Prodigality and Meanness, 2 but the prodigal man and the mean man exceed and fall short in opposite ways to one another: the prodigal exceeds in giving and is deficient in getting, whereas the mean man exceeds in getting and is deficient in giving.[44]

With growing satisfaction of wishes and increase in enjoyment, reason is turned off and moderation made impossible.[45] For that reason, a wasteful person appears to be flawed with numerous vices, due to his lack of abstinence. Generosity, on the other hand, is the right virtue in the management of riches. Consequently, the one who gives will be shown more gratitude and praise than the one who takes.[46] The wrong use of giving and taking leads to greed, which is characterised by too little giving and too much taking.

The medieval Aristotelian Thomas Aquinas holds that for rational beings private property is an addition to natural law, because it serves the common good, individual interests and the common interest.[47]

With reference to the just price, Thomas Aquinas takes, as the patristics did before him, the procurement costs as a starting point, but adds that it further depends on the cost of living befitting one's social standing. The estate-based medieval society thus understood that they had to assume a higher or lower cost of living according to their estate, and that the amount of gain varied according to the maintenance of the house. The situation was more complicated when a traveling merchant, being

---

[42] Aristotle (1944), 1257b, p. 45.

[43] Aristotle (1934), 1107a, pp. 97–98.

[44] Aristotle (1934), 1107b, p. 99.

[45] Aristotle (1934), 1119b, p. 185.

[46] Aristotle (1934), 1120a, p. 191.

[47] Cf. Thomas Aquinas (2006), q. 66, a. 2–3, pp. 65–70.

a foreigner, could not be positioned in the local estate hierarchy. How could one decide about an appropriate cost of living, proceeds and price then?

Whether or not a just price was to be fixed by the State or free market forces, was already discussed in the Middle Ages, for as early as the twelfth century there was long-distance trade, which reached from Scotland to Southeast Asia, from Portugal to Central Russia and from Scandinavia to sub-Saharan Africa.[48] According to Thomas Aquinas, the just price was the result of the interplay between supply and demand without manipulations by the State or monopolies,[49] and hence subject to fluctuations, because prices change depending on time and place. Nominalists, such as Johannes Gerson or Gabriel Biel adopted a contrary position, pleading for a fixed price by the authorities. This, of course, has to take into account the general need, the total quantity and shortage of goods.[50]

In the writings of Aristotle, the profession of the merchant was considered useful, in the light of a positive reevaluation of this life; acquisition and management of property are natural, provided that they show moderation and restrictions. In that case, they accord with the virtue of generosity, which distinguishes the merchant. If the just price of goods is not only determined by supply and demand, but also serves to finance the merchant's cost of living according to his status, more or fewer riches are justified, depending on the social standing. This position, based on Aristotle, is taken up, as is known, not only by the medieval Scholasticism, but also in the Late Spanish Scholasticism in the Siglo de Oro by the School of Salamanca, which kept it alive.[51] In the following, two texts will be presented which impressively bear witness to the merchant's prestige in seventeenth century France.

1.3 The Appraisal of the Merchant: Nanteser und Savary

The first text was published in the middle of the century, when the French mercantilism had not yet been fully developed and France had still to catch up.

The anonymous author, who calls himself simply "un habitant de la ville de Nantes", publishes his book in 1646, entitled "Le commerce honorable ou considerations politiques" "pour les utilités de la France, et qui regarde en particulier les avantages du Pais".[52] He works "à l'établissement de quelque bien commun" and his book, "qui regarde le bien general de la France, & de la Bretagne en particulier"[53] cannot be countered, he affirms, by enemies other than enemies of the State. Accordingly, he considers the welfare of the State as being dependent on trade. He attributes the bad situation of France to the fact that trade is in the hands of foreigners,

---

48 Cp. Goez (1982), p. 22.

49 Cp. ibid., p. 24.

50 Cp. ibid., p. 27.

51 Cp. Strosetzki (2015, 2016).

52 Anonymus (1646), *Epitre*.

53 Ibid., *Au lecteur*.

who had drawn the French into slavery and seized the cities. To him they are like sheep, who obediently allow their opponents to shear their fur without any resistance. Firstly, he wants to expose this unfortunate situation and its causes, in order to encourage secondly the French to improve it by establishing trade with the help of commercial partnership and stock exchange. In his view, the heroic deeds of Hercules or the Argonauts are comparable to a "noble et glorieux commerce [...] nous avons aussi besoin d'un puissant Chef pour la conduitte de cette entreprise: notre Navigation est. exposée aux tourmentes & aux tempêtes".[54] He holds that supporting trade is "un des premiers devoirs & des plus importans au bien de l'Etat".[55] When trade flourishes, the State also prospers. If the state can be compared to the human body, the king is the head, the hands are aristocracy and princes, the belly is the military, ordinary people the thighs, but the feet are the merchants: "Car comme les jambes & les pieds supportent toute la machine du cors humain, & font mouvoir la personne ca là pour l'exercice de ses actions; en sorte que sans ce mouvement le corps seroit comme un tronc immobile inutile à toutes choses".[56] Referring to Aristotle, he differentiates between sea trade, overland trade and moneylending. As long as foreigners are in charge of import and export in the French wholesale trade, the state cannot prosper.[57] Accordingly, the first necessary step is to establish a French shipping fleet for trade.

The author compares himself to the Samaritan from the Gospel of Luke, who, on the way from Jerusalem to Jericho, takes care of the badly injured and robbed traveller, when he helps the French state, which equally lies broken on the ground. Where he cannot find appropriate quotes from the Bible, he invents them, just like in the following quote from Psalm 106: "Ceux qui voguent dans la mer en des vaisseyux, et qui negocient en plusieurs traits de mer, ont veu les oeuvres du Seigneur, & ses merveilles en l'étendue & profondeur des eaux."[58] Elsewhere, with reference to Matthew, chapter 23, he compares the kingdom of God to a good and wise merchant and considers the apostles as particularly talented merchants, bearing to cross the sea in order to convert others.[59] The Biblical verse that two are better than one, serves him to illustrate the advantage of commercial partnership over retailers.[60]

[54] Ibid., *Epitre*.

[55] Ibid., p. 3.

[56] Ibid., p. 6.

[57] "Car comme il est. certain que le trafic est. la veritable la plus feconde source de toutes sortes de biens de commoditez necessaires à la vie, qui par un flux reflux continuel, fournist ce qui nous est. necessaire, restablist ce qui est. consommé; il ne faut point s'étonner de ce que nous tombons dans l'indigence, puisque à present cette souce nous est. tarie même nous est. ôtée par les étrangers. Eux seuls ont les facultés necessaires, les vaisseaux en abondance, les intelligences habitudes dans tous les pais, les pouvoirs les privileges pour exercer le Commerce avec avantage; [...] la ruine du Commerce de la France est. la veritable cause de toutes les incommoditez du peuple."Ibid., p. 124–126.

[58] Ibid., p. 132.

[59] Ibid., p. 141.

[60] Ibid., p. 246.

He thus considers seafaring as the greatest marvel which has been given by God. It refines morals, serves as a preparation of arts and science and is able to transport various types of goods in order to serve the needs of every country.

The first can be observed with the savage people from Brazil or Canada, who became civilised as a consequence of trade: "Par le moien du Negoce on forme peu à peu les hommes sauvages à la raison; de la raison à la bien-seance civilité des moeurs; & de l'un & de l'autre à la douceur de la vie."[61] Aristotle, the "Prince des Philosophes" gives a proof of this, as he had defined man as a social being and had held that there was no better way of achieving sociability than by trade and seafaring. And because different parts of the world had generated different arts and sciences, trade secondly serves for their distribution across all borders, in which they would otherwise be enclosed. Even Plato had gone to Egypt in order to discover the wisdom of that place. Which nation in the worlds would be better suited than France "qui possede comme en propre la gloire des lettres & des armes, l'honneur des arts, & la politesse des mœurs", at opening seafaring "& contribuer par ce moien à l'instruction & politesse des nations barbares & étrangeres"?[62]

In practice, trade can be conducted well or badly. Therefore, avarice is perfectly permissible, but it needs to be controlled by "le motif de l'utilité publique".[63] Trade as such does not have lower or ignoble aspects which could be harmful to honour and reputation. Quite the contrary, "il a le vrai caractere de la vertu & de la noblesse", so that „le bon, loial & fidel marchand [...] fait des actions d'un grand esprit & d'un grand cœur, qui meritent un des premiers rangs d'honneur & d'estime parmi toutes les nations du monde."[64] In order to counter the general prejudice of trade and aristocracy being incompatible, the author refers to a royal enactment, which explicitly assures the maintenance of aristocracy to those aristocrats in charge of seafaring. Even commoners, the enactment further reads, could be granted titles of nobility under special circumstances because of their seafaring.[65] In earlier times, the author states, it was up to the kings and princes to doing business. An invented quote from the Old Testament again serves as a proof for this: "Demeurés avec nous, vous jouirez de cette terre, vous labourerez & ferez Negoce."[66] It is remarkable how much importance this anonymous author from Nantes attaches to proving his arguments by Biblical quotes. His obvious inventiveness and efforts to find convincing proofs, wherever he is not able to find any, underlines his endeavour to adequately counter the positions of the patristics. He debunks the notion of the dishonourable when he claims that commoners were able to become aristocrats through trade, princes and kings were doing business and trade did not serve the personal interest but the common good instead. Without merchants the state would remain paralysed and merchants are heroes like Hercules and the Argonauts.

[61] Ibid., p. 134.

[62] Ibid., p. 138.

[63] Ibid., p. 189.

[64] Ibid., pp. 192 f.

[65] Ibid., p. 262.

[66] Ibid., p. 280 f.

One senses an apologetic attitude behind this hyperbolic acclaim, for a trade that still has to be advertised.

By the second half of the seventeenth century, it has seemingly become more natural to enumerate the occupations, merits and areas of knowledge in trade. This is, at least, the impression one gets when reading Jacques Savary's introduction. Savary (1622–1690) lived during the reign of Louis XIV and gained wealth in cloth wholesale trade, before he began to work for the famous Finance Minister Colbert, in the *Conseil de Réforme* at the *Ordonnance de Commerce*, an extensive codification of capitalist trade law. In his preface, Savary underlines that both his book and trade are not about self-interest, but rather about the common good. He does not consider it harmful to this purpose, however, if the young merchant‘s chance of accruing much wealth for himself or of guaranteeing his descendants the most distinguished judicial offices -certainly meaning the „noblesse de robe“, the aristocratic offices-, might be his actual motivation. The entrepreneur's objectives are diverse and can be summarized as follows: 'the common good; responsibility before God; social responsibility; profit; protection; reputation; work satisfaction; social recognition.'[67]

When Savary (I, 3) focusses on the merchant's negative and positive characteristics and ways of behaving, he is convinced that the entrepreneurial personality is the central factor for the prosperity and ruin of a company. Apart from the innate characteristics, he should possess the inclination to the commercial profession and physically, a handsome appearance, combined with politeness and amiability. (I, 4) Furthermore, a successfully completed education with an experienced merchant is essential, since ignorance in business life leads to overconfidence, imprudence and ambition, and finally to bankruptcy. He has to learn about the importance of having a good reputation as a skilful und respectable merchant, places and ways of producing goods, accounting, sales behaviour, market research and the assessment of the customer's creditworthiness.[68] All these fields of knowledge provide the merchant with prudence and security in management policy, in the light of varying monetary, measurement and weighting systems, of hazardous land and sea routes, of harvest fluctuations and of wars. The merchant and his family should avoid excessive spending in order to guarantee the solvency and internal protection of a company.

"J'ai commencé dès ma jeunesse de m'instruire de la plupart de toutes ces choses, et j'en ai acquis l'expérience par une longue et forte application que j'ai eue à me render capable dans toutes les différentes négociations."[69] Savary explains the reasons why trade is necessary and useful right at the beginning of his book, pointing out the God-given realities of the world. Not everything that is needed can be found in one place, but rather scattered all over the world, which in turns makes mutual friendship and support necessary, so that goods can be brought wherever they are needed. "C'est cet échange continuel de toutes les commodités de la vie qui fait le commerce, et c'est ce commerce aussi qui fait toute la douceur de la vie: puisque par ce moyen il y a par tout abondance de toutes les choses."[70] Consequently, the merchant makes

---

[67] Cp. Savary (2010), p. 64.

[68] Cp. ibid., p. 33.

[69] Savary (2011), p. 196.

[70] Ibid., p. 213.

abundance and joy of living possible. According to Savary, overabundance in some places could lead to harmful idleness, if goods were not carried away in order to provide balance. Not only is trade useful to the consumers, but also to the merchants themselves, as they accrue remarkable riches and give their children the chance of holding distinguished posts.[71] Even the kings benefit from trade, for it provides not only with taxes, but also with credits, which they need for larger enterprises, such as wars for example, all of which suggests that merchants can stand above kings. Travelling merchants eventually provide the king with valuable information about foreign countries and people. Savary particularly singles out King Louis XIV as laudable, because he had reinforced the trade of the country by means of his authority and laws, which avoid abuses and deceitful bankruptcies. In his work "Le parfait négociant" he accompanies the merchant from apprentice to wholesaler, who exports and imports goods across the continents, presenting not only his practical knowledge, but also the maxims of behaviour which are to be followed. The merchant has to avoid three things: "l'ignorance, l'imprudence et l'ambition".[72] He has to be at the service of an experienced merchant for a sufficiently long time, in order to acquire all the skills and rules needed for his commercial affairs. "Car il est. constant que quelque honnête homme que soit un marchand, s'il ne sait toutes ces choses, et qu'il ne tienne un fort bon ordre, il sera toujours aveugle dans les affaires, ne les conduira jamais comme il faut".[73] Exaggerated ambition, excessive spending on celebrations, household and clothing result in bankruptcy in much the same way as negligence in debt collection. Especially in case of the latter, prudence is required: "elle consiste à ne dire que les choses nécessaires pour parvenir à la fin que l'on se propose, qui est. de recevoir la dette dont on sollicite le paiement".[74] Without order, ruin is imminent.That is why the destiny of a trading company depends on the accountant: "En effet, c'est sur la conduite et le bon ordre de celui qui tient les livres et la caisse, d'où dépend tout le bonheur de la société."[75]

When educating a future merchant, who has to distinguish himself by ingenuity and a pleasant outward appearance by nature, it is necessary to ensure that university studies do not distract him from his plans. Then he can become as rich as to attain "jusque dans les plus hautes dignités de la robe".[76] For Savary, the *honnête homme* is succesful, amiable and competent, unlike the malicious and incompetent persons, who ruin the business.[77] In his *Dictionnaire universel de commerce*, Savary explains the word "placer" using the example of a young man, sent to be apprentice: "J'ai bien placé mon fils, je l'ai obligé à un Mercier aussi honnête homme qu'habile Marchand."[78]

[71] Ibid.: „mettre leurs enfants dans les premières charges de la robe".

[72] Ibid., p. 240.

[73] Ibid., p. 241.

[74] Ibid., p. 593.

[75] Ibid., p. 700.

[76] Ibid., p. 245.

[77] Ibid., p. 240, 542.

[78] Savary (1726), p. 1112.

It has been shown that Savary underlines the usefulness of trade, pointing out the necessity of redistributing unevenly distributed goods and approving of trade, capable of increasing joy of life and avoiding abundance that could lead to harmful idleness. Further, trade promotes friendship and provides the king with information about foreign countries. In the first place, the merchant as an entrepreneurial personality distinguishes himself by his knowledge, for instance about places and ways of production, before he is required to have indispensable character traits such as prudence, caution, discipline and orderly bookkeeping. Nonetheless, additional exterior features, such as a good reputation, a pleasant outward appearance, kindness and politeness, are of particular importance. It is especially these latter characteristics that make a merchant an *honnête homme*, as in the France of the seventeenth century he is not characterised, unlike the *homme honnête*, by honesty, *honnêteté*, but rather by perfect manners and conversation skills in business and social interaction. At about the same time, the philologist and Jesuit Dominique Bouhours characterises the *honnêteté* of the skilful businessman as follows: "Dans les négociations ils se conduisent avec beaucoup d'habilité et d'une manière fort délicate: ils découvrent d'abord les pensées de celui avec qui ils traitent sans se découvrir eux-mêmes; ils s'insinuent dans son esprit; ils l'engagent par ses propres intérêts."[79] In this sense also the *parfait négociant* described by Savary appears to be not primarily morally perfect, but perfectly efficient. That the merchant can behave morally as well as immorally has been undisputed since Aristotle, Thomas Aquinas and Neo-Scholasticism. The question of the dignity of the materiality and of this world, which the patristics disputed, has been acknowledged just as long. For Savary it is more important, when promoting the perfect merchant, to underline his function in society, his position and reputation, his character traits and ways of behaving, as well as his necessary commercial knowledge. Nevertheless, there are also definitions of the *honnête homme*, which consider him a model of righteousness and performance of duties, the King being the best example. In this sense, Armand de Gérard holds that "le Roy est le plus honneste homme de son Roiaume."[80] If the merchant is also viewed as an *honnête homme*, he seems, at least in seventeenth century France, to have reached the top of the social hierarchy.

Works Cited

Anonymus. 1646. *Le commerce honorable ou considerations politiques*. Nantes.

Aristotle. 1934. *The Nicomachean ethics*. In: *Aristotle in 23 Volumes*, Vol. 19. Trans. Harris Rackham. Cambridge MA: Harvard University Press. London.

———. 1944. *Politics*. In: *Aristotle in 23 Volumes*, Vol. 21. Trans. Harris Rackham. Cambridge, MA: Harvard University Press. London.

———. 1962. *The metaphysics. Books X–XIV*. Trans. Hugh Tredennick. Cambridge, MA: Harvard University Press. London.

---

[79] Bouhours (1671/1920), p. 172f.; cp. also Strosetzki (2013).

[80] Gérard (1682), p. 220 f.

Basil the Great. (Homilia in divites, Sermon to the Rich) PG 31: 293.
Beierwaltes, Werner. [3]2014. *Platonismus im Christentum* (Philosophische Abhandlungen 73). Frankfurt am Main.
Bouhours, Dominique. 1671/1920. *D'Ariste et d'Eugène* hrsg. René Radouant. Paris.
Brentano, Lujo. 1923. *Der wirtschaftende Mensch in der Geschichte*. Leipzig: Meiner.
Clement of Alexandria. 1885. Paedagogos (The instructor) Books II and III. In *Ante-Nicene Fathers: The writings of the fathers down to A.D. 325*, Vol. II, ed. Philip Schaff.
Gérard, Armand de. 1682. *Le caractère de l'honneste homme moral*. Paris.
Drecoll, Volker. 2012. Middle platonic elements in Augustine's De Civitate 8. In *Religion and philosophy in the Platonic and Neoplatonic traditions. from antiquity to the early medieval period* hrsg. Kevin Corrigan, 183–193. Sankt Augustin.
Geyer, Bernhard (Hrsg.). 1951. *Die patristische und scholastische Philosophie*. Basel: Schwabe.
Goez, Werner. 1982. Das Ringen um den "gerechten Preis" in Spätmittelalter und Reformationszeit. In *Der "Gerechte Preis"*, Beiträge zur Diskussion um das "pretium iustum", ed. Johannes Herrmann, 21–32. Erlangen: Universitätsbund.
Gurjewitsch, Aron J. 2004. Der Kaufmann. In *Der Mensch des Mittelalters*, ed. Jacques Le Goff, 268–311. Essen: Magnus Verlag.
Savary, Jacques. 1726. Dictionnaire universel de commerce. *Tome* II. Amsterdam: Jansons.
Savary, Jacob. 2010. *Der vollkommene Kauff- und Handelsmann*, Nachdruck der Ausgabe von 1676, hrsg. Fritz Klein-Blenkers. Bergisch: Gladbach.
Savary, Jacques. 2011. Le parfait négociant. *Tome* I hrsg. Édouard Richard. Genf: Droz.
St Ambrose. 1890. On the duties of the clergy. In *A select library of Nicene and post-Nicene fathers of the Christian church. Second series*, Vol. 10, ed. Philip Schaff, Henry Wace. New York.
St. Augustine. 1950. The city of God. Trans. Marcus Dods, with an introduction by Thomas Merton. Random House Publishing Group.
———. 1959. *Of true religion* (De vera religione). Trans. J.H.S. Burleigh and with an introduction by Louis O. Mink. Chicago.
———. 2007a. The confessions and letters of St. Augustine. In: *Nicene and post-Nicene Fathers.* First series, Vol. 1, ed. Philip Schaff. New York.
———. 2007b. On Christian Doctrine (De doctrina christiana). In: *Nicene and post-Nicene Fathers.* First series, Vol. 2, ed. Philip Schaff. New York.
Strosetzki, Christoph. 2013. *Konversation als Sprachkultur. Elemente einer historischen Kommunikationspragmatik*. Berlin: Frank & Timme.
———. 2015. Le négociant: entre générosité, justice et "pretium iustum". In *Actes pour une économie juste*, hrsg. Dominique de Courcelles, 247–252. Paris: Lemieux Éditeur.
———. 2016. Zum Kaufmann bei Aristoteles und im Spanien der Frühen Neuzeit. In *Ethik und Politik des Aristoteles in der Frühen Neuzeit* hrsg. Christoph Strosetzki in Verbindung mit Walter Mesch und Christian Pietsch, 303–311. Archiv für Begriffsgeschichte, Sonderheft 12. Hamburg: Felix Meiner Verlag.
Taylor, Charles. 2012. *Ein säkulares Zeitalter*. Frankfurt am Main: Suhrkamp.
Thomas Aquinas. 1955. *Summa Contra Gentiles, 2: Book two:* Creation. Trans. James F. Anderson. Michigan.
———. 2006. *Summa Theologiae*: *Volume 38, Injustice: 2a2ae. 63–79,* ed. Thomas Gilby. Trans. Marcus Lefébure. Cambridge University Press.
Weber, Max. 2010. *Die protestantische Ethik und der Geist des Kapitalismus*, hrsg. Dirk Kaesler. München: Beck.
Wyrwa, Dietmar. 1983. *Die christliche Platonaneignung in den Stromateis des Clemens von Alexandrien* (Arbeiten zur Kirchengeschichte 53). Berlin.

Chapter 2
The Honorable Merchant and the Corporate Social Responsibility Movement

Christoph Lütge

Abstract The Honorable Merchant as an ideal of business ethics has a long-standing tradition. However, this ideal focusses a lot on the individual person and less on situational conditions, constraints and incentives under which people act. The Order Ethics approach helps conceptualize and justify why business ethics for the globalized market economy might shift this focus and put situational conditions on top of the agenda. This holds within companies as well: Instead of insisting on the ideal of the honorable merchant, companies should change structural incentives and conditions, by way of mechanisms such as Corporate Social Responsibility and others.

2.1 Introduction

The model of the honorable merchant has been taught in commercial manuals in Europe since at least the twelfth century, especially in Northern Italy and the Hanseatic League. Even though written much later, the corresponding piece of advice from Thomas Mann's "Buddenbrooks," which the elder Buddenbrook shares with his son, has become famous: "My son, show zeal for each day's affairs of business, but only for such that make for a peaceful night's sleep."

This quote expresses two things: on the one hand, a warning about undertaking certain actions, but, on the other hand, an encouragement to do others "with zeal." The entrepreneurial spirit, the calculated (not unconsidered) taking of risks is part of the ideal of the honorable merchant as well as the responsible handling of capital and resources of every kind. The entrepreneurial spirit, though, is often misconstrued as an essential element of the honorable merchant. In his famous essay "The Protestant Ethics and the Spirit of Capitalism" from 1905, Max Weber already drew this connection: According to Weber, modern capitalism needed a certain kind of

C. Lütge (✉)
Technical University of Munich, Munich, Germany
e-mail: luetge@tum.de

C. Lütge, C. Strosetzki (eds.), *The Honorable Merchant – Between Modesty and Risk-Taking*, Ethical Economy 56, https://doi.org/10.1007/978-3-030-04351-3_2

entrepreneur. Not everyone can endure the capitalist economy: An unusually firm character is required to prevent such an entrepreneur of the new capitalist style from experiencing moral and economic collapse. Along with clarity of vision and drive, he or she also needs certain ethical qualities.

Incidentally, the origin of similar models is not limited to Europe. They also originated (in different forms) in non-European regions such as Japan[1] and China.[2]

In recent years, various organizations of small and medium-sized enterprises in particular have been trying to revive this model, such as the German chambers of commerce and industry.[3] I do not believe, however, that it is possible to *directly* transfer the merchant virtues and traditional customs to the modern economy under globalization. While models are to be welcomed in principle, they must be placed within a larger framework of theoretically based business ethics as well as structurally oriented and implementable corporate social responsibility. Therefore, the question of whether the idea of the honorable merchant is applicable to today's situation is above all a question of business ethics.

To be sure, business ethics can be pursued in two fundamentally different ways. Firstly, as *individual ethics*[4]: Such an approach, which largely dominates public debate, focuses primarily on the individual, inquires about the moral motivation of the individual, and looks for individual culprits, e. g. greedy managers or selfish investors. Nevertheless, here the question is neglected concerning the incentives available to the actors and the extent to which they can act freely under these incentives. Dilemma situations such as the prisoner's dilemma or the stag-hunt game model exactly those situations in which the individual cannot act freely and cannot escape the logic of a given situation.

By contrast, the second approach of *order ethics*[5] focuses on the conditions and incentives of the respective situation. In Anglo-American regions, this approach is known as the "moral market model." Some of its core elements are described below.

2.2 Order Ethics: Pre-modern and Modern

The term "order ethics" (*Ordnungsethik*) deliberately recalls the German term "order politics" (*Ordnungspolitik*), as well as the Freiburg School and the tradition of the social market economy. Both order politics and order ethics are concerned with structural conditions, institutions, and incentives. Thus, order ethics primarily

---

[1] See Shibusawa (1916) and Shimazu in this volume, as well as the writings of Chikuro Hiroik on "Moralogy" (Institute of Moralogy 1987).

[2] Chun (2012).

[3] See e.g. IHK für München und Oberbayern (2012).

[4] In English-speaking countries, it is known as the "moral manager model"; see e.g. Boatright (1999)

[5] Homann and Lütge (2004/2013); Homann and Kirchner (1995); Lütge (2012a, b, 2015 and 2019), Lütge et al. (2016), as well as Lütge and Mukerji (2016).

deals with the implementation of norms, not just their justification. And this implementation must be conceived under the relevant social conditions, i. e. the conditions of modernity. A business ethics for *modern* society is thus fundamentally distinguishable from an business ethics for the pre-modern era.

In pre-modernity – indeed for the vast majority of cultural history – human beings mainly lived in small groups. Until the year 1000, there were only about ten cities in the world that could be described from today's perspective as major cities (with more than 100,000 inhabitants). These societies were governed by conditions that can be clearly distinguished from today's societies: Above all, they were zero-sum societies without systematic, sustainable growth. Interestingly, the only exception was perhaps the Roman Empire. The Roman Empire, according to some scholars, managed to maintain stable economic growth for several centuries. And, indeed, this may also have been grounded in Roman thought. In "De Officiis" (I, 151) Cicero gives a positive assessment of wholesale trade, entirely in contrast to other traditions of ethical thinking:

> The following branches of activity, for example, are conventionally viewed as appropriate for the free man, but nonetheless vulgar: Firstly, all those trades are frowned upon which aimed at earning the spite of one's fellow human beings like usury and tax collecting. The gainful employment of all unskilled day laborers is also considered ignoble. Among the vulgar trades, one further counts the middleman. [....] All craftsmen, moreover, belong to the impure guild; what can a workshop have in itself that is noble? It is the least possible to approve of professions that only serve sensual pleasures such as herring tamers, butchers, cooks, chefs, chicken masters, fishermen. [...] Retail trade is one of the impure businesses, *whereas the wealthy wholesale trade, which honestly allows the masses from all over the world to benefit from consumer goods, is perfectly blameless.*[6]

But that was an exception. For thousands of years, the zero-sum society formed the stable background of human sociality. The successful Florentine merchant Giovanni Rucellai put it in a nutshell when he who wrote in his memoirs of 1450: "By being rich, I am making poor others whom I may not even know."[7] In fact, this was the case at that time: Since the economy as a whole did not grow, it was only possible to differently distribute its gains. The gain of one was necessarily the loss of another.

The reaction of ethics to this situation was the demand for moderation. The ethics of the mean or the ethics of moderation[8] arose against the background of pre-modern society. Some of the particularly drastic consequences of this doctrine are the ban on interest payments in antiquity, the Middle Ages and Islam as well as the doctrine of the just price (prominently from Thomas Aquinas). Even the honorable merchant seems to have originated from this logic.

The social situation has fundamentally changed in the modern age, however. We are dealing with a growth society: In the industrialized countries, there has been a long-term average of real income growth of only about 1.5% per year – but this has been the case for 200 years.[9] Since the beginning of industrialization and the

---

[6] Cicero (1959), I, 150f.

[7] Rucellai (1772).

[8] Lütge (2009, 2019).

[9] See e.g. McCloskey (2006).

accompanying economic growth, we have been living in a situation entirely without historical precedent. In recent decades, it has spread with globalization to many, if not most, of the world's regions (or at least started to do so). This applies in particular to the African continent, which for a long time was written off as "lost," but now has a steadily growing number of countries on the upswing (e.g. Angola, Ghana, Mozambique, Ethiopia, etc.).

In the modern age, zero-sum games are systematically no longer played, but positive-sum games. As the overall economic return grows, it is now possible to increase one actor's profit without having to do so at the expense of another. This is also and especially true of globalization, which, with its considerably more intense competition, does not represent a continuation of the exploitation of the "poor" by the "rich" countries, but rather brings advantages to all sides.[10]

That said, ethics – to put a finer point on it – only takes note of these new social and economic qualities to a limited degree. An ethics of growth or competition[11]still needs to be developed. Our moral concepts and categories instead remain oriented toward the situation of the pre-modern era. They lag behind the intervening social and economic developments. Our moral expectations can be described with the term "moral mesocosmos": As in the mesocosmos of natural science, our everyday categories fail if we apply them beyond the usual dimensions of our everyday world. We can reliably calculate with millimeters or miles, but on a large scale and on a very small scale, our everyday physics breaks down. In order to fly to the moon, we need the theory of relativity, and in quantum physics there are phenomena such as absolute coincidences, which can no longer be grasped by everyday physics.

We have no reason to believe that morality is any different.[12] Indeed, experimental studies by Joshua Greene and others confirm this.[13] For business ethics, this means that the pre-modern morality, which demands the systematic deferral of one's own interests, can in fact be dysfunctional in the global competition of modern society and lead to counterproductive results. If you want to hold onto the honorable merchant as a pre-modern ideal, the model must be applied in a fundamentally different way. Above all, it is necessary to comprehend question of implementing norms differently than in pre-modernity.

2.3 Ethics in Competition

The central problem of business ethics in the modern age is the question of how ethical concerns can be implemented in competition. The conditions of competition pose the following fundamental ethical problem:

---

[10] See e.g. Homann et al. (2005).

[11] Lütge (2019).

[12] On the concept of mesocosm, see Vollmer (1975/1998), 161ff.; on that of "moral mesocosm," Lütge (2007), 121f.

[13] See Greene et al. (2001), Greene and Haidt (2002), and Greene (2012).

Those actors who, for moral reasons, provide costly advance and additional services risk being placed at a disadvantage in competition with their competitors – which can lead to their elimination. The market cannot differentiate between companies that produce too much for moral reasons or simply because they are inefficient. A classic example of this is the incorporation of environmental protection measures in a business: the entrepreneur who unilaterally installs a filtering system without a legal basis puts herself at a cost disadvantage vis-à-vis her competitors. These, in turn, benefit from the slightly improved air quality, without having to pay for it.

This logic, which can also be formally represented with the help of the prisoner's dilemma,[14] can be found in many of the socio-economic contexts of modernity. Many earlier authors, such as Max Weber and by Marx in the nineteenth century, already recognized it. According to Marx, in the long term, the moral actors must leave the market – even if they are capitalists. Even the capitalists, as individual entrepreneurs, are only prisoners of the larger capitalist system. Whether they intend to exploit and alienate their workers is completely irrelevant.

From this situation, Marx drew the – albeit too radical and counterproductive – conclusion that the entire market-economy system with competition needed to be abolished. This is not sensible from an ethical point of view, however, as competition offers many – not just economically but also ethically relevant – advantages.

- Competition provides incentives for creativity. It rewards successful innovations (beyond mere inventions and "ideas") with pioneer profits. The successful innovator (e.g. Apple with the iPad) gets the lion's share of the gains.
- Competition, however, also exerts discipline over other vendors. It forces them to adapt to what the customers actually want. A world without competition produces only Trabants and Wartburgs (the sub-standard automobiles produced in the former East Germany).

But this also means that markets are not simply free (as Friedman said[15]), but also subject to considerable pressure and coercion. Market players, whether companies or employees, experience this pressure continuously – and many believe it is only increasing. Yet, as consumers, we all benefit.

- Competition processes information in a decentralized way that no central planning authority could ever manage on its own. It can thus provide every individual with exactly what they desire. F. A. Hayek stresses this point in particular.[16]
- The market eventually destroys positions of power, especially those of large companies that want to achieve (near) monopolies. Examples include Microsoft and at least in part the Deutsche Bahn (which, however, has been competing,

[14] See Homann and Lütge (2004/2013); for an example of the problem of anti-corruption, see Lucke and Lütge (2011), and for the corresponding analysis of the financial crisis, Münch (2015).

[15] See Friedman (1962).

[16] See Hayek (1968/1994).

though to a limited extent, with long-distance buses since 2013). F. Böhm called the market the "best instrument of disempowerment" that history has ever invented.[17]

- D. McCloskey has pointed out – with many historical examples and parallels – that competition creates considerable more opportunities for self-realization of broad sections of the population than other economic forms. The competition also supports a pluralistic society and the rights of minorities or disadvantaged groups (diversity).[18]

In order to exploit the advantages of competition and to limit the disadvantages of ethics, the basic logic of competition must remain in place and take effect. On the other hand, ethical standards have to be incorporated into the rules of the competition – but they cannot directly control the motivations of the actors. Competitors cannot be asked to directly apply morality in their daily actions at the risk of competitive disadvantage or even ruin. This is why there are formal and informal rules for competition and its institutions. All competitors are subject to the same rules, so that no one can benefit from having lower moral standards. In other words, morality becomes resistant to exploitation by actors who are less moral.

An analogy to sport presents itself: We do not expect the players to behave morally in their individual actions; we rather set the rules in such a way that no one benefits from having lower standards. The ultimate goal is that viewers (here: the consumers) can watch an exciting (here: useful) match.

Real economic examples are found in formal, legal regulations such as antitrust bans in antitrust law, prohibitions on fraud, extortion, corruption, and others. Here, however, new rules should also lead to more intense – and simultaneously more efficient – competition. To cite one example: In recent decades, the costs of nursing care in Germany have skyrocketed in a way that cannot be limited to extended lifespans or an aging population. Instead, they are mostly due to a lack of supply and competition in the nursing-care market. The new mobility of workers in the EU (not completely introduced in Germany and Austria until 2011) has changed this situation. No one is forced to employ nurses from other countries. But it is only through the supply of new workers from other EU countries that care providers have come under pressure in the nursing care market. What's more, if they want to maintain their prices, they must deal with corresponding improvements in service, quality, and other factors. Of course, as in other markets, certain minimum standards must be established for the quality of nursing care. But beyond such a minimum standards, there must be room to maneuver (again as in other markets) and price-conscious behavior encouraged – which is not the same thing as miserliness or the search for the cheapest offer. In any case, the opponents of competition have yet to show that competition tends to reduce quality in the nursing care sector.

---

[17] Böhm (1961).

[18] See McCloskey (2006).

2.4 Morality in a Company: Corporate Social Responsibility

Traditionally, the regulations envisaged by order ethics are established at the legislative level. This does not necessarily have to be the case, however, especially under globalization. Here, regulations beneath the statutory framework can also play a significant role. At the corporate and industry level, too, agreements can be reached on rules that have ethical characteristics.

Regulations at the sector level, for example, can be highly effective: One success story is the ethics management of the Bavarian construction industry, which has been in existence since 1996 and has since expanded outside of Germany.

The economic basis for such actions is quite simple: moral behavior must be an investment for companies. Companies cannot afford to forego profits on an permanent and systematic basis; they cannot sacrifice revenue on the "altar of morality." Companies, however, can certainly invest – which they do continuously and to a significant degree anyway. If morality becomes a production factor for companies, there is nothing to prevent such investments from being made in morality.

Ethics, however, must then abandon the notion that morality is necessarily not in the interest of those who practice it, but rather always entails a burden – a disadvantage for the benefit of others. Morality *can* be worthwhile for companies. In the long run, it even *must* be worthwhile, otherwise it won't survive in the market.[19]

Morality can strengthen various factors for the company; in particular, it can support the long-term safeguarding of a company's reputation and social capital.[20] Such factors and others are frequently discussed in the ongoing debate on Corporate Social Responsibility (CSR).

2.5 Corporate Social Responsibility and the Honorable Merchant

One of the longest-established definitions (from the European Commission's Green Paper of 2001) called CSR "a concept that serves as a basis for companies to integrate social and environmental concerns on a voluntary basis into their business activities and interactions with stakeholders." This definition, however, was simplified and broadened in 2011. Now, CSR is defined as "the responsibility of enterprises for their impacts on society."

The term has been discussed for decades, especially in Anglo-American countries.[21] In Germany, the concept has been increasingly dealt with since the mid-2000s, specifically regarding the following developments:

---

[19] Lütge (2013b).

[20] See Homann and Lütge (2004/2013).

[21] See e.g. Crane et al. (2009).

- Article 30 of the Administrative Offences Act (OWiG), which now also guarantees the liability of companies, not only of individual persons;
- EU directive and strategy on CSR from 2011;
- UN Global Compact from 1999;
- OECD Guidelines for Multinational Enterprises, which have been repeatedly revised;
- United Nations Principles of Economy and Human Rights from 2011;
- Guidelines of the Global Reporting Initiative (GRI) from 2002;
- ISO 26000 as a guideline for corporate social responsibility (published in Germany in 2011).

All these regulatory efforts have contributed to the fact that CSR is a widely known concept in Germany today. According to a survey conducted by the Chair of Business Ethics at the Technical University of Munich, 74.5% of the polled German SMEs were familiar with the CSR concept. What's more, as many as 58% of SMEs said that they consider CSR to be either highly relevant or very relevant.

It would seem natural to assume that CSR measures can be a modern form of implementing the classical ideal of the honorable merchant under conditions of globalization. CSR is not a concept focused on individuals, but emphasizes structures and incentives within a company. This means that it can also play a leading role in competition and become a long-term competitive advantage for companies – without running counter to the concerns of ethics.

In the meantime, an alternative (although perhaps not entirely new concept), has been developed that draws on Porter and Kramer: Creating Shared Value (CSV).[22] This article ties in with Porter's work on strategic CSR and has provoked a significant critical response.[23] CSV's goal is to give companies a more active role in (also) pursuing social goals than is the case – from Porter's point of view – in (at least some parts) of CSR. This also means that the creation of "shared value" is seen as a central activity of a company, and not just as a disconnected "add-on." Whether this is a sustainable long-term concept will be demonstrated in further debate. Just the same, it is perfectly compatible with the dual character of the honorable merchant.

2.6 Conclusion

The usefulness of the honorable merchant may be questioned. It certainly has not been fully exploited. Nonetheless, in the globalized economy it will be primarily realized as an ideal through structural measures such as CSR or CSV and less through individual, personal virtues.

[22] See Porter and Kramer (2011).

[23] See i.a. Lütge and v. Liel (2015).

Literature

Boatright, John R. 1999. Presidential address: Does business ethics rest on a mistake? *Business Ethics Quarterly* 9: 583–591.

Böhm, Franz. 1961. Demokratie und ökonomische Macht. In *Kartelle und Monopole im modernen Recht: Beiträge zum übernationalen und nationalen europäischen und amerikanischen Recht. Bd.*, ed. hrsg. Institut für ausländisches und internationales Wirtschaftsrecht, vol. 1, 3–24. Karlsruhe: Müller.

Chun, Shan. 2012. *Major aspects of Chinese religion and philosophy: Dao of inner saint and outer fing*. Heidelberg/New York: Springer.

Cicero, Marcus Tullius. 1959. *Vom pflichtgemäßen Handeln. "De officiis"*. Übersetzt und erläutert von Karl Atzert. München: Goldmann.

Crane, Andrew et al. hrsg. 2009. *The Oxford handbook of corporate social responsibility*. Oxford: Oxford University Press.

Friedman, Milton. 1962. *Capitalism and freedom*. Chicago: Chicago University Press.

Greene, Joshua D. 2012. Reflection and reasoning in moral judgment. *Cognitive Science* 36 (1): 163–177.

Greene, J.D., and J. Haidt. 2002. How (and where) does moral judgment work? *Trends in Cognitive Sciences* 6 (12): 517–523.

Greene, J.D., R.B. Sommerville, L.E. Nystrom, J.M. Darley, and J.D. Cohen. 2001. An fMRI investigation of emotional engagement in moral judgment. *Science* 293: 2105–2108.

Homann, Karl, und Christian Kirchner. 1995. Ordnungsethik. *Jahrbuch für Neue Politische Ökonomie* 14: 189–211.

Homann, Karl, und Christoph Lütge (2004/2013). *Einführung in die Wirtschaftsethik* (3. Aufl.). Münster: LIT.

Homann, Karl, Peter Koslowski, und Christoph Lütge, hrsg. 2005. *Wirtschaftsethik der Globalisierung*. Tübingen: Mohr Siebeck.

IHK für München und Oberbayern, hrsg. 2012. *Den Ehrbaren Kaufmann leben: Mit Tradition zur Innovation*. In Zusammenarbeit mit Christoph Lütge. München.

Institute of Moralogy. 1987. *An outline of moralogy: A new approach to moral science*. Chiba-ken: Reitaku University: The Institute of Moralogy.

Lucke, Eva-Maria, und Christoph Lütge. 2011. Moralisches Verhalten in einem korrupten Markt: Anreize und Erfolgsfaktoren anhand einer Fallstudie aus Argentinien. *ORDO* 62: 297–320.

Luetge, C., T. Armbrüster, and J. Müller. 2016. Order ethics: Bridging the gap between contractarianism and business ethics. *Journal of Business Ethics* 136: 687–697.

Lütge, Christoph. 2007. *Was hält eine Gesellschaft zusammen? Ethik im Zeitalter der Globalisierung*. Tübingen: Mohr Siebeck.

———. 2009. Gegen eine Ethik der Mäßigung. In *Abschied von der Gerechtigkeit: Für eine Neujustierung von Freiheit und Gleichheit im Zeichen der Krise*, hrsg. K. Gentinetta und K. Horn, 99–106. Frankfurt: Frankfurter Allgemeine Buch.

———. 2012a. *Wirtschaftsethik ohne Illusionen: Ordnungstheoretische Reflexionen*. Tübingen: Mohr Siebeck.

———. 2012b. Fundamentals of order ethics: Law, business ethics and the financial crisis. *Archiv für Rechts- und Sozialphilosophie Beihefte* 130: 11–21.

———, hrsg. 2013a. *Handbook of the philosophical foundations of business ethics*. Heidelberg/New York: Springer.

———. 2013b. Moral muss sich auch am Markt durchsetzen. *Interview mit Deutschlandradio Kultur* 6: 02. http://www.dradio.de/dkultur/sendungen/thema/2001973/. Zugegriffen: 02. April 2016.

———. 2015. *What holds a society together? Order ethics vs. moral surplus*. Lanham: Lexington.

———. 2019. *The ethics of competition: Why a competitive society is good for all*. Cheltenham: Elgar.

Lütge, Christoph, und B.V. Liel. 2015. Creating Shared Value und seine Erfolgsfaktoren – ein Vergleich mit CSR: Was macht Creating Shared Value aus und wie kann man es am besten fördern? *Zeitschrift für Wirtschafts- und Unternehmensethik* 16 (2): 182–119.

Lütge, Christoph, und N. Mukerji, hrsg. 2016. *Order ethics: An ethical framework for the social market economy*. Heidelberg/New York: Springer.

McCloskey, Deirdre. 2006. *The bourgeois virtues: Ethics for an age of commerce*. Chicago: University of Chicago Press.

Münch, Philipp A. 2015. *Die Ordnungsethik der globalen Finanzkrise: Eine Analyse anhand von Dilemmastrukturen*. Heidelberg: Springer. (Reihe: Wirtschaftsethik in der globalisierten Welt).

Porter, M.E., and M.R. Kramer. 2011. Creating shared value – How to reinvent capitalism and unleash a wave of innovation and growth. *Harvard Business Review* 89 (1/2): 62–77.

Reiff, Antonia. 2011. *CSR im deutschen Mittelstand*. München.

Rucellai, Giovanni. 1772. *Ricordanze*. Padua.

Shibusawa, Eiichi. 1916. *Rongo to soroban*. Tokio: Toado Shobo. ("The Analects and the Abacus").

Vollmer, Gerhard. 1975/1998. Evolutionäre Erkenntnistheorie. 7. Aufl. Stuttgart: Hirzel.

von Hayek, Friedrich August. 1968/1994. Der Wettbewerb als Entdeckungsverfahren. In *Freiburger Studien: gesammelte Aufsätze*, 2. Aufl., 249–265. Tübingen: Mohr.

Chapter 3
The Legend of Excellent Businessman. A Neuroethical Perspective

Adela Cortina

Abstract If the question about the causes of the crises has generated a good deal of literature in Spain, the key issue in recent times has been how to create that tangible and intangible wealth that only companies can give. One of the proposals that specialists agree upon is to *revitalise the business entrepreneurial spirit,* presenting the entrepreneurs' way of life as an attractive option, due to the good they produce and the social recognition they enjoy. Accepting the suggestions of the so-called "narrative turn", the article analyses the virtualities of business narratives in order to enhance the role of entrepreneurs. To this end, the article aims to cover three stages: (1) narratives are necessary because they are brain-based, (2) it is advisable to find out why entrepreneurs are not usually considered in Spain as the main characters of good narratives, (3) good narratives, the ones that convince, are the ones that have the capacity to show the *meaning* of the entrepreneurial activity and the *truth* of what we have been doing.

3.1 The Business Entrepreneurial Spirit

The crises that we have been suffering since at least 2007 have generated a good deal of bibliography and encounters aimed at reflecting upon their possible causes.[1] Economists, politicians, sociologists, philosophers have spent time and energy wondering what has occurred at a global and at a local level to reach the precarious situation, which, in the countries of the South of the European Union, has become

[1] This study is contained within the Scientific Research and Technological Development Project FFI2013-47136-C2-1-P, financed by the Spanish Ministry of Economy and Competitiveness, and within the activities of the Group of Excellence for Research PROMETEO/2009/085 of the Generalitat Valenciana.

A. Cortina (✉)
University of Valencia, Valencia, Spain
e-mail: Adela.Cortina@uv.es

C. Lütge, C. Strosetzki (eds.), *The Honorable Merchant – Between Modesty and Risk-Taking*, Ethical Economy 56, https://doi.org/10.1007/978-3-030-04351-3_3

especially painful.[2] But at the same time, and above all lately, the major question is what to do, how to create tangible and intangible wealth that will enable us to advance with our plans for life, counting on the asset base that only economic activity and enterprises can provide. The reason why it is important to ask about the aetiology of the crises and the diagnosis of the situation is, above all, to formulate well-based suggestions to leave such a bad situation behind.

Obviously, something that is unavoidable in all proposals is the creation of employment, above all youth employment both in the private and public sectors, and to achieve this, different measures are suggested. There is one measure that all specialists agree about, and that is, *revitalising the entrepreneurial spirit* in the economic world.

Of course, the necessary formalities to create enterprises must be simplified, providing facilities so that they can be created without insurmountable difficulties. But it is also necessary to foster the creative spirit of those who are willing to assume risks and face up to the challenge of taking decisions in situations of uncertainty, to provide society with goods and services that would be lacking without that initiative, and to achieve this by obtaining a business profit. We will address this in this article.

The incentives that arouse the desire to create enterprises may and must be economic and social, of course. But that is not enough, as it is also necessary to present the businessman's or the entrepreneur's way of life as a project that is worthwhile committing to, as an attractive option for the good that it produces and because it enjoys social recognition. This latter point is also of major importance. As Hegel points out, the basis of social life is not the isolated individual, but the mutual recognition of individuals who know they are, in some way, related and who need the esteem of others to be able to go ahead with their plans for life.[3] Personal self-esteem depends to a great extent on the esteem that others have of our person, projects and capacities, and we can say that if the business option is not one of the options that are socially recognised as valuable, it is very costly to opt for it.

Some specialists advise introducing a different image of the businessman than the one that appears in Spanish manuals in primary and intermediate education, where presenting the businessman with a worse image would be practically

[2] A good example of this are works such as those included in AAVV, *Empresas éticas ante la crisis actual*, ÉTNOR Foundation, Valencia, 2009; AAVV, *Revitalizar las empresas para construir una buena sociedad*, ÉTNOR Foundation, Valencia, 2011; RACMYP, *Crisis económica y financiera: intervenciones en la RACMYP 2000–2010*, (Spanish) Royal Academy of Moral Sciences and Politics, Madrid, 2010; Antón Costas (coord.), *La crisis de 2008. De la economía a la política y más allá*, Cajamar Foundation, 2010.

[3] G.W.F. Hegel, *Grundlinien der Philosophie des Rechts*, Felix Meiner, Hamburg, 1955 (4. Auflage); Karl-Otto Apel, *Transformation der Philosophie*, Suhrkamp, Frankfurt a.M., 1973, 2 Bd.; Jürgen Habermas, *Moralbewusstsein und kommunikatives Handeln*, Suhrkamp, Frankfurt, 1983; Adela Cortina, *Ética mínima*, Tecnos, Madrid, 1986; Jesús Conill, *El crepúsculo de la metafísica*, Anthropos, Barcelona, 1988; Domingo García-Marzá, *Ética de la justicia*, Tecnos, Madrid, 1992; Axel Honneth, *Kampf um Anerkennung*, Suhrkamp, Frankfurt a.M., 1992; Paul Ricoeur, *Parcours de la reconnaissance*, Éditions Stock, 2004.

impossible. And, by the way, this is a good piece of advice, which, perhaps, should be accompanied by that even more important task proposed by those who wish to introduce *storytelling* into the business world.

3.2 Telling Stories and Not Just Giving Accounts

Indeed, as from the 1990s of the twentieth century, what has been called the "narrative turn" was introduced into the United States, both in the management world and in the world of political communication.[4] Back in the 1980s, the economist, McCloskey, had already stated that economy is an essentially narrative discipline,[5] it is an art of storytelling and thus, from the 1990s onwards, storytelling or the art of telling stories, spread as a way of both internal and external communication. A narrative era is established, therefore, in the world of social sciences, which affects, among others, the world of business sciences.

As we have gradually learnt, good communication is essential to generate a good reputation, and therefore, for the success of the enterprise. And, in principle, it is the annual reports and ethical codes that are responsible for informing about the business activity. However, in the 1990s of the last century, the advisability of telling the story of the enterprise as a way of informing about its identity and about its objectives was added to the traditional way of communication: who we are, where we are going and where we want to go. In the end, it is a way of inviting citizens to consider the enterprise as an ally that is worthwhile having alongside us. Faced with the growing number of offers, it is essential to create confidence to enhance customer loyalty and to conquer new customers, and a good resource to achieve this is to make them part of the actual story and integrate them into it. Based on this perspective, it has been said that enterprises are stories, and the brands, on their part, are stories that people consider to be their own.[6]

Faced with this proposal of storytelling, which seeks to generate reputation and recognition for the enterprises, in my opinion at least *three basic considerations* become necessary.

Firstly, we must gauge to what extent narrative is important; that is, if it is a fairly ingenious occurrence that has become fashionable and which, like all fashions, will become outdated or if, on the contrary, it is a need for enterprises to survive, because we people live in stories and from stories, and if the good story is not told, the bad one will be.

Secondly, as at this volume we are dealing with the figure of the "honest businessman" in ethics from the perspective of different cultures and countries, I would

---

[4] Christian Salomon, *Storytelling. Bewitching the Modern* Mind, Verso, London, 2017.

[5] Donald N. McCloskey, *The Rhetoric of Economics*, The University of Wisconsin Press, 1985.

[6] Jonathan Haidt, *The Righteous Mind: Why People are Divided by Politics and Religion*, Pantheon Books, 2012, chap. 12.

like to ask myself why, in Spain, the businessman is not usually considered a main character of good stories, why he does not appear as a person to be copied.

And, *last*, but not least, I would like to recall that good stories are the ones that have the ability to show the *meaning* and the *truth* about what we do. Stories are reconstructions, but they are good if they are able to highlight those episodes that bring to light who we really are, where we want to go and, above all, why we do what we do, and what is the meaning of our activity. Meaningless and deceitful stories lead to the narrator losing all credibility and reputation. Today, we will deal with these three points.

3.3 We Live from Stories and in Stories

According to those who defend the proposal of storytelling as an unavoidable way of communication, in order to be effective, stories must transmit values that can tune in with the public; values that, in some way, are heroic, such as hope, drive to improve or sacrifice.[7] But what those who insist on the importance of stories do not usually say is that if the stories have that power, it is because there are some neural bases that give them that power, as shown by cognitive sciences. And this consideration is, in my opinion, essential for our topic.

Indeed, advances in cognitive sciences show that the human mind is a story processor, more than a logic processor, which amazes those who insist on presenting human beings as calculators of the maximum profit. On the other hand, our brains are vast networks of neurons that work to generate our experience of the world and to this end, they draw up maps, they draw up value frameworks.[8] The frameworks are present in the brain synapses and unconsciously influence our decisions, to the extent that we integrate the facts, the data that we know about, in those value frameworks that we have been emotionally generating since childhood, and we interpret them based on these.

And it happens that we know those value frameworks through language; the words are defined in connection with the frameworks and, when a word is heard, the relative framework is activated in the brain. It is not surprising that hermeneutics have triumphed in the philosophical world, convinced that we live from interpretations.[9] There are no pure facts in the human world, but rather, we always reach them through interpretations. The positivist school ideal that Thomas Gradgrind proposed to reach in Charles Dickens's famous novel, *Hard Times,* is totally preposterous.

[7] Joseph Campbell, *The Hero with a thousand faces*, Princeton University Press, Princeton and Oxford, 1949.

[8] George Lakoff, *Don't Think of an Elephant*, Chelsea Green Publishing Company, 2004; *The Political Mind*, Penguin Books, 2009; Drew Westen, *The Political Brain*, Public Affairs, New York, 2007; Adela Cortina, *Neuroética y neuropolítica*, Tecnos, Madrid, 2011, Kap. 4.

[9] Jesús Conill, *Ética hermenéutica*, Tecnos, Madrid, 2009.

Now, what I want is Facts –said Thomas Gradgrind at the start of the work–.

> Teach these boys and girls nothing but Facts. Facts alone are wanted in life. Plant nothing else, and root out everything else. You can only form the minds of reasoning animals upon Facts: nothing else will ever be of any service to them. This is the principle on which I bring up my own children, and this is the principle on which I bring up these children. Stick to Facts, sir.[10]

The end of the novel is instructive, because the author shows that facts are always interpreted based on evaluations.

But, in addition, the frameworks are structures of *meaning*, linked to the language, and the data and facts that we know about take on a meaning in the framework as a whole. And it turns out that stories are structures of meaning, linked to the language, which are emotionally integrated into the brain synapses. Thus, all cultures educate their children by telling them stories, which is why religions and the different versions of the philosophy of history tell the story of salvation, the story of indefinite progress, the story of the Absolute Spirit, that of the universal class, that of the autonomous and supportive individuals. By incorporating these stories from very early ages, we gradually learn to place the facts and the data in the stories as a whole so that they become meaningful. And we read them in the light of that meaning so, by interpreting them, they take on a value.

So, it can be said that human beings learn more about themselves through *stories* than through *accounts,* more through *metaphors* than *concepts,* more through *legends* than *reports*. It is a mistake to believe that the mind is an impartial calculator of interests. On the contrary, the real truth is that it is so closely linked to emotions and to values that it is impossible to transmit a message without connecting with either of them. Rhetoric has known this since ancient times, but now it is confirmed by cognitive sciences and neurosciences.[11] Stories have a communicative and pedagogical capacity. And, insofar as the topic of this contribution is concerned, in order to revitalise the entrepreneurial spirit, good stories about the business world must be told, because if the good ones are not told, the bad ones will take control of the minds. The story of the "honest businessman" must be told.

But, if this is true, one question prevails: have enterprises known how to tell good stories, or, absorbed by their eagerness to crunch numbers, have they ignored the communicative and pedagogical capacity of good stories that are essential to acquire a reputation?

At a global level, they do not seem to have been able to do this, as shown, among other things, by the fact that the World Social Forum generates much more sympathy and adhesions than the World Economic Forum. And as far as Spain is concerned, the situation is identical; the businessman is not seen as an ally in the construction of a better world, as the necessary travel companion to reach Ithaca. What has happened?

---

[10] Charles Dickens, *Hard Times*, Penguin Books, London, 1995, 9.

[11] Aristotle, *Ars Rhetorica*, ed. W.D. Ross, Oxford University Press, 1959.

3.4 In Spain the Businessman Is Not a Moral Ideal

MacIntyre, in his book *After Virtue*, said that the distinctive morality of an era can be detected, in a certain place, through what he called "its characters".[12] Seemingly, in the Japanese Noh theatre and in the performances of English morality plays, a series of characters appear who are immediately recognised by the spectators, because they are the moral representatives of their culture. They play a major role in the plays, in such a way that all the other actors define their roles in relation to them. It is as if the moral ideas of an era were incarnated in them, and the people value them because they provide them with a cultural and moral ideal. The specific aspect of a culture would be, then, the specific aspect of its characters.

As an example of these statements, MacIntyre mentions those who, in his opinion, are distinctive characters of two eras in two different countries. According to him the culture of Victorian England was partially defined by three characters: the Public Headmaster, the Explorer and the Engineer. Whilst, the culture of Wilhelm's Germany was defined by the Prussian Officer, the Professor and the Social Democrat.

When I read this text some time ago I wondered what the characters of a crucial period in Spanish history, such as the Golden Age, would be. And I reached the conclusion, a disputable one, of course, that there could also be three: the Warrior (either the Third of Flanders, the Conqueror or even the knight errant), the Saint and the Rogue. The Warrior seeks glory and fortune; the Saint, the salvation of his own and other's souls; the Rogue is an anti-hero who makes every effort to live without working. Curiously, none of them have any relationship with the production of material wealth or with the trading of goods, not even considering that a benefit for the community would be achieved with this.[13]

It is true that some ethical trading principles were present in Spanish society, and proof of this are texts like the one that appears, in Latin, in the *Lonja de los Mercaderes* (Merchants' Exchange) of the city of Valencia, around the four walls of the *Sala de Contratación* (Hiring Hall). In the text, which dates from the end of the fifteenth century, the *Lonja* talks to the citizens and tells them this, translated into English: "I am a magnificent house, constructed in fifteen years. Enjoy and observe, fellow citizens, how good is trade that does not scheme with its tongue to defraud; that vows for its fellow men and does not defraud them; that does not give money to usury. Merchants, whoever acts in that vein will abound in riches and, in the end, will enjoy eternal life".[14]

On reading these words, it is easy to think that it would have been a good thing for these basic ethical principles to have been satisfied since the fifteenth century

---

[12] Alasdair MacIntyre, *After Virtue*, Duckworth, 1985 (second corrected edition with Proscript), 27–31.

[13] Luis Perdices also insists on "the abandonment of production activities, which derived from contempt for work, as living off the capital that is not the result of work was a thing of nobles", *La Economía Política de la Decadencia de Castilla en el siglo XVII*, Síntesis, Barcelona, 1996, 42.

[14] The translation into Spanish is by Josep Corell, Professor of Latin Philology of the University of Valencia.

until our days, in trade and in the production of wealth, in the banks, but also in political and social life, as a whole. That hopefully, swindle, fraud and usury would have been eradicated from daily life.

Even so, the tradesperson is not a moral character, he is not the incarnation of a moral ideal or the producer of material wealth. It is not surprising that Ramiro de Maeztu, after returning from a trip to the United States in 1925, enthusiastic about its economic prosperity, stated in *The reverential sense of money*: "My ideal would consist of multiplying the leaders of industry, the model farmers, the great bankers, the businessmen (…) in Spanish-speaking countries. It is much harder to set up a business creating wealth than to distribute our fortune amongst the poor and go into a convent".[15]

Perhaps this is one of the reasons why Spain, although it has an excellent geo-strategic position for trade, did not prosper economically as other nations did. Its much appreciated ways of life were not associated with the creation or with the exchange of wealth.

And it is true that, rummaging in the literary world, hardly any novels or plays can be found whose characters are businessmen or bankers, and who become heroes that are worth emulating. As far as I remember, *El señor Esteve* by Santiago Rusiñol (1907) or the five parts of *La ceniza fue árbol* by Ignacio Agustí (1943–1972) are exceptions. As is, more recently, that Peruvian businessman, Felícito Yanaqué, whose story is told by Mario Vargas Llosa in *El héroe discreto*. Felícito Yanaqué, the owner of a small transport company, Narihualá, appears as the honest businessman, who is willing to risk his life and the lives of the people who are dearest to him so as not to be extorted by the gangsters of his hometown, Piura. The motto that governs his life "never let yourself be trampled on" was learnt from his father and he never forgets it. That is why he is worthy of the opinion that Doctor Castro has of him, that he is an ethical man, ethical to the tips of his toes, one of the few that he has ever met. Felícito Yanaqué, who, in a broad sense, is in line with the Spanish world, is one of the exceptions of a literature that does not usually tell tales about exemplary businessmen.

And the fact is that things have not improved much lately in Spain, in this regard. Progressive thinking does not include businessmen or bankers among its characters, among its heroes, in its stories. Neither have Marxism, anarchism or progressive Christianity in our country. But, the conservatives have not made an effort, either, to write stories that present the positive part of the business world. And the crises that we have been suffering since 2007 are writing the last chapter of a story in which those heroic tales have been rejected.

If we were to take the pulse of our society, the characters of present-day Spain could be the Athlete, such as Rafael Nadal, or indeed, Lionel Messi or Cristiano Ronaldo, the Singer, which a lot of young people would like to be due to their social success, the unavoidable Rogue, who is a white-collar worker today, and as someone very rightly told me, the Civil Servant. Not so much because civil servants are

[15] Ramiro de Maeztu, *El sentido reverencial del dinero*, Editora Nacional, Madrid, 1957, p. 139.

a moral ideal worth imitating, but precisely because they have a secure job that prevents them from running business risks.

Certainly, the businessman or – even less so – the Banker, would not form part of those moral ideals, of those characters who incarnate the ethical core of an era. Does the business activity not provide society with any good things?

3.5 The Meaning of Business Activity

"Life is not the one that you lived –said Gabriel García Márquez at the start of his autobiography –, but the one that you remember and how you remember it to narrate it".[16] And, it is true that stories are selective reconstructions of the past, often connected to an idealised vision of the future. But it is no less true that the essential part of those narrations, to be good stories, include two things, at least: (1) they should try to transmit values that are able to be in tune with the people, with the values embedded in the brain synapses of its target public, giving *meaning* to the facts and data, and (2) those stories should be true, should respond to the reality, in this case, of the business activity.

That is why it is essential to ask what is the meaning of business activity in modern society, what is the goal whereby it claims social legitimacy, and tell stories whose argument places axiological emphasis on the good work of the company, aimed at reaching that goal.

The goal of business activity in the modern world, the goal whereby it takes on a meaning and social legitimacy, consists in giving the profit from its products and services to all those who are affected by it, thus helping construct good societies, by obtaining the business profit that is comprised of tangible and intangible goods. It is obvious that enterprises must obtain profits to be competitive in an environment of uncertainty, but the legitimate way of doing this and also the most intelligent, because it increases the probability of the enterprise's survival in the mid and long term, consists in seeking a profit for all those affected by its activity.

Societies expect enterprises to generate real tangible and intangible wealth, to create jobs, to carry out technological transfer, to train professionals, to be a source of innovation, to strengthen social capital networks. And, recently, a new suggestion now complements the above, a suggestion aimed at enterprises of any size: to actively collaborate in the defence of human rights and in the empowerment of the basic human capabilities.[17]

Because it is impossible to achieve respect for human rights everywhere on earth if enterprises do not join in with that task, it is impossible to reach the constantly

[16] *Vivir para contarla*, Mondadori, Barcelona, 2002, p. 7.

[17] Adela Cortina, "Empresa y Derechos Humanos", Real Academia de Ciencias Morales y Políticas, Madrid, 2011.

postponed Sustainable Development Goals without them; in short, it is impossible to achieve fair societies without the cooperation of enterprises.[18]

In fact, in countries with a high level of corruption, good enterprises help break the vicious circle of malpractices and start the virtuous circle of good practices, fostering compliance with contracts, showing that it is possible and advisable to integrate workers into the running of the enterprise, trying to satisfy the legitimate expectations of those affected by its activity, making transparency a habit of daily life and making trust a well-known value.

And, the fact is that without the necessary trust for banks, savings banks and enterprises to operate, without the know-how provided by those who work in the organisations, without an ethical climate, without cohesion, without awareness of one's own identity, and without veracity, enterprises do not operate well, with the subsequent harm for society. On the other hand, enterprises that provide those tangible and intangible goods, create a new culture, they tap into their "moral resources" and benefit their environment with this.[19] As Sen correctly says, an ethical enterprise is a public good.[20]

This series of goods that enterprises can and must provide, seem to be synthesised in some way in the strategic management proposal that R.E. Freeman put forward for discussion in 1984 with his stakeholders approach. With this approach, the game of the enterprise would be a positive-sum game, not a zero-sum game: the more stakeholders benefit from the enterprise, the better the enterprise will operate.[21] Our working group interprets this approach as "that of those affected by the business activity", and one must acknowledge that it has triumphed in the discourse of business ethics, in the discourse of corporate social responsibility, in the discourse of shared values of Porter and Kramer,[22] and in the discourse of the Sustainable Development Goals.[23] And it is clear that, if it were to be taken seriously, it would make the businessman a collaborator in the task of constructing good societies.[24] Taking this seriously would mean presenting businessmen as allies of the States and of the citizens in the task of constructing a more human world.

---

[18] Onora O'Neill "Agents of Justice", en Thomas Pogge (comp.), *Global Justice*, Blackwell, Oxford, 2001.

[19] Domingo García-Marzá, *Ética empresarial*, Trotta, Madrid, 2004.

[20] Amartya Sen, "Does business ethics make economic sense?", *Business Ethics Quaterly*, 3/1 (1993), 45–54; "Ética de la empresa y desarrollo económico", en Adela Cortina (ed.), *Construir confianza*, Trotta, Madrid, 2003, 39–53; Jesús Conill, *Horizontes de economía ética*, Tecnos, Madrid, 2004.

[21] R.E. Freeman, *Strategic Management: A Stakeholder Approach*, Pitman, Ballinger, Boston; José A. Moreno, "Responsabilidad social corporativa y competitividad: una visión desde la empresa", en *Revista Valenciana de Economía y Hacienda*, n° 12, III (2004), 9–50.

[22] M.E. Porter & M.R. Kramer, "Creating shared values", *Harvard Business Review*, 89 (February), 62–77.

[23] Jeffrey Sachs, *The Age of Sustainable Development*, Columbia University Press, 2014.

[24] Adela Cortina, Jesús Conill, Agustín Domingo, Domingo García Marzá, *Ética de la empresa*, Trotta, Madrid, 1994.

And, as it is the task of ethics to ask, in the case of each social activity, which is the goal whereby it is socially legitimised and what practices are appropriate to pursue it, it would be advisable to introduce professional and trade ethics into the curricula as a subject, in this case, in business sciences and economics. Indeed, a society shows that it believes a type of knowledge is essential to exercise a profession -as is the case of ethics- when it includes it in the curricula so that future professionals can reflect upon the goals of their profession, on how to attain those goals in a more honest and cautious manner, what ethical problems they may encounter in their daily work. In short, what converts them into professionals and not into simple technicians, even less into manipulators.

3.6 From Statements to Actions. True Stories

However, and as we have mentioned, the businessman is not perceived as an ally to change the world for the better either in the global or in the local environment. Perhaps because, despite the fact that since the 1970s of the last century the business world has been flooded with ethical expressions –value management, ethical codes, ethical audits, corporate social responsibility, good governance codes, ethical banking, supportive banking, fair trade, responsible consumption, responsibility and ethics observatories, ethical certifications, shared values–, the crises that we have been suffering have spoken volumes of the *statements* not having been reflected in *actions*. Therefore, people do not perceive enterprises, and even less banking institutions, as allies in the construction of a better society.

Insofar as bank institutions are concerned, the astronomical wages of their directors, which have been sustained despite the institutions having received public money and even having been put into administration, the enormous gap between declared assets and the assets that really exist, creative accountancy, opaque products, the refusal to loan money, have gradually created the image of really immoral institutions and people. Not only would they not be heroes, but they would be antiheroes, not arousing the sympathy prompted by the humble rogue of the Golden Age, not moving to compassion, like Lazarillo de Tormes or Don Pablos, the Buscón, because now they are white-collar workers and we are talking about millionaire amounts.

Enterprises, on their part, have often been forced to close or reduce personnel to their regret; but on other occasions, they have resorted to unnecessary collective dismissals, they have taken advantage of the moment to get rid of workers without trying to relocate them, without prior notice and under legally doubtful, if not to say illegal, conditions.

There is no doubt that these actions are harmful for those who are directly affected and for society as a whole, but they are also harmful for enterprises and for banking institutions, which need to generate a good reputation to survive in the mid and long term.

On the other hand, these malpractices frustrate any attempt to enhance the figure of the businessman, to convert him into a moral character, whose work deserves recognition.

According to the 2013 Eurobarometer, 50% of Spanish people consider that the influence of enterprises in the country is positive, and 46% consider that it is negative. But those polled distinguish between large enterprises and SMEs. Forty-three percent positively rate large companies and 53% rate them negatively; whilst 76% positively rate SMEs and only 19% rate them negatively. These data coincide with the METROSCOPIA survey, published in the newspaper *El Pais* on 10 January 2013. According to the survey, SMEs deserve the approval of 89%, whilst large enterprises deserve the approval of only 49%. These data are very similar to those of neighbouring countries. And the fact is that a large percentage of Spanish people understand that the actions of businessmen are motivated exclusively by selfish interest and that they benefit from the work of others.

By way of conclusion then, we can say that if we want enterprises to form part of the organisations that the citizens consider as allies in order to leave the crises behind and to form good societies, storytelling is necessary, but the stories told must be good. This means the narrations must have axiological frameworks of societies that consider that human rights and environmental sustainability cannot be waived. *But, above all stories must be told that, through narration, express the meaning of the business activity and they also must be true.*

Because, when the actions do not match the statements, when there is constant disagreement between what is done and what is told, mistrust prevails, and all meaning is lost. A loss that is suicide for the people and for the enterprises.

If one of the indications to leave the crises behind and construct a fair economy consists of enhancing the figure of the businessman, of making him one of the characters of our era, then it is a wise thing to recover that phrase that once became famous: *in search of excellence,* but giving that word, "excellence" the strength that it had in the Homeric world.[25]

The excellent, the virtuous character of the Homeric poems of the *Iliad* and the *Odyssey,* were outstanding in terms of skills and abilities, such as Priamus in prudence, Hector in value, Achilles in speed, Ulysses in wisdom, Andromache in loyalty. But above all, they placed these skills at the service of the community, which needed them to live and to live well. Thus, the people admired the feats of their heroes. And thus they remained gratefully in their memories.

[25] Homer, *Iliad, Odyssey*; Tom J. Peters und Robert H. Waterman, *In Search of Excellence*, Harper & Row, New York, 1982.

Chapter 4
The Honest Businessperson: Cosmopolitan Theory and Cultural Praxis (The Example of Denmark and Scandinavia)

Jacob Dahl Rendtorff

Abstract This paper discusses the relationship between a Kantian, cosmopolitan economic ethics and business ethics and the theory and practice of the honest businessperson in Scandinavia. A cosmopolitan business ethics is the prerequisite for accountability, ethics and legitimacy of companies in the global social and economic system. Accordingly, the need for a cosmopolitan business ethics in a complex and hypermodern society is considered as a basis for the theory and practice of the honest businessperson and merchant. Consequently, it is possible to formulate a philosophical theory of corporate governance in the global context of economic business. This raises the question of how such an idea of the cosmopolitan economics ethics and business ethics is expressed in the different cultural practices of the ideals of the respectable businessperson in different countries and regions in the world. In the present article, the author discusses the example of Denmark and Scandinavia. With this investigation, we can see that cosmopolitan business ethics is realized with the concepts of trust, transparency and integrity through corporate governance and with a focus on integration of accountability into corporate strategy of business firms. The values of the Protestant ethics of equality and asceticism are important aspects of this institutionalization business ethics. The economic ethics of the Scandinavian economy is very closely connected to the values of sustainability and corporate social responsibility in Denmark and Scandinavia.

4.1 Cosmopolitan Theory of the Honest Businessperson

Today, society is experiencing major challenges of business ethics. We can for example mention the financial crisis, the climate crisis and the ecological crisis. In addition, history shows the social and economic change from modernity to postmodernism

J. D. Rendtorff (✉)
Department of Social Sciences and Business, University of Roskilde, Roskilde, Denmark
e-mail: jacrendt@ruc.dk

C. Lütge, C. Strosetzki (eds.), *The Honorable Merchant – Between Modesty and Risk-Taking*, Ethical Economy 56, https://doi.org/10.1007/978-3-030-04351-3_4

and hypermodernity. In this context, society experiences the emergence of the experience economy and the search for authenticity, as the American authors Pine und Gilmore demonstrate in their Monography *Authenticity. What consumers really want!*[1] This social condition can also be described as an anesthetization of the economy with a concomitant generalization of consumption and hedonism. In political theory, we can speak of the movement from the welfare state to the competition state, as it has been analyzed by the Danish political scientist Ove Kaj Pedersen.[2] This development is further influenced by the international confrontation of cultures as a "Clash of Civilizations" in global society[3] and this intensifies the challenge of mutual understanding in global society. Globalization is a challenge for business ethics and makes a global cosmopolitan responsibility of business corporations necessary.

In this context, we can say that we need a cosmopolitan and Kantian business ethics.[4] Consequently, the theory of the honest businessperson must be cosmopolitan, because such an economic ethics implies a new formulation of the concept of the venerable businessperson and merchant in today's context. A cosmopolitan business ethics is the prerequisite for accountability, ethics and legitimacy of the companies of the global social and economic system. Thus, the need for a new business ethics in this context implies that business ethics and economic ethics must be cosmopolitan in order to meet the international challenges of contemporary social and economic developments.

The understanding of such a need arose above all in the context of my research on the subject of the balanced company, which has been published in our book *The Balanced Company Organizing for the 21st Century*.[5] The concept of balance moves here in the foreground. Balance refers to the need to develop environmental and sustainability-oriented corporate governance and the art of controlling complex relationships, with ethical principles playing an important role in business management and organization.

The focus of the present contribution on the concept of the honest businessperson is therefore an effort to contribute to the formulation of ethical principles that can function as the basis for a cosmopolitan business ethics. In this sense, this research on the balanced company and cosmopolitan business ethics can be considered as a development of the argument of the monograph on *Power and Principle in the Market Place: On Ethics and Economics*.[6]

The tendencies of the present towards a more deep economic and social crisis, for example the current experience of poverty crisis, the financial crisis or the ecological crisis, illustrate very clearly that the crisis is a crisis of the system and

---

[1] Pine und Gilmore (2007).

[2] See Pedersen (2011, 2014).

[3] Huntington (1997).

[4] Rendtorff (2009, 2018).

[5] This was a part of the research of the research group *Management in Transition* at Roskilde University, Denmark (2008–2013). The book was a publication about business ethics and social responsibility of business. See Jensen et al. (2013).

[6] Rendtorff (2010).

emphasize the urgency of developing a cosmopolitan business ethics.[7] Efforts to find alternative ways out of the crisis are for example facing the difficulty to find a capitalist growth society in times of environmental and climate crisis; the "green growth" does not really exist, as you may say: "Green growth may not help – is it to have your cake and eat it too". Thus, we need "a great transition" from the systemic crisis to a green economics, that is, an economically sustainable society, as the Danish journalist Jørgen Steen Nielsen has proposed.[8]

In other words, we are confronted with the need for an economy of scarcity dealing with limited resources. World society and international businesses need to take this into account when formulating business and management plans. Indeed, the questions are Do we need new concepts of economics when we face the global challenges that we need to solve? Do we need another economy? Is another economy possible? What are the constituents of such another more sustainable economy? To answer these questions we must not only look at economic answers, but must discuss the questions in economic, philosophical and ethical perspectives.

Nevertheless, what is business or management philosophy? The business or management philosophy can be considered as a combination of ethics, leadership and philosophy.[9] The task of business or management philosophy includes the responsibility, ethics and legitimacy of business corporations.[10] Accordingly, economic philosophy can be considered as the political philosophy of business and management. Economic actions do not only imply an instrumental legitimacy, but also a democratic legitimacy. Applied business and management philosophy seeks a functional legitimacy with regard to areas that lie outside economic activity (democracy and politics). With this turn of economics, business and management, philosophy also deals with topics of political theory of organization and leadership of companies.

What does a global business or management philosophy mean? It deals with ethical values and moral management of companies, with the conditions for developing an integrity-based leadership, with the meaning of individual judgment and with the ability the leaders to ethically assess moral dilemmas, with complexity and balance in leadership as well as with the relevance of sustainability for entrepreneurial decisions and decision-making.[11] Global business ethics is based on the development of global ethics management where companies are considered as global economic responsible actors, which follow various codes of conduct for companies such as compliance codes, corporate governance or corporate social responsibility (CSR). In addition, various theories of social philosophy provide an important guide for the answer of ethical questions in the global context. Here we can mention theories of power (biopower and global governmentality) by Foucault; Theories of capitalism, like the concept project society and the new spirit of capitalism by Boltanski; theories of social development, such as hypermodernity

[7] Rendtorff (2009, 2018).

[8] Nielsen (2012).

[9] Rendtorff (2009, 2013, 2018).

[10] Rendtorff (2009, 2018).

[11] Rendtorff (2013, 2018).

and the aesthetic capitalism by Lipovetsky; Theories of universal and global responsibility by Levinas and Sartre; and finally theories of deconstruction by Derrida, where justice as such is an ideal that cannot be deconstructed, but opens for critique of injustice in particular social and organizational contexts.[12] These philosophical theories are on the one hand a helpful support of the economic philosophy and philosophy of management; on the other hand, they document the need to rethink business ethics in a cosmopolitan way.

Then what is cosmopolitan business philosophy and business ethics? A cosmopolitan business ethics can contribute to analyze the different theories of the business ethics by placing the philosophy of Immanuel Kant in a global perspective in order to give legitimacy to the economic ethics of global, political and democratic aspects of the global economic market. At the same time, this cosmopolitan approach includes an integrative business ethics that seeks to make the link of the current problems of business ethics in connection with sustainability issues, human rights and global responsibility. The need such an analysis is illustrated by concrete examples from economic practice including: the oil drilling platform "Deep Water Horizon" with the oil spill in the Gulf of Mexico; the fashion industry and its misfortune in the factory in Bangladesh; the shipping company Maersk and the attempts to blackmail governments to get new oil fields; IKEA and the question of cultural differences with regard to discrimination against women (the company has taken out all women from its sale catalog in Saudi Arabia to avoid to give them a veil or show them without a veil). It is the task of a cosmopolitan business ethics is to shape and define concepts and theories that lead to a responsible contribution to solve such conflicts in a sustainable perspective. Two important terms in this context would be the responsibility and integrity, for example, the integration of human rights in leadership and management in order to help to legitimize the leadership of international companies. In addition, the concept of the political corporation and its global economic citizenship must be defined and understood in a cosmopolitan way.

The historical basis of cosmopolitan business ethics is the philosophical concept of cosmopolitanism (Individual freedom and global governance). In the context of a global economy, the concept of cosmopolitanism is defined as a global citizenship, as "world citizenship", which determines the application of this term companies in the sense of a "global and world citizenship of business and corporations". Kant's political philosophy and ethics as well as the concept of the cosmopolitan responsibility of human beings and business is central for developing a philosophical rational ground for global business ethics. In his founding of the metaphysics of morals, *Grundlegung zur Metaphysik der Sitten*, Kant formulates the categorical imperative and he grounds his ideas in the universal norms. This can be used as the basis for the institutionalization of responsibility in world citizenship and in the democratization of economic markets with the help of reflective judgment as the basis for ethical decision-making in business organizations.

The various German theories of business ethics can be analyzed in the perspective of these theories of cosmopolitanism.[13] When the order ethics according to

[12] See Rendtorff (2014).

[13] See Rendtorff (2016, 2018).

Homann and Lütge (2004/2013) criticizes Kant's image of humankind and human morality in many ways, it affirms the need for institutional and legal regulation of the economy. On the other hand, Steinmann's republican economic ethics of corporate citizenship and peace tries to use a business ethics as a republican philosophy of peace, according to which the business companies should establish moral leadership and contribute to a global peace order. Even the philosophers Maring and Heidbrink understand business ethics as a universal ethics of responsibility, according to which corporate responsibility is given a great deal of importance. The Kantian business ethics, according to Dierksmeier, postulates that we should think universal norms serve as the basis of cosmopolitanism. Added to this we can mention the integrative business ethics according to Peter Ulrich, that tries to give and ethical foundation for economic action and ethics and economic rationality are united with each other in a socioeconomic rationality of the communicative ethical rationality in society. In Koslowski's theory, the principles of an ethical economy are developed and formulated as the basis of cosmopolitanism, and Wieland sets up a governance-ethics in the service of a global value management. With Küng, finally, economic ethics can be formulated as a global ethos of the world community.[14]

The basics of cosmopolitan business ethics can, as Matthias Kettner argues, also be justified by critical theory. Here, we can refer to the critique of market capitalism and the search for communicative recognition, as suggested by critical theory. A critical cosmopolitanism implies, according to the somewhat other critical perspective of the post-structuralism Michel Foucault, an analysis of the genesis of the liberal and neo-liberal concepts of cosmopolitanism and global world politics that shows that we are currently in a situation of a global economic freedom of free action on capitalist markets without political freedom. The global inequality between rich and poor has risen sharply, as the French economist, Piketty has demonstrated it in his book about capital in the twenty-first century.[15] Accordingly, the capitalist economy gives rich countries power over of the poor countries and maintains them in an economic dependency relationship with each other. The result is a greater inequality between all the countries in the world.

As suggested the cosmopolitan dimension of business ethics can be developed with Kant's philosophy. The existential dimension of business ethics, on the other hand, can be based on the work of the Danish philosopher Søren Kierkegaard. Nevertheless, what is really the existential dimension of business ethics? In Denmark, different business philosophers have tried to justify the reflective dimension of corporate governance existentialistically based on different interpretations of the philosophy of Søren Kierkegaard. Existentialist thinking about leadership means to integrate Kierkegaard's philosophical categories into the ethical discourse of economics. In this sense, Kierkegaard provides us with a horizon of reflection that makes it possible for us to get a better understanding of business philosophy and ethics.[16]

---

[14] See Rendtorff (2016, 2018).

[15] Piketty (2014).

[16] Rendtorff (2008).

The connection between Kant and Kierkegaard is important for understanding ethics in organizations. We can illustrate this by looking at Hannah Arendt's *Eichmann in Jerusalem. An Essay on the Banality of Evil* (1964) that can be read as a book about the lack of existential choice and responsibility in organizations. In this book, Arendt analyzes the relationship of administration and leadership, showing that leadership is a matter of personal integrity and moral judgment. The problem in Eichmann's case was that he had no understanding of morality and humanity. He could only follow and obey the ideological and bureaucratic rules and precepts of National Socialism, but without being able to judge the justice and morality of these rules and commandments. In this sense, he was "banal", because he was incapable of moral thinking. And this is the basis for Arendt's formulation the problem of the banality of evil in the context of the organization's bureaucracy: "It was as though in those last minutes he was summing up the lesson that his long course in human wickedness had taught us – the lesson of the fearsome, word-and-thought-defying banality of evil".[17]Arendt and Kierkegaard discuss the need for moral integrity and identity. Arendt connects Kantian philosophy with existentialism and raises the problem of personal responsibility in organizations. From this ethical and philosophical perspective, it becomes apparent that Eichmann is a person who cannot think morally: he is a bureaucrat and a manager who knows no personal responsibility and he is (morally) dumb, blind and deaf.

How can we apply the thinking and the categories of Søren Kierkegaard in management thinking and business philosophy? As you know, Kierkegaard distinguishes between the "petit bourgeois," the esthetician, the ethicist, and the religious. These names are categories of life as well as of personal existence and they can serve as analytical tools for business ethics and business philosophy.[18] The understanding of the manager as "petit bourgeois" means: The manager is not really aware of his position as a manager and maybe he is not himself as an authentic person, but alienated because he does not really want to be himself. In the case of the aesthetic manager, the manager lives and acts like a hedonist; he is looking for fun and entertainment – management is a game for him. The ethical manager understands love and the relationship to other people as essential for the development of the company – ethics is here an expression of love. The religious Manager does his work with the utmost commitment and he controls his company with sincerity and respect for God and his faith, despite his deep knowledge of the absurdity of life where God is transcendent and a kind of paradox for human reason and rationality. The religious manager A has his faith, but he is without deep reflection about the foundations of his company. For the religious manager assuming leadership responsibility means, however, really to bear Jesus' cross. Here leadership is, as opposed to the figure of Eichmann's really a matter of personal existence and of the ability to connect existence and working life. In this sense, the honest businessperson or honorable merchant can only act with integrity when he or she is moving from the aesthetics and ethic levels to the deeper and more reflective level of religious existence.

[17]Arendt (1964), p. 252.

[18]Rendtorff (2008).

It becomes clear that business ethics and economic ethics are grounded in ethical theories and principles that have a deep philosophical foundation.[19] Thus, a concrete application of philosophy and terminology of Kant and Kierkegaard on business ethics is possible, especially in relation to the concepts of cosmopolitanism and existential dimensions of management. Now in order to formulate such a theoretical business ethics or to be able to formulate an applied philosophy we must consider business ethics theories in the framework of different ethical theories such as deontology, virtue ethics, utilitarianism, communitarian ethics, existentialism, etc. These theories concern the foundation of application of ethical analysis in relation concrete actions and areas of action within ethics and philosophy of management. In this context, we can formulate a theory of integration of the cosmopolitan dimension of ethical principles and with principles and ideas of respect for the human person. The principles of respect for the human person are autonomy, human dignity, integrity and vulnerability. Although these terms originally were established within bioethics, they can have an important application within business ethics.[20] Thus, in ethical analysis, the application of ethical principles and theories is used in specific cases in order to solve and address real-life action dilemmas of business ethics.

Furthermore, a cosmopolitan business ethics requires a critical assessment of the accountability of the various stakeholders (interest groups) from the perspective of cosmopolitan philosophy of management.[21] Such a stakeholder analysis needs to consider different stakes or interests, such as: for example: (a) Global corporate governance: Shareholder responsibility, (b) Responsibility for employees, (c) Responsibility for consumers, (d) responsibility for local governments and (e) responsibility for the environment and climate protection. The term of responsibility used here follows with Hans Jonas the Kantian approach to cosmopolitanism. Power and responsibility are closely connected, but in this approach, we also experience a moralization of responsibility; we are responsible for the whole world, as the famous existentialist philosopher Jean Paul Sartre has said.

With this application of cosmopolitan business ethics to issues of stakeholder management, it is also possible to use philosophy of management to contribute to the development of a global theory of stakeholder justice. In addition, the development of a decision model for cosmopolitan business ethics is an important part of this effort to develop such a global theory of philosophy of management. To do this we can develop a model of ethical theories and principles for the important dimensions of analysis in an ethical decision-making model. This includes analysis of interpretation and explanation of ethical dilemmas; Analysis of the consequences of social responsibility and civic duties; Analysis of laws and ethical rules (Codes of conduct) that lead to a decision and evaluation as the final result of the ethical analysis of possible decision-making in ethical management.[22]

---

[19] Rendtorff (2009).

[20] Rendtorff and Kemp (2000), Rendtorff (2009).

[21] Bonnafous-Boucher and Rendtorff (2014).

[22] Rendtorff (2009, 2018).

The cosmopolitan business ethics can be determined more closely with the development of the concept of reflective judgment. The reflective judgment is the ability to apply ethical principles and ethical theories to new concrete decision-making situations. With the French Philosopher Paul Ricoeur we can define three levels of application of judgment: (1) the level of wisdom and practical knowledge; (2) the level of universal deontological norms; and (3) the level of reflective judgment. This analysis allows in addition to work with a combination of ethical and legal norms of judgments.

Thus, judging is considered as a major point of development of the ethical strategy of the cosmopolitan business ethics, economic ethics and philosophy of management. Such a cosmopolitan approach to economic ethics in the field of leadership, business administration and organization work with strategies of sustainability development and stakeholder dialogues combined with the general integration of economy, environment and leadership on a global level. Thus, the strategies of a cosmopolitan economic ethics as a theory of the honest businessperson or merchant contribute to the establishment of the values of global responsible management, social responsibility, stakeholder management and global economic citizenship as fundamental values of cosmopolitan philosophy of management.

4.2 Cultural Practice of the Honorable Businessperson: Perspectives from Scandinavia

This raises the question of how such an idea of cosmopolitan business ethics is realized in the cultural practice of the ideals of the honorable businessperson and merchant in different countries and regions of the world. This can be discussed with the example of Denmark and Scandinavia. However, we will begin with a small digression to America. The reason for this is that the spirit of the honorable businessperson fits well with the example of the so-called "Warning Flags" that have been used in corporate business ethics education in the US to illustrate ethical and as economic warning signs for ethical problems in big American companies: "Well, may be just this once", "No one will ever know", "It doesn't matter how it gets done as long as it gets done", "Everyone does it", "Shred that document", "We can hide it", "No one will get hurt", "What' in it for me?", "This will destroy the competition", "We didn't have that conversation", "This is a 'non meeting'". An ethical quick quiz in order to make businesspeople aware of ethical problems contains important questions of such ethical warning signs:

> 1. Are my actions legal? 2. Am I fair and Honest? 3. Will my action stand the test of time? 4. How will I feel about myself afterwards? 5. How will it look in the newspaper? 6. Will I sleep soundly to night? 7. What would I tell my child to do? 8. How would I feel if my family, friends, and neighbors knew what I was doing?"[23]

[23] Rendtorff (2009, 2018).

With this idea of honesty and integrity as the basic concept of the honorable businessperson and merchant the question that arises is, how can the honest businessperson be "studied"? In a historical perspective, we can go back in the tradition of economic theory and philosophy in modern times. Adam Smith formulated a theory of moral feelings in 1759, even before the culmination of his economic theory with *The Wealth of Nations*. For Smith moral feelings and indeed our moral sentiments can indeed be proposed as the foundation of economic action and thus we can say that the ethics of honorable businessperson function as an integrated parts of the capitalist economic system. With the economic sociologist Marc Granovetter we can speak of the idea of embeddedness of economic activities in social and cultural systems and norms.[24] The sociologist Jens Beckert joins this theory by explaining the institutionalization of action as patterns of integrity and trust that can be understood as the foundation of the economic systems.[25] The social conditions of economic action imply the virtues of the honorable businessperson that are important to ensure their functionality. With this is it possible to be critical and refute the thesis of separation of economy and morality that among others the sociologist Niklas Luhmann has proposed. In contrast to Luhmann authors like Axel Honneth and his associates try to capture the social conditions of the economic system, when they propose critically to discuss the moralization of the market as an important aspect of effective economic action.[26] Terms such as trust, integrity and mutual respect for each other represent the foundation for this institutionalization and socialization of economic action. In this sense, mutual recognition is an important dimension of the rules of successful economic action and represents a normative condition of possibility of the efficiency of economic markets.[27] Thus, with the norms of the integrity we find the possibility of the institutionalization of the connection between economics and ethics in economic life. Perhaps this institutionalization of ethical norms function as a new interpretation of the cultural order of the economy, which is an important element of a general system of economic order in society. Accordingly, the connection between economics and ethics is institutionalized in economic life with the norms of the integrity and trust. This institutionalization of ethical norms as a new interpretation of the cultural order of the economy can perhaps be interpreted within the concept of order economy as an expression of the social and economic system of society.

The idea of the honorable businessperson and merchant in Scandinavia and Denmark can in this perspective be considered as an element of an ethical turn of order liberalism. In contrast to the German order liberalism, dealing with the order of legal framework of the economic interactions, we can say that the ethical norms in the Scandinavian countries are based on the concepts of integrity and trust and it also gives integrity a very special importance for the functionality of the economic interactions. In the Scandinavian countries Denmark, Norway and Sweden, the con-

[24] Granovetter (1995, 2000).

[25] Beckert (1997).

[26] Luhmann (1999).

[27] Herzog und Honneth (2014).

cept of the honorable businessperson and merchant is not so much to be seen as based on the individual level. Rather the figure of the honest businessperson can be considered as a part of collective and institutional involvement of individuals in the institutions of society and business. In the Scandinavian countries, trust and integrity are considered as very important elements of a collective, social capital. The term of social capital designates in this context the basis for the social conditions for market interactions.[28] Accordingly, we can say that research on social capital helps to understand the concept of the honest businessperson and merchant in the economic and social institutions of society. Trust and social capital are essential aspects of the institutional basis of economic interactions in Scandinavian welfare states. As stakeholder societies, they are dependent on democratic equality and the democratic foundation of decisions in market and society are central elements that characterize the welfare institutions – despite a certain movement of these societies in the direction of becoming more competitive states, where social interactions are accomplished by social competition.

Scandinavian welfare states are characterized by an institutional inclusion and integration of the idea of the honest businessperson in the fundamental values of society. For example, transparency is an important value, which is reflected in the almost complete absence of corruption in state and society and from a transaction-economic perspective, we can say that commercial transactions are passing almost without corruption. Honesty, integrity and trust are considered as an institutionalized part of society and of the cultural and social values of the economic system. Historically, we can thus mention social solidarity of consumer organizations as something that has had particular importance for the emergence of a society of equality and transparency. In this way, the welfare state has been important historically as the basis of a general negotiation economy with a large element of a dynamics of self-regulation of the participants and citizens in society in the economic interactions. This idea of the negotiation economy is developed by by Ove Kaj Pedersen and Klaus Nielsen in an important book with the title *The Negotiation Economy*.[29]

The values of trust and integrity are in Scandinavia and Denmark closely linked to the concept of equality. This is called the "Law of Jante"(Janteloven), which means that no one should be considered as better than others and that everyone are equal and that no would should be different from the others. Equality is also understood as being equal in culture, identity and this is the basis for equal rights. Consequences of this is the idea of strong equality in the business life and economic systems are based on this strong equality as the informal structure of business and economic life. We can for example mention the informal structure of business companies and the abandonment of rigid hierarchies in society as a result of this culture of equality. Moreover, the Scandinavian understanding of equality implies a behavioral structure of valuing group equality over the individual different, for example with regard to the critical and negative attitude to individual success on the dispense

[28] Fukuyama (1995) and Putnam (2000).

[29] Nielsen und Pedersen (1989).

of the group which leads to negative reactions and sanctions by the group towards the individual. in the economy we see that this cultural sanctioning of inequality means that a successful businessperson and merchant always is very modest and avoids to show off or talk too much about his economic success in business life.

This combination of equality law, trust and integrity can be considered the ideal of Protestant ethics in Scandinavia. The values of equality, trust and integrity are closely connected in business life with the requirement of a strict work ethic. This is also, where the seriousness of Kierkegaard's philosophy plays a role. Thus, it is a commandment and divine demand to live authentically, which is an important part of the Protestant business ethics in Scandinavia. The commandment of Protestantism is to work hard to protect yourself and to take care of your own family. In traditional Protestant ethics this commandment and demand is also associated with a Protestant work ethic. The money should not always be spent, but donated, saved and used rationally. Such values are historically seen very strong in the Scandinavian countries. With this, we see how the welfare states follow the idea of Max Weber, who maintained that there is a close connection between Protestantism and capitalism.[30] In the Protestant ethic, hard work, work ethic and asceticism are very important. In addition, the ascetic life can accordingly be considered as integrated part of the life of honest businessman and merchant in Scandinavia.

In contemporary economic life, this Protestant conception of business ethics deals with the dictates of sustainability and corporate social responsibility has been institutionalized.[31] We see the development of this with initiatives of sustainability corporate governance, ethical business management, value management and corporate social responsibility in corporate governance. In the current economic life this Protestant conception of business ethics has been institutionalized with the dictates of sustainability and corporate social responsibility. We see this development in initiatives of sustainability and corporate responsibility in management, ethical business management, value management, governance ethics and emphasis on corporate citizenship, stakeholder management and corporate governance with respect for social dimensions and environmental conditions (triple bottom-line management). Examples of companies who seek to implement such values of social responsibility and sustainability in their management and leadership of their corporations are Novo Nordisk, Maersk, Westas, IKEA and Carlsberg. These companies try to incorporate social responsibility into their models of business management and corporate governance. Accordingly, we can formulate the thesis that the notion of the honest businessperson is not just to be considered as an individual virtue, but that it also has to be defined as an institutional dimension of economic activity in society.

In Denmark, for example, it is significant that the practice of the honest businessperson today is closely connected with corporate social responsibility (CSR). Since the 1990s, CSR has played a major role in society and good business is closely linked to it in the social perception of the good business behavior by the citizens and customers. CSR is not only strategic and economically defined, but it is also under-

[30] Weber (1934).

[31] Rendtorff (2009).

stood as ethical, international and global dimension of the honest businessperson and good merchant. Thus, there is a clear link between CSR and cosmopolitan business ethics and the concept of responsible corporate management. The legislation concerning CSR in Denmark is based on a reporting practice in which the largest companies must report on their CSR activities, even though it is not specified what kind of activities business should have. Accordingly, in order not to lose face these companies need to set up CSR activities to produce good reports about the subject. These reports on CSR are based on the importance of self-regulation as an important instrument to govern the business firm. In this respect, the honest business is also institutionalized.

In conclusion, it can be said that cosmopolitan business ethics with the terms of trust, transparency and integrity are realized through corporate governance with the focus on CSR. The values of the Protestant ethics of equality and asceticism are important aspects of this institutionalization of ethical values of responsibility and honesty in economic life. Accordingly, the cosmopolitan ideals of business ethics and economic ethics are, in Denmark and Scandinavia, closely linked to the values of sustainability and CSR.

References

Arendt, Hannah. 1964. *Eichmann in Jerusalem. Essay on the banality of evil.* New York: Viking Press.

Beckert, Jens. 1997. *Grenzen des Marktes. Die Sozialen Grundlagen wirtschaftlicher Effizienz.* Frankfurt/New York: Campus Verlag.

Bonnafous-Boucher, Maria, und Jacob Dahl Rendtorff. 2014. *La théorie des parties prenantes*, La Collection Reperes. Vol. 627. Paris: Editions La Decouverte.

Fukuyama, Francis. 1995. *Trust. The social virtues and the creation of prosperity.* New York: Free Press.

Granovetter, Marc. 1995. *Getting a job. A study of contacts and careers.* Chicago: University of Chicago Press.

———. 2000. *Le marché autrement, sociologie contemporaine.* Paris: Descleede Brouwer.

Herzog, Lisa, und Axel Honneth (Hrgs). 2014. *Der Wert des Marktes. Ein ökonomisch-philosophischer Diskurs vom 18. Jahrhundert.* Frankfurt: Suhrkamp Verlag.

Homann, Karl, und Christoph Lutge (2004/2013). *Einführung in die Wirtschaftsethik* (3. Aufl.). Munster: LIT.

Huntington, Samuel P. 1997. *The clash of civilizations and the remaking of world order.* London: Simon and Schuster.

Jensen, Inger, John Damm Scheuer, und Jacob Dahl Rendtorff (Hrg.). 2013. *The balanced company: Organizing for the 21st century.* Farnham: Gower Publishing Ltd

Luhmann, Niklas. 1999. *Die Wirtschaft der Gesellschaft.* Frankfurt: Suhrkamp Verlag.

Nielsen, Jorgen Steen. 2012. *Den store Omstilling. Fra Systemkrise til gron Okonomi.* Kobenhavn: Informations forlag.

Nielsen, Klaus, und Ove K. Pedersen (Hrgs). 1989. *Forhandlingsokonomi i Norden.* Kobenhavn: Jurist og Okonomforbundets forlag.

Pedersen, Ove Kaj. 2011. *Konkurrencestaten.* Kobenhavn: Hans Reitzels forlag.

———. 2014. *Markedsstaten.* Kobenhavn: Hans Reitzels forlag.

Piketty, Thomas. 2014. *Capital in the twenty-first century.* Cambridge, MA: Belknap Press.

Pine, Joseph P., and James H. Gilmore. 2007. *Authenticity – What consumers really want*. Boston: Harvard Business School Press.
Putnam, Robert D. 2000. *Bowling alone. The collapse and revival of American community*. New York: Touchstone Books.
Rendtorff, Jacob Dahl. 2008. La sagesse pratique et l'ethique: Kierkegaard et le management. In *Le Singulier. Pensées kierkegaardiennes sur l'Individu*, hrsg. Peter Kemp und Karl Verstrynge, 95–105. Bruxelles: Vubpress – Academic and Scientific Publishers.
———. 2009. *Responsibility, ethics and legitimacy of corporations*. Copenhagen: Copenhagen Business School Press.
———. 2010. *Power and principle in the market place: On ethics and economics*. London: Ashgate.
———. 2013. Basic concepts of philosophy of management and corporations. In *Handbook of the philosophical foundations of business ethics*, hrsg. Christoph Luetge, 1361–1386. Dordrecht: Springer.
———. 2014. *French philosophy and social theory: A perspective for ethics and philosophy of management*, Ethical Economy 49. Niederlande: Springer.
———. 2016. Towards a global ethical economy. Different concepts of ethical economy in a cosmopolitan context. In *International Symposium Philosophies in Dialogue: Bridging the Great Philosophical Divides*. Chulalongkorn University in March 2015.
———. 2018. *Cosmopolitan business ethics. Towards a global philosophy of management*. London: Routledge.
Rendtorff, Jacob Dahl, and Peter Kemp. 2000. *Basic ethical principles in European bioethics and biolaw. Autonomy, dignity, integrity, vulnerability I-II*. Copenhagen/Barcelona: Center for Ethics and Law.
Weber, Max. 1934. *Die protestantische Ethik und der Geist des Kapitalismus*. Tubingen: Mohr.

Chapter 5
Voluntary Business Regulation for Sustainability: Intends, Norms and Motivations of Building Public Trust of Corporate Managers

László Fekete

Abstract Although tackling climate change and the environmental degradation are the shared responsibility of the global community for averting catastrophic consequences and the likelihood of severe welfare losses on global level, the majority of the states are not willing to give up their short-term economic interests and to pool their sovereignty to make legally binding international environmental agreements. Therefore, the implementation and enforcement of a comprehensive and coercive international regulatory regime have been stalled in the international fora for a long time. At the same time, private regulation, voluntary environmental assessment and reporting framework initiated by business, civic and professional organizations have been proliferating since the beginning of the 1990s. The question is whether these private self-regulatory initiatives of assessing and monitoring environmental performances, especially, of the large corporations are the adequate and proper substitute of mandatory multilateral environmental agreements; whether those regarding global environmental outcomes can counterbalance the unwillingness of the majority of the states to comply with a stringent international regulatory regime.

5.1 From Stockholm to Paris: Failures of International Environmental Treaty-Making

Since the United Nations Conference on the Human Environment held in Stockholm in 1972 2294 bilateral and 1311 international environmental treaties, agreements, conventions, protocols and amendments have been drafted and signed in which the contracting parties agreed upon mitigating human impacts on environment, natural resources, and water reservoirs, banning the use of persistent organic pollutants,

L. Fekete (✉)
Business Ethics Center, Corvinus University of Budapest, Budapest, Hungary
e-mail: lfekete@ella.hu

C. Lütge, C. Strosetzki (eds.), *The Honorable Merchant – Between Modesty and Risk-Taking*, Ethical Economy 56, https://doi.org/10.1007/978-3-030-04351-3_5

preventing and minimizing the causes of climate change, and conserving biodiversity (Mitchell 2003, 429–461, 2010, 894–895; IEA 2002–2016). The contracting states recognize the majority of these international and bilateral environmental agreements as legally binding and declare their commitment to preventing the overuse and degradation of natural resources, set up the effective national regime of regulating the processes of environmental protection, and enforce stringent environmental policies in accordance with the newly established international or bilateral legal provisions. Despite the endless profusion of international and bilateral treaties, agreements, conventions, and protocols agreed upon the last four decades – about 50 and 29 per year, respectively – the writ commitment of the contracting states and their self-proclaimed responsibility do not precisely attune to their actual conducts, well-designed and useful environmental policies, programs and institutions, measurable and verifiable outcomes. As the authors of the *UNDP Fifth Global Environment Outlook* (2012) state: "Out of 90 goals and objectives assessed, significant progress could only be shown for four. Of equal concern, progress could not be appraised for 14 goals and objectives simply because data were lacking (GEO-5 2012, xvii.)."

The UN Climate Change Conference held in Copenhagen in 7–18 December 2009 was supposed to replace the expiring Kyoto Protocol in 2012 with a new comprehensive and legally binding agreement for all countries is a case in point. The refusal of legally binding commitments and the short-term economic interest of the biggest emitter countries at the conference simply frustrated the recognition and the implementation of a new comprehensive agreement (Vidal and Watts 2009; Broder 2010). The final document of the Copenhagen Summit, the so-called Copenhagen Accord (2009), was drafted by the representatives of the United States, China, India, Brazil, and South Africa which countries either declined to sign the Kyoto Protocol (1997) and to comply with its aims and objectives, or were not the parties of its legally binding obligations to reduce the greenhouse gas emissions due to the endorsement of corrective justice principle for the developing and newly industrialized countries in the original protocol.

It is noticeable that the Copenhagen Accord emphasized the solid scientific basis of the impacts and the anthropogenic causes of climate change and the urgent need of the shared climate policy of the global community, however, the big emitter countries, especially, its drafters did not want to sign a legally binging agreement which imposes quantitative performance standards of greenhouse gas emissions on all major economies including the developing and newly industrialized countries, as well. Besides, the Copenhagen Accord also failed to deal with the reform of the Clean Development Mechanism and emissions trading system, financing and facilitating the diffusion and transfer of advanced clean technologies to developing countries and many other innovative business approaches. These market-based solutions have been frequently criticized during the last few years because they do little to stop the decline of environmental quality (Barrett 2005, Chs 4, 15; Stiglitz 2006; Schatz 2008, 704–742; Nakhooda et al. 2014, 28–31; Ni 2015,709–719). The Clean Development Mechanism and the European emissions trading scheme (EU ETS) clearly illustrate the failures of these business approaches which were initially invented to serve as effective market-based solutions of climate change mitigation as the substitutes of a direct regulatory regime. The aggravated greenhouse gas emissions prove that the EU ETS emissions trading scheme is a cost-effective instrument for the polluters than to provide strong market-based incentives for the deployment of the new and costly carbon-neutral technologies. Under the recent market condition, stagnant and weak economies keep the relative price of tradable emission allowances low; therefore the use of old technologies is more economical for the polluters than investing cleaner production, eco-efficient, and renewable energy technologies. Paradoxically, underpricing environmental externalities in carbon market improves the cost-effectiveness of the use of old polluting technologies, meanwhile, impairs the implementation of advanced eco-friendly ones and the decarbonization of the energy sector (Egenhofer et al. 2012, 21–26; Lohmann 2010; Aldred 2012; Emblemsvåg 2016, 52–59).

The advocates of the market-based solutions of the climate change mitigation usually refer to the Coase Theorem as the highest instance which is thought to buttress their strong arguments against the costly regulatory imposition and restrictions on the greenhouse gas emissions and the exploitation of natural resources. Needless to emphasize that the Coase Theorem works perfectly well in a small-scale bilateral contractual situation when transaction cost is zero, the limited number of contracting parties are involved, who are symmetrically informed and rational, their property rights are initially well-defined, and the third party is not affected. In case of the private exploitation of global public goods, however, none of these Coasean preconditions could be applied. When the states and private corporations trade with emission allowances in the carbon market, it is quite problematic to suppose that the state would be the initial rights holder of global public goods or a part of them who is entitled to allocate the property rights to pollute the planet's atmosphere by selling and assigning it to who is concerned to buy. Even if the rights of the contracting parties are initially well-defined, the property rights do not include *ius abutendi*, namely, the right to destroy (Stone 2007, 310). Still, emission allowances permit the harmful use of global public goods and natural resources. For this reason, the current practice of emission trading – one party who does not have legitimate ownership rights sells the rights to pollute global public goods, the other buys it in order to gain entitlement to private economic benefits from pollution – does not seem to be very well-founded from the legal as well as moral point of view. Coaseans would undoubtedly object this way of arguing for emissions trading system. Carbon market at most regulates and manages the allocation of the rights to pollute in order to maximize the economic efficiency of the use of global public goods and natural resources, but does not bring about the sustainable use of these resources (Driesen 2008, 21–69; Caney 2010). In addition, *Directive 2003/87/EC of the European Parliament and of the Council of 13 October 2003* entitled the EU member states to allocate about 95% of their tradable emission allowances for the most significant domestic emitters operating in the fields of oil refinery, aviation, aluminum, pig iron and steel, cement, glass, ceramic, chemical, pulp and paper productions free of charge (Directive 2003/87/EC 2003). Because carbon market does not contribute to improve the quality of the planet's atmosphere and the environmental sustainability of production and consumption and instead makes the use of the old technologies more profitable than the implementation of eco-efficient technologies, the coalition of more than hundred civic organizations petitioned the European Parliament on 1 July 2013 to abolish the European Union Emissions Trading Scheme (Böhm 2013).

Despite the successive failures of achieving substantial progress at the United Nations Climate Change conferences since Copenhagen, the major international political and economic organizations endeavor to make reassuring sustainability narratives to demonstrate their commitment to an action plan for tackling climate change and environmental degradation. As Jim Yong Kim, the president of World Bank pointed out at Davos Press Conference on 23 January 2014: "A year ago, I said at this meeting that we needed a plan for tackling climate change, a plan fit for the challenge that we face. A year later, we've seen great leadership on climate from countries and companies, but emissions are still rising and the poor are still suffering."[1] Aaditya Mattoo and Arvind Subramanian, the researchers of the World Bank, described the current situation as follows: "International negotiations on climate change have been dogged by mutual recriminations between rich and poor countries, constricted by the zero-sum arithmetic of a shrinking global carbon budget, and overtaken by shifts in economic and hence bargaining power between industrialized and developing countries (Mattoo and Subramanian 2012, Ch. 1)." The authors underlined the need for international cooperation to prevent climate change catastrophe. However, they turn down any differentiation regarding the respective economic and environmental responsibilities, the principles of corrective or distributive justice, economic need and capability among the industrialized, the newly industrialized and the developing countries. The Paris Climate Agreement (2015) seems to abandon the principles of corrective or distributive justice in burden-sharing arrangements among the industrialized, the newly industrialized and the developing countries as if those would have been the primary impediment of the effectiveness of international environmental treaties (Young 2011).

On December 12, 2015, the representatives of 195 countries adopted the Paris Climate Agreement. World leaders, politicians, and many prominent environmentalists acclaimed it as a significant leap for humankind, historic moment which secures our planet for many, many generations to come, the end of the era of fossil fuels and so forth. However, the Paris Climate Agreement is instead a diplomatic manifesto, a kind expression of good intentions than the consistent global strategy of ensuring global sustainability. Sustainable development objectives and mechanisms, proper deadlines, binding and robust commitments, effective coordinating mechanism, quantitative performance standards of greenhouse gas emissions, or climate finance architecture are absent from the Paris Climate Agreement (Morseletto et al. 2016, 13–16; Spash 2016, 70–71). It reiterates the call of Copenhagen Accord (2009) and Cancún Agreement (2010) again for "holding the increase in the global average temperature to well below 2 °C above pre-industrial levels and pursuing

[1]World Bank Group President Jim Yong Kim Remarks at Davos Press Conference. January 23, 2014. http://www.worldbank.org/en/news/speech/2014/01/23/world-bank-group-president-jim-yong-kim-remarks-at-davos-press-conference

efforts to limit the temperature increase to 1.5 °C above pre-industrial levels, recognizing that this would significantly reduce the risks and impacts of climate change (Paris Climate Agreement 2015, art. 2a)." Despite these common objectives of the participant countries, the Paris Climate Agreement is not legally binding. It provides no means – besides the naming and shaming of underperforming countries – to hold an individual party responsible if these objectives were failed to meet. Well before the Paris conference, the United States and China did insist upon the precondition of their participation at the conference that the countries should be allowed to set their emission targets, environmental policy and to tackle climate change on their self-determined basis. As Alan Boyle elucidates the general character of the international environmental agreements: "No one has yet successfully identified any specifically environmental rules or principles with a *ius cogens* status (Boyle 2007, 136.)" Meanwhile the draft proposals and preparatory documents of the climate agreement dealt with the development and implementation of market-related mechanisms, like global carbon tax, carbon labeling scheme, tax on aviation, reducing emissions from deforestation and forest degradation (REDD+), Sustainable Development Mechanisms (SDM) etc., the final text of the Paris Climate Agreement lacks in the specification of the new market-based mechanisms of climate change mitigations. The Paris Climate Agreement also repeats the unfulfilled voluntary pledge of the developed countries made in Copenhagen to mobilize USD 100 billion per year by 2020 for financing the climate adaptation of the developing countries. As reported by different financial studies and estimations, the developed countries have managed to provide about 10–50% of this global climate finance funding per year for the developing countries since 2009 (OECD-CPI 2015; Dasgupta et al. 2015; Weikmans et al. 2016, 10–15; Skovgaard 2017, 98–104). As George Monbiot characterized the Paris Climate Agreement: "By comparison to what it could have been, it's a miracle. By comparison to what it should have been, it's a disaster" (Monbiot 2015).

As the majority of the states so the GATT and later the WTO were not particularly supportive of promoting effective environmental regulations, programs, policies and initiatives which may challenge the vested interest in the *status quo* of international trade system. Even though the Marrakesh Agreement Establishing the World Trade Organization (1994) put particular emphasis on the importance of "… the optimal use of the world's resources in accordance with the objective of sustainable development, seeking both to protect and preserve the environment…(WTO 1994)". Since the establishment of the World Trade Organization, the Committee on Trade and Environment have frequently discussed the issues of the ban, quota, licensing arrangement, environmental labeling on processes, products, services, and other environmental measures. As a matter of fact, the Marrakesh Agreement instead authorized the WTO Committee on Trade and Environment to control the environmental measures of the states on the basis of non-discriminatory principle than gave equal concern for trade and the environment (Nissen 1997, 901–928; Eckersley 2004, 24–50; Horn and Mavroidis 2014, 162–164). The stringent environmental regulation always creates the relatively high entry and exit barriers for the enterprises, because it tends to drive the environmentally inefficient polluters out of the market. Nonetheless, the advocates of the free trade are predisposed to regard the stringent environmental protection as restrictive trade measure and underline that it increases welfare losses as if the harmful environmental externalities would not have far-reaching detrimental effects on human welfare. The environmental measures initiated and implemented by different states in order to promote sustainable production and consumption were frequently considered as the violation of the underlying trade principles of the Marrakesh Agreement in arbitration processes. As the decisions of the WTO Committee on Trade and Environment demonstrate, it especially considers the environmental labeling, regulations and measures of the member states about processes, products, and services as discriminatory and unnecessary trade barriers and forced them to adhere to the WTO agreements. For instance, the GATT and the WTO scrutinized and decided the case of mandatory timber labeling initiated by Austria requiring eco-labels on all tropical timber imports in order to certify that the timber products being marketed are from sustainably managed forests and to curb the abuse of tropical deforestation as the protectionist barrier to free-trade. For this reason, the GATT and later the WTO Committee on Trade and Environment forced Austria to revoke its eco-labeling law (1992). As the recent cases of US-Clove Cigarettes, US-COOL, US-Tuna II, and EC-Seal Products before the WTO Trade and Environment Commission demonstrate, the proliferation of private and governmental initiatives of carbon labeling requirements on products, process and production methods is still in opposition of the non-discrimination principle of GATT/WTO law (WTO 2010; Appleton 2015, 4–5; Duran 2015, 6–10). The Japanese government introduced voluntary carbon labeling scheme on food packaging, detergents and electrical appliances in 2008. Recently, the environmental labels pilot project of the French government and the Green Economy Program of Switzerland launched in 2010 were investigated in October 2013 by the Committee on Trade and Environment whether these two initiatives are compatible with the basic WTO legal norms and principles. The French initiative about the dispute resolution is especially problematic because the French government aims to introduce a compulsory carbon labeling rule which applies to imported as well as French products, and subsequently to require labels on all kind of products including other environmental data as the product's water footprint, impact on biodiversity and so forth according to the different product categories in order to provide information about the environmental and social dimensions of business and consumption.

In lack of cooperative international directive in common environmental policy about tackling climate change and environmental degradation, the countries which adopt higher environmental standards to create more stringent national regulatory regime and set higher domestic target for greenhouse gas emissions must face the political, economic and social risks of free-ridings and parasitic corporate and governmental behaviors on global level. In these countries, the business organizations have to internalize the high costs of the imposition and enforcement of the more stringent environmental regulation about processes, products and services and the deployment of the new carbon-neutral technologies, waste management, resources conservation and recycling requirements and many others, meanwhile, their competitors who operate under more relaxed regulatory regimes can externalize the significant portion of the costs of their excessive use of global public goods and natural resources. The responsible countries with substantial environmental commitments – as the cases of tropical timber trade and many other environmental disputes at the WTO Committee on Trade and Environment demonstrate – sometimes must face with the unfavorable international rulings and state-supported boycotts if they try to impose high tariffs on the imports of energy-intensive products and consumer goods in the domestic market, or to ban them altogether. The recent feeble and legally non-binding environmental regulation does not sanction the overuse and depletion of the natural resources; therefore, the major emitter industries and corporations can exploit their comparative advantages of economizing the costs of production, particularly, in less regulated industries. Race to the top in environmental issues is still not a general rule in business. Briefly, the global market without comprehensive and coercive international regulatory regime or hard law tends to undercut domestic regulatory efforts and allocates the costs and benefits of the prodigal and frugal uses of natural resources unevenly, namely, it rewards the prodigal producers and punishes the frugal ones at least in short and medium terms (Daly and Farely 2011, 256–257). Besides, the more stringent sustainable environmental policy of the responsible countries cannot offset the disruptive effects of the corporate and governmental negligence of the most significant emitter countries on the global environment.

In conclusion, the weak political, economic and social commitments to sustainability, the underlying disaccord among the countries about bearing and sharing the cost burden of the green transformation of the global economy, the fundamental flaws and ineffectiveness of Clean Development Mechanism and other market-based initiatives, and the high costs and short-term risks of the clean technology investment resulted that the recognition and the implementation of an international environmental agreement on greenhouse gas emissions which is comprehensive, consistent, timely, operational and enforceable cannot be expected in the near future.

5.2 Voluntary Business Regulation for Sustainability: Objections and Approvals

Although tackling climate change and the environmental degradation are the shared responsibility of the global community for averting catastrophic consequences and the likelihood of severe welfare losses on global level, the majority of the states are not willing to give up their short-term economic interests and to pool their sovereignty to make a comprehensive and coercive international environmental agreement (Fligstein 2005, 199–201). Therefore, the implementation and enforcement of a comprehensive and coercive international regulatory regime have been stalled in the international fora for a long time. At the same time, private regulation, voluntary environmental assessment and reporting framework initiated by business, civic and professional organizations have been proliferating since the beginning of the 1990s (Bartley 2007, 301–306). The question is whether these private self-regulatory initiatives of assessing and monitoring environmental performances, especially, of the large corporations are the adequate and proper substitute of mandatory multilateral environmental agreements; whether those regarding environmental outcomes can counterbalance the unwillingness of the majority of the states to comply with a stringent international regulatory regime.

Because of the disapproved decisions of the GATT and the WTO Committee on Trade and Environment in the environmental regulation of tropical timber trade and many other environmental cases,[2] the value-based enterprises and their international membership associations frequently adopt and operate their own, higher quality, social and environmental responsibility standards beyond compliance with compare to legal rules and well-established international and domestic industry regulation. For instance, the failure of launching an International Forest Convention in the Earth Summit of Rio de Janeiro in 1992 inspired the colorful coalition of business enterprises, civic and professional organizations to create the Forest Stewardship Council (1993) which has practically become the global standard-setting institution of sustainable forest management during the last two decades (Dudley et al. 1995; Lipschutz and Rowe 2005, 99–121; Dingwerth 2008; Pattberg and Widerberg 2015, 687–688). Because of the commitment of the member organizations to the principles of sustainable forest management are voluntary, standards, certification processes, and environmental labeling are not subjects to either the WTO or national jurisdiction and approval, although, the WTO makes some effort to interfere with and regulate voluntary environmental labeling, as well (Doha Declaration 2001, para 32(iii); Charnovitz 2002; Fliess et al. 2007, 22–24, 58; Öko-Institut e.V. 2009; Baddeley et al. 2012, 71–80; Kudryavtsev 2015, 118–122). In any case, private sector voluntary environmental initiatives have been proliferating, voluntary environmental and social labeling organizations like Bio Suisse, Blue Angel, Bonsucro, Breeam, Bre Global, Clean Clothes Alliance, EarthCheck, EKOenergy, Fair Trade, Fair Flowers and Plants, GlobalGAP, GOTS, GreenGlobe, Leaf, Minergie, MSC, NoCO2, Rainforest Alliance, RSPO, UTZ Certified and many others have become the internationally recognized standard settlers in managing natural resources and the environment for the different branches of industries (Sethi 2011, Ch. 1).

The business, civic and professional initiators of private sector standards and the self-regulatory regime in environmental protection are quite successful in building and advancing international cooperation in particular environmental issues, however, the states or international political organizations do not delegate any legal authority to them. In some measure, they seem to be quite capable of bringing their cause in on the agenda. Many political documents, for instance, the European

[2] See for example, Mexico v. USA (1988) restrictions on imports of tuna; Venezuela, Brazil v. USA (1996) gasoline environmental standards; India etc. vs. USA (1998) import prohibition of certain shrimp and shrimp products from non-certified countries; Peru v. EC (2002) marketing and labeling preserved sardines; EC v. Brazil (2009) Brazil's import prohibition on retreaded tires.

Union's *Promoting a European Framework for Corporate Social Responsibility* (2001), modestly applaud the importance and effectiveness of self-regulatory environmental regimes in business. The document as mentioned above underlines that "[c]orporate social responsibility should nevertheless not be seen as a substitute to regulation or legislation concerning social rights or environmental standards, including the development of new appropriate legislation (European Commission 2001, 8)." This statement seems to indicate that the environmental policy, private voluntary initiatives initiated by the corporate stakeholders could have only a limited and follow-up role. The *Sustaining Forests: A Development Strategy* (2004) features the outstanding performance of the World Bank's forest strategy and passingly mentions third-party involvement and the role of business, civic, and professional organizations in sustainable forest management (World Bank 2004, 10–14). The European Commission's *Contributing to Sustainable Development: The Role of Fair Trade and Nongovernmental Trade-Related Sustainability Assurance Schemes* (2009) instructs the private actors that voluntary private regulation and labeling schemes initiated by Fair Trade and International Social and Environment Accreditations and Labeling Alliance should be consistent with the WTO rules and regulations. The authors of the communication of the European Commission are convinced that the recent international regulatory framework, especially, the WTO's and the EU's, creates opportunities for accomplishing sustainable development objectives, and the acceptance of more stringent environmental regulatory regime could be damaging rather than beneficial (European Commission 2009). The majority of The States, or the European Union, tend to regard voluntary standards, certification and labeling systems mainly as niche market phenomena doing for the informed choices of consumers and completing the public policy objectives and not as a necessary correction of the shortcomings of international and domestic regulatory regimes. Briefly, the initiators of private regulatory schemes could be pathbreakers but not rule makers in environmental regulation.

Needless to emphasize that the private voluntary initiatives only prove out if they outperform the legal norms and principles of the current domestic and international regulatory framework and encourage the business organizations to adopt and develop best practices, innovative technologies, methods and standards in their corporate environmental policy. So the vanguard initiatives ratchet up the environmental standards of processes, products and services, and those in the long run come to displace the old and ineffective environmental rules generally used in business practices. Therefore, the quoted official opinion that the work of these businesses, civic and independent professional organizations is useful to popularize and complete the public environmental policy objectives of the governments, which are loose and insufficient, is somewhat meaningless.

The corporate actors habitually express their discontent over government intervention and regulation in business affairs. Many large corporations distrust the interference of the government and its ability to regulate the market and advocate the priority of the voluntary regulation in environmental issues. They usually belittle the environmental and social welfare losses of relaxed market regulation, market failures, race to the bottom, and regulatory shopping, meanwhile, incline to magnify the extensiveness of government failure, its bureaucratic costs and perverse effects of state regulation (Cassidy 2009, 82–110). (Honestly speaking, they have some reason to think so.) For instance, as the authors of the General Motors' *Our message: 2005/2006 Corporate Responsibility Report* assert: "GM believes the most effective way to improve energy efficiency and reduce greenhouse gas emissions is the voluntary development… […] Policy initiatives that encourage advanced technology development are best addressed through voluntary initiatives and market-oriented measures, not government mandates (General Motors 2007a, 3–6, 3–7)." In other words, only the voluntary, market- and technology-driven approach based on the cutting-edge corporate practice could bring about the formation of „technically sound and financially responsible environmental laws and regulations (General Motors 2007a, 6–1)". Interestingly, the Board of Directors counselled the stockholders attending at the 2007 annual meeting to vote against one of the stockholder proposals which demanded to "improve the environmental performance of their products" from the management, because General Motors is "the largest product 'carbon burden' of automakers selling vehicles in the U.S. today (General Motors 2007b, 57–58)." Non-governmental environmental organizations usually grade General Motors and the largest automobile manufacturers in general as the worst greenwashers in business. Despite asserting the green credentials in their advertising campaign and mission statements, the greenwasher corporations make the world neither cleaner, nor greener (Green Life 2006; Delmas and Burbano 2011, 64–87; Horiuchi et al. 2009; Lyon and Maxwell 2011, 3–41; Terrachoice 2007, 2009, 2010; White 2015; Rhodes 2016, 1506–1509). Without taking sides for or against in public versus private regulation debate, it is better to keep Adam Smith' instruction in mind: "The proposal of any new law or regulation of commerce which comes from […] an order of men, whose interest is never exactly the same with that of the publick, […] ought always to be listened to with great precaution, and ought never to be adopted till after having been long and carefully examined, not only with the most scrupulous, but with the most suspicious attention (Smith 1976, Vol. I, 278)."

It stands to reason that large corporations could do a lot to mitigate the environmental degradation and greenhouse gas emissions, because more than 90% of global capital assets, large pool of mobilizable human and financial resources, expertise as well as political leverage to advance the paradigmatic change in the environmentally efficient resource use of industries are at their disposal. However, the majority of large corporations use their capability instead to weaken the progressive environmental initiatives and the endeavors of the upward harmonization of the national and multilateral regulations than to make efforts to set up and enforce stringent industry standards in order to mitigate the social and environmental externalities of production. For instance, the hostile criticism and lobbying of the European and American chemical producers against the EU's new regulatory policy on industrial chemicals and dangerous substances (REACH Regulation 2007) are cases in point (Waxman 2004; Ackerman et al. 2006, 3–4; Michaels 2008, 208; Gerstetter 2014, 30–31; Myant and O'Brien 2015, 23). Despite significant structural shifts in production and technology in the last decades, about 60% of the annual greenhouse gas emissions still come from the generation of power and heat, transport, manufacturing and construction industries, therefore, the environmental policy, corporate behavior, technological and organizational advancement of the large emitter corporations profoundly influence the pace of the transition to the sustainable development (Stern 2007, Part III; Bernstein et al. 2007, 451–454; CAN Europe 2010).

Even though many progressive environmental programs also come from large corporations like publishing audited sustainability reports, voluntary compliance with higher environmental standards, and setting voluntary carbon reduction targets, it is not surprising that laudatory opinion about the virtues of private governance and self-regulation in the environmental protection and business affairs, in general, is not very frequent in the legal and economic literature, lately. Strong criticism against the idea of the self-regulating markets is particularly manifest in social theories. As Karl Polányi put it sharply, a self-regulating market "…could not exist for any length of time without annihilating the human and natural substance of society; it would have physically destroyed man and transformed his surroundings into a wilderness (Polányi 1957, 3)." The devastating economic and social consequences of the deregulatory furor in banking and financial industries since the beginning of the 1980s worldwide do not win over skepticism about the effectiveness of voluntary compliance and market-driven solutions in preventing the environmental degradation. Many case studies and survey researches prove that the outcomes of voluntary environmental programs initiated by business organizations are quite shallow; some of them – like BP's Beyond Petroleum advertising campaign to proclaim its leadership in environmental responsibility – is rather impertinent (Vogel 2005, 123–132). Moreover, as Nicole Darnall and Stephen R. Sides come to a provoking conclusion in their essay after studying the data of over 30,000 firms, the environmental performances of the companies which participate in the ISO 14001 and other voluntary environmental programs are less satisfying than the non-participant companies. Other critical studies also draw our attention to the fact that obtaining ISO 14001 certificate is frequently a symbolic action, a relatively low-cost tool for corporate environmental image advertisements without attaining measurable change in environmental performance (Darnall and Sides 2008, 95–117; Schwartz and Tilling 2009, 293; Welford 1997, Ch. 2; Wright and Nyberg 2015, Ch. 4). Briefly, the obtainment and formal approval of environmental management systems do not necessarily lead to the companies' better environmental performance. Nevertheless, a few authors are convinced that the expansion of self-regulatory environmental regimes in business is inevitable because the development of economic globalization has gradually shifted the regulatory functions from the national regulatory authorities and established international treaty-making bodies to alternative regulatory arrangements and private sector institutions (Sassen 2003, 241–248, 2005, 20–23; Cafaggi 2015, 878–879).

Besides the lack of measurable outcomes of many environmental programs initiated by business organizations, their opportunistic behavior, rampant noncompliance, and the unreliability of self-reporting, further objections are usually raised against private environmental regulation. Private environmental regulation without monitoring compliance and enforcing higher environmental standards only encourages the value-based corporations and niche market providers to comply and does not stimulate incentives for mainstream business. Private regulation usually does not create a legally binding obligation for business organizations to obey, but it mostly imposes the moral obligation upon them to fulfill stringent voluntary standards. If government delegates the authority to private standard-setting organizations to monitor and compel business enterprises to comply with stringent environmental rules, it sometimes serves beneficiaries' interests and gives free scope for economic rent-seeking, cartels and baseless entry restrictions into the market. Besides, legally empowered private regulation always causes constitutional problems and generates legal disputes if private interest and industry groups endeavor to enforce not only their members and affiliates who voluntarily bring themselves under the control of private regulatory regime but unconsented third-party actors to comply with the norms and rules of private standard settlers. (Although, these conflicts in environmental regulation is less prevailing than in case of banking and finance industries, self-regulatory organizations, statutory public bodies, professional associations.) As Joseph E. Stiglitz expressed it in using informal, arresting language to make the point: "Self-regulation is preposterous… (Stiglitz 2009)" Briefly, private regulatory regime initiated, monitored and enforced by the most influential private interest and industry groups may cause significant social deadweight loss. The conflicts as mentioned above are especially imminent if independent supervisory institutions are not accredited to oversee and assess the impacts of the activities and decisions of private standard-setting organizations on fundamental rights, natural or business environment, economic competition, and social welfare. (That is why the UN International Labor Organization discords with ISO 26000 voluntary non-certifiable guideline which may impair the established international labor standards and binding legislation.)

The involvement of civic and independent professional organizations in supervising and evaluating the environmental performances of economic organizations indeed assures the credibility of the corporate commitment to comply with voluntary standards as well as mandatory environmental laws. They can quite effectively correct the frequent unconcern and incompetence of the official enforcement mechanisms by using the variety of legal and non-legal tools and sending positive and negative market signals like approvals, certifications or massive publicity campaigns, stakeholder activism, public pressures, consumer boycotts, and citizen suits against the disobedient enterprises, respectively. If the integrity of civic and independent professional organizations is generally recognized by society, their evaluation and approval about the environmental performances of business enterprises which subject themselves to higher standards count for more than their formal compliance with environmental laws. Nevertheless, the paradox of civic and independent professional organizations fostering sustainable development lies in that they can inspire the value-based corporations and their devoted leadership, meanwhile, their efforts do not have considerable effect on correcting the misconducts of corporations which take advantages of relaxed regulatory regime and use their adoption of voluntary regulatory standards and their sustainability reporting just for brand building and public relations tactics. It seems that Say's Law cannot be applied to the market for virtue (Vogel 2005), namely, the governance failure of international and national environmental regulations creates a market for the vast supply of recommendations, guidelines, standards, credits and certifications for environmental performance initiated by civic and professional organizations, however, it does not necessarily generate sufficient demand for corporate environmental responsibility. For this reason, private environmental regulations and standard settings of the economic organizations grounded on voluntarism can only be complementary and not an alternative to a comprehensive and legally binding international environmental agreements.

The further question is why many large corporations make considerable efforts to exceed the requirements of the established environmental rules and to comply with higher voluntary standards. Some explanation refers to the pragmatic concerns of corporate management over the risks of adjusting the long-term corporate business strategy to relaxed environmental regulation. The endless profusion of international and bilateral treaties, agreements, conventions, and protocols does not only demonstrate the failures of integrating the different political interests of the states for the common purpose, but it also reflects the pressing need of global environmental agenda about sustainability. In the situation of regulatory uncertainty, the cutting-edge corporations endeavor to improve their productive capacities by introducing and using advanced environmental technologies, methods, and standards to protect their long-term economic advantages in the global market. It is better to lead the inevitable paradigmatic change in the use of natural resources, business methods and production processes than to be an unprepared and exposed economic actor of a stringent environmental regulatory regime in the future. Voluntary environmental standards fill these regulatory gaps what are left by the unsuccessful attempts of drafting, signing, implementing and enforcing a comprehensive international environmental agreement, indeed. Voluntary environmental regulation and greenhouse gas emissions reductions represent Pareto improvements over the status quo when the environmental degradation is not constrained by comprehensive and coercive international regulatory regime even if corporate self-regulation is only the second best solution (Maxwell et al. 2000, 583–617).

The other possible explanation for the proliferation of corporate voluntarism in environmental protection comes from the central concepts of behavioral economics, game theory, and experimental economics. The recent studies do not support Michael Jensen's theories about corporate behavior and single-valued objective function which means that managers can only maximize either current profit, or market share, or R&D expenditure for future growth in profit, respectively. As Jensen states: "Thus, telling a manager to maximize current profits, market share, future growth in profits, and anything else one pleases will leave that manager with no way to make a reasoned decision.", alternatively, "Without the clarity of mission provided by a single-valued objective function, companies embracing stakeholder theory will experience managerial confusion, conflict, inefficiency, and perhaps even competitive failure (Jensen 2001, 9–11)." Environmental concerns merely appear in Jensen's essay as one of the private causes and personal interests of corporate managers like "art, cities, and medical research" which must be detached from the firm's primary function, to wit, profit-maximizing activity (Jensen 2001, 14).

The results of the recently conducted survey researches based on large samples of face-to-face interviews with corporate managers contravene Jensen's view on managerial conducts and motivations. The managers of large corporations think of corporate objectives quite differently. First of all, corporate value maximization is a comprehensive notion for them which cannot be reduced to a single-valued objective function. For instance, the authors of the *Global 500 Climate Change Report* (CDP 2013, 2014, 2015) show that the majority of the managers of the largest corporations operating in different branches of industry regards climate change and environmental degradations as the most pressing issues for business, today. About 60–70% of them believes that their genuine commitment to effective climate policy, environmental program, and emission reductions have significant consequences for their public reputations. Briefly, good environmental performance in environmentally-friendly products, carbon emissions reduction, and energy and water usages has a reputational opportunity, but corporate negligence has severe reputational risk. Losing public reputation could cause about 30% devaluation of the shares of the disfavored company in the stock market. Reputational damage is considered almost as severe business risk as global financial crises, political breakdowns, or nuclear catastrophes. As many business cases like Johnson&Johnson, GE, Chiquita, Xerox, Mattel, and others demonstrate that if public reputation is impaired its regain takes at least 3-year hard work for the company (Kelly et al. 2005, 5; CDP 2013; Dunbar and Schwalbach 2001, 115–123; Schwaiger 2004, 46–71; Dowling and Moran 2012, 23; Sahai 2014). The latest *CDP Global Climate Change Report* (2015) which surveyed more than 5500 companies and investors demonstrates that these leading-edge business organizations and investors assess the climate risks of their business activities and investments conforming to the main findings of climate science.

The global survey of *Navigating the Reputation Economy* (2013) also shows that the majority of managers – 83% of respondents – "believe we live in a Reputation Economy, a world where who you are matters more to consumers than what you sell (Reputation Institute 2012, 4)." For fostering their public reputation and trust in their business operation, corporations often use personification metaphors like honest, trustworthy, cordial, open-minded, innovative, environmental-friendly, meticulous and so forth, to build corporate identity and to delineate their commitment to pressing social and environmental issues (Davies et al. 2001, 113–127; Campbell 2007, 946–967; Tonello 2007; Dietz and Gillespie 2012; Weng and Chen 2017). Beyond environmental mission statements communicated by corporations, the ethical and sustainability indices and rankings initiated by business, professional and research organizations – the ARESE Sustainable Performance Indices, the *Newsweek* Green Rankings, the Dow Jones Sustainability Index, the Ethisphere Most Ethical Companies, the *Fortune* 100 Best Companies to Work for, the FTSE4Good Index, the S&P Global 100 Index, the Domini 400 Social Index, the MSCI ESG Environmental Indexes, and many others – could substantiate whether those are factual or just intend to send false market signals on the corporate behavior.

In conclusion, a good reputation or public trust in sound environmental policy is rightly recognized as one of the most important intangible assets of the corporation which drives economic performance and corporate valuation.

References

Ackerman, F., E. Stanton, and R. Massey. 2006. *European chemical policy and the United States: The impacts of REACH*. Medford: Tufts University.

Aldred, Jonathan. 2012. The ethics of emissions trading. *New Political Economy* 17 (3): 339–360.

Appleton, Arthur E. 2015. Product labeling: What has the Appellate Body wrought? *BIORES* 9 (8): 4–5.

Baddeley, Shane, Peter Cheng, and Robert Wolfe. 2012. Trade policy implications of carbon labels on food. *Estey Centre Journal of International Law and Trade Policy* 13 (1): 59–93.

Barrett, S. 2005. *Environment and statecraft: The strategy of environmental treaty-making*. Oxford: OUP.

Bartley, T. 2007. Institutional emergence in an era of globalization: The rise of transnational private regulation of labor and environmental conditions. *American Journal of Sociology* 113 (2): 297–351.

Bernstein, L., et al. 2007. Industry. In *Climate change 2007: Mitigation*, Contribution of Working Group III to the Fourth Assessment Report of the Intergovernmental Panel on Climate Change, ed. B. Metz et al. Cambridge/New York: CUP.

Böhm, S.. 2013. Why are carbon markets failing? *Guardian Professional*. Friday, 12 April, 11.50 BST.

Boyle, Alan. 2007. Relationship between international environmental law and other branches of international law. In *Oxford handbook of international environmental law*, ed. Daniel Bodansky, Jutta Brunnée, and Ellen Hey, 125–146. Oxford: OUP.

Broder, J. M.. 2010. Remember the Copenhagen Accord? *The New York Times*. June 8, 2:02 pm.

Cafaggi, Fabrizio. 2015. The many features of transnational private rule-making: Unexplored relationships between custom, Jura Mercatorum and Global Private Regulation. *University of Pennsylvania Journal of International Law* 36 (4): 875–983.

Campbell, J.L. 2007. Why would corporations behave in socially responsible ways? An institutional theory of corporate social responsibility. *Academy of Management Review* 32 (3): 946–967.

CAN Europe. 2010. *Think globally sabotage locally*. Brussels: Climate Action Network Europe.

Caney, S. 2010. Markets, morality and climate change: What, if anything, is wrong with emissions trading? *New Political Economy* 15 (2): 197–224.

Cassidy, J. 2009. *How markets fail: The logic of economic calamities*. New York: Farrar, Straus and Giroux.

CDP. 2013. *Global 500 climate change report 2013: Sector insights: What is driving climate change action in the world's largest companies?* New York: CPD-PwC.

———. 2014. *CDP S&P 500 climate change report 2014: Climate action and profitability*. New York: CPD.

———. 2015. *CDP Global 500 climate change report 2013: At the tipping point?* New York: CPD.

Charnovitz, Steve. 2002. The law of environmental "PPMs" in the WTO: Debunking the myth of illegality. *Yale Journal of International Law* 27 (1): 59–110.

Daly, H.E., and J. Farely. 2011. *Ecological economics: Principles and applications*. 2nd ed. Washington, DC: Island Press.

Darnall, N., and S.R. Sides. 2008. Assessing the performance of voluntary environmental programs: Does certification matter? *Policy Studies Journal* 36 (1): 95–117.
Dasgupta, Dipak, et al. 2015. *Climate change finance, analysis of a recent OECD report: Some credible facts needed*. New Delhi: Ministry of Finance, Government of India.
Davies, G., et al. 2001. The personification metaphor as a measurement approach for corporate reputation. *Corporate Reputation Review* 4 (2): 113–127.
Delmas, M.A., and V.C. Burbano. 2011. The drivers of greenwashing. *California Management Review* 54 (1): 64–87.
Dietz, G., and N. Gillespie. 2012. *The recovery of trust: Case studies of organisational failures and trust repair*. London: Institute of Business Ethics.
Dingwerth, Klaus. 2008. North-South Parity in Global Governance: The affirmative procedures of the forest stewardship council. *Global Governance: A Review of Multilateralism and International Organizations* 14 (1): 53–72.
Directive 2003/87/EC of the European Parliament and of the Council of 13 October 2003. Establishing a scheme for greenhouse gas emission allowance trading within the Community and amending Council Directive 96/61/EC Annex I.
Doha Ministerial Declaration. 2001. Adopted on 14 November 2001.
Dowling, Grahame, and Peter Moran. 2012. Corporate reputations: Built in or bolted on? *California Management Review* 54 (2): 25–42.
Driesen, D.M. 2008. Sustainable development and market liberalism's shotgun wedding: Emissions trading under the Kyoto protocol. *Indiana Law Journal* 83 (1): 21–69.
Dudley, N., J.-P. Jeanrenaud, and F. Sullivan. 1995. *Bad harvest? The timber trade and the degradation of the world's forests*. London: Earthscan.
Dunbar, R.L.M., and J. Schwalbach. 2001. Corporate reputation and performance in Germany. *Corporate Reputation Review* 3 (2): 115–123.
Duran, Gracia Marin. 2015. Carbon labeling schemes at the WTO: Real or imagined conflict? *BIORES* 9 (8): 6–10.
Eckersley, R. 2004. The big chill: The WTO and multilateral environmental agreements. *Global Environmental Politics* 4 (2): 24–50.
Egenhofer, Christian, et al. 2012. *The EU emissions trading system and climate policy towards 2050: Real incentives to reduce emissions and drive innovation?* Brussels: CEPS.
Emblemsvåg, Jan. 2016. *Reengineering capitalism: From industrial revolution towards sustainable development*, 52–59. Cham: Springer.
European Commission. 2001. *Promoting a European framework for corporate social responsibility*. Luxembourg: EU.
———. 2009. *Contributing to sustainable development: The role of fair trade and nongovernmental trade-related sustainability assurance schemes. Communication from the Commission to the Council, the European Parliament and the European Economic and Social Committee*. Brussels: EC COM(2009) 215 final.
Fliess, B., et al. 2007. *CSR and trade: Informing consumers about social and environmental conditions of globalised production*, OECD Trade Policy Working Paper No. 47 – PART I. Paris: OECD.
Fligstein, N. (2005) The political and economic sociology of international economic arrangements. Handbook of economic sociology, N. Smelser, R. Swedberg (Princeton, N.J.: Princeton Princeton University Press) 183–204.
General Motors. 2007a. *Our message: 2005/2006 corporate responsibility report*. Detroit: General Motors.
———. 2007b. *Proxy statement for annual meeting of stockholders to be held June 5, 2007*. Detroit: General Motors.
GEO-5. 2012. *Global environment outlook: Environment for the future we want*. New York: United Nations Environment Programme.
Gerstetter, Christiane. 2014. *Regulatory cooperation under TTIP – a risk for democracy and national regulation?* Berlin: Ecologic Institute.
Green Life. 2006. *Don't be fooled 2005: Americas 10 worst greenwashers*. Boston: Green Life.

Horiuchi, R., et al. 2009. *Understanding and preventing greenwash: A business guide*. London: Business for Social Responsibility.
Horn, Henrik, and Petros C. Mavroidis. 2014. Multilateral environmental agreements in the WTO: Silence speaks volumes. *International Journal of Economic Theory* 10 (1): 147–165.
IEA. 2002–2016. *International environmental agreements database project (2002–2016)*. http://iea.uoregon.edu/page.php?query=home-contents.php.
International Energy Agency. 2016. *World energy outlook 2016*. Paris: OECD/International Energy Agency.
Jensen, M.C. 2001. Value maximization, stakeholder theory, and the corporate objective function. *Journal of Applied Corporate Finance* 14 (3): 8–21.
Kelly, Ch., et al. 2005. *Deriving value from corporate values*. Washington, DC: The Aspen Institute and Booz Allen Hamilton.
Kudryavtsev, A. 2015. *Private-sector standards as technical barriers in international trade in goods: In search of WTO disciplines*. Oisterwijk: Wolf Legal Publishers.
Lipschutz, R.D., and J.K. Rowe. 2005. *Globalization, governmentality and global politics: Regulation for the rest of us?* London: Routledge.
Lohmann, Larry. 2010. Uncertainty markets and carbon markets: Variations on polanyian themes. *New Political Economy* 15 (2): 225–254.
Lyon, Th.P., and J.W. Maxwell. 2011. Greenwash: Corporate environmental disclosure under threat of audit. *Journal of Economics and Management Strategy* 20 (1): 3–41.
Mattoo, A., and A. Subramanian. 2012. *A greenprint for international cooperation on climate change*. Washington, DC: Center for Global Development.
Maxwell, J.W., Th.P. Lyon, and S.C. Hackett. 2000. Self-regulation and social welfare: The political economy of corporate environmentalism. *The Journal of Law and Economics* 43 (2): 583–617.
Michaels, D. 2008. *Doubt is their product: How industry's assault on science threatens your health*. Oxford: OUP.
Mitchell, R.B. 2003. International environmental agreements: A survey of their features, formation and effects. *Annual Review of Environment and Resources* 28: 429–461.
———. 2010. Compliance theory: Compliance, effectiveness, and behavior change in international environmental law. In *Oxford handbook of international environmental law*, ed. Daniel Bodansky, Jutta Brunnée, and Ellen Hey, 893–921. Oxford: OUP.
Monbiot, Georg. 2015. Grand promises of Paris climate deal undermined by squalid retrenchments. *The Guardian*. Saturday 12 December, 15.53 GMT, https://www.theguardian.com/environment/georgemonbiot/2015/dec/12/paris-climate-deal-governments-fossil-fuels.
Morseletto, Piero, Frank Biermann, Philipp Pattberg. 2016. Governing by targets: Reductio ad unum and evolution of the two-degree climate target, *International environmental agreements: Politics, Law and Economics*. online.
Myant, Martin, and Ronan O'Brien. 2015. *The TTIP's impact: Bringing in the missing issue*. Brussels: ETUI aisbl.
Nakhooda, Smita, et al. 2014. *Climate finance: Is it making a difference? A review of the effectiveness of multilateral climate funds*. London: Overseas Development Institute.
Ni, Kuei-Jung. 2015. Legal aspects (barriers) of granting compulsory licenses for clean technologies in light of WTO/TRIPS rules: Promise or mirage? *World Trade Review* 14 (4): 701–719.
Nissen, J.L. 1997. Achieving a balance between trade and the environment: The need to amend the WTO/GATT to include multilateral environmental agreements. *Law and Policy in International Business* 28 (3): 901–928.
OECD-CPI. 2015. *Climate finance in 2013-14 and the USD 100 billion goal*. Paris: OECD.
Öko-Institut e.V. 2009. *Product carbon footprint memorandum*. Freiburg: Öko-Institut e.V.
Paris Climate Agreement. 2015. Adopted on 12 December 2015.
Pattberg, Philipp, and Oscar Widerberg. 2015. Theorising global environmental governance: Key findings and future questions. *Journal of International Studies* 43 (2): 684–705.
Polányi, K. 1957. *The great transformation: The political and economic origins of our time*. Boston: Beacon Press.

Reputation Institute. 2012. *Navigating the reputation economy: A global survey of corporate reputation officer*. New York: Reputation Institute.
Rhodes, Carl. 2016. Democratic business ethics: Volkswagen's emissions scandal and the disruption of corporate sovereignty. *Organization Studies* 37 (10): 1501–1518.
Sahai, Neeraj. 2014. *Climate change: What are the risks to corporations?* http://fortune.com/2014/07/09/climate-change-what-are-the-risks-to-corporations/.
Sassen, S. 2003. The state and globalization. *Interventions* 5 (2): 241–248.
———. 2005. The ecology of global economic power: Changing investment practices to promote environmental sustainability. *Journal of International Affairs* 58 (2): 11–32.
Schatz, A. 2008. Discounting the clean development mechanism. *Georgetown International Environmental Law Review* 20 (4): 704–742.
Schwaiger, M. 2004. Components and parameters of corporate reputation: An empirical study. *Schmalenbach Business Review* 56 (1): 46–71.
Schwartz, B., and K. Tilling. 2009. 'ISO-lating' corporate social responsibility in the organizational context: A dissenting interpretation of ISO 26000. *Corporate Social Responsibility and Environmental Management* 16 (5): 289–299.
Sethi, S.P. 2011. Self-regulation through voluntary codes of conduct. In *Globalization and self-regulation: The crucial role that corporate codes of conduct play in global business*, ed. S.P. Sethi. New York: Palgrave Macmillan.
Skovgaard, Jakob. 2017. Limiting costs or correcting market failures? Finance ministries and frame alignment in UN climate finance negotiations. *International Environmental Agreements: Politics, Law, and Economics* 17 (1): 89–106.
Smith, A. 1976. *An inquiry into the nature and causes of the wealth of nations*. Vol. 1. Chicago: UCP.
Spash, Clive L. 2016. The political economy of the Paris Agreement on human induced climate change: A brief guide. *Real-World Economics Review* 75: 67–75.
Stern, N. 2007. *The economics of climate change: The stern review*. Cambridge: CUP.
Stiglitz, J.E. 2006. A new agenda for global warming. *Economists' Voice*. July, www.bepress.com/ev.
———.. 2009. *Capitalist fools*. http://www.vanityfair.com/magazine/2009/01/stiglitz200901-2.
Stone, Christopher D. 2007. Ethics in international environmental law. In *Oxford handbook of international environmental law*, ed. Daniel Bodansky, Jutta Brunnée, and Ellen Hey, 291–312. Oxford: OUP.
Terrachoice. 2007, 2009, 2010. *Greenwashing reports*. http://sinsofgreenwashing.org/findings/index.html.
Tonello, M. 2007. *Reputation risk: A corporate governance perspective*. New York: Conference Board.
Vidal, J., and J. Watts. 2009. Copenhagen closes with weak deal that poor threaten to reject. guardian.co.uk. Saturday, 19 December, 15.54 GMT.
Vogel, D. 2005. *The market for virtue*. Washington, DC: Brookings Institute Press.
Waxman, H.A. 2004. *A special interest case study: The chemical industry, the bush administration, and European efforts to regulate chemicals*. Washington, DC: United States House of Representatives.
Weikmans, Romain, et al. 2016. *Toward transparency: The 2016 adaptation finance transparency gap report*, White Paper, 10–15. London: Adaptation Watch.
Welford, R. 1997. *Hijacking environmentalism: Corporate responses to sustainable development*. London: Earthscan.
Weng, Pei-Shih, and Wan-Yi Chen. 2017. Doing good or choosing well? Corporate reputation, CEO reputation, and corporate financial performance. *North American Journal of Economics and Finance* 39: 223–240.
White, Rob. 2015. Climate change, ecocide and crimes of the powerful. In *Routledge international handbook of the crimes of the powerful*, ed. Gregg Barak. New York: Routledge Ch. 14.
World Bank. 2004. *Sustaining forests: A development strategy*. Washington, DC: World Bank.

Wright, Christopher, and Daniel Nyberg. 2015. *Climate change, capitalism, and corporations: Processes of creative self-destruction*. Cambridge: CUP.
WTO. 1994. *Marrakesh agreement establishing the world trade organization*. 15 April 1994.
———. 2010. Summary report of the information session on product carbon footprint and labeling schemes. WT/CTE/M/49/Add.1, 28 May.
Young, Oran R. 2011. Effectiveness of international environmental regimes: Existing knowledge, cutting-edge themes, and research strategies. *Proceedings of the National Academy of Sciences of the United States of America* 108 (50): 19853–19860.

Part II
The Image of the Merchant in Europe from Late Middle Ages Until Early Modern Times

Chapter 6
The Honest Merchant Before Adam Smith: The Genesis and Rise of a Literary Prototype in Britain

Laurenz Volkmann

Abstract This contribution outlines the genesis and rise of the merchant in British literature from the Middle Ages to the eighteenth century. It charts a chequered history of early rejection, lingering skepticism with regard to the mercantile life and a slow, gradual, though never uncontroversial acceptance of merchants. This growing acceptance is mainly tied to the evolving positive image of trade and its function of promoting national as well as global wealth. By means of a literary *tour d'horizon* significant phases of this development up to Adam Smith's *homo oeconomicus* are sketched out, with reference to texts by key authors such as Langland, Chaucer, Shakespeare, Marlowe, Bunyan and Mandeville.

6.1 Adam Smith's *Homo Oeconomicus* as Point of Reference

When it comes to popular images or representations of merchants and their profession, certain passages in the works of Scottish moral philosopher and economist Adam Smith quickly come to mind. The *homo oeconomicus*, originating in the land of sea trade companies and the Industrial Revolution, seems to have been first fashioned in much-quoted passages from Smith's key publications *The Theory of Moral Sentiments* (1759) und *An Inquiry into the Nature and Causes of the Wealth of Nations* (1776). It is interesting to observe from the onset, though, that Smith's reception has been rather lopsided over the decades, with a select number of passages reiterated in secondary literature and in references to economic liberalism. Frequently they have been instrumentalized to bolster up one's own economic position (see Volkmann 2001, 2007). It was Adam Smith who in the era of neoliberalism, Thatcherism and Reagonomics was used regularly to back up ideological stances in favour of unfettered market forces, individual entrepreneurship and non-intervention by the state. Simultaneously, an opposing position evolved around the

L. Volkmann (✉)
University of Jena, Jena, Germany
e-mail: l.volk@uni-jena.de

C. Lütge, C. Strosetzki (eds.), *The Honorable Merchant – Between Modesty and Risk-Taking*, Ethical Economy 56, https://doi.org/10.1007/978-3-030-04351-3_6

turn of the millenium, whose proponents claim to have discovered or rediscovered the "true" Adam Smith, who was wrongly appropriated by the neoliberals.

The gist of the debate, which economist Onken dubbed the Adam-Smith-Problem as early as in 1898, centers on Smith's alleged view of humans as basically traders and merchants, of man (or woman) as *homo oeconomicus* and society as a network of trade and exchange. A first line of argument detected in Adam Smith is his pivotal insight into the universal nature of the *homo oeconomicus*, expressed in the famous words of "the propensity to truck, barter, and exchange one thing for another" as a trait "common to all men" (Smith 1981, II.ii.1, p. 25 and II.ii.2, p. 25). What follows from this basic insight is the assumption that humans are innately inclined to be self-interested. This basic human disposition is expressed in a frequently quoted aphorism: "It is not from the benevolence of the butcher, the brewer, or the baker that we expect our dinner, but from their regard to their own interest" (Smith 1981, II.ii.2, p. 26f.).

From this follows a third line of argument concerning the social dynamics of this inherent human trait. Unchained and unrestricted by society and the state, propelled on by the division of labour, this propensity can generate a dynamic, mutually beneficial network of interdependence. In turn, it is this very network which creates a system of checks and balances, an "enclosure" (Kant would call it a *Gehege*) of mutual interdependence. In the end, this would serve as a social cohesive. Simultaneously, the mechanisms of give and take create material wealth on the macroeconomic level – for communities, societies and finally the globe. As the argument continues, each member of society will in the end benefit from this exchange, with wealth spreading in sometimes unpredictable and random ways. At the time of Reagonomics, for example, this effect became known as the "trickle-down effect" and was, of course, linked to the economic theories of Adam Smith. The standard image for such a distribution of wealth through the non-interference of the state was encapsulated in the famous metaphor of the "invisible hand," which incidentally was first introduced in Smith's study on moral philosophy, *The Theory of Moral Sentiments*. It was used to explain the paradox of beneficial results of unpurposive actions. Interestingly, the metaphor is used in a context which describes the affluent lifestyles of "the rich" in a rather derogatory manner.

> They are led by an invisible hand to make nearly the same distribution of the necessaries of life, which would have been made, had the earth been divided into equal portions among all its inhabitants, and thus without intending it, without knowing it, advance the interest of the society, and afford means to the multiplication of the species (Smith 1984: IV.I.10, p. 184f.).

The Wealth of Nations rephrases the same paradox, which is that someone who is only interested in their own interest "[…] is in this, as in many other cases, led by an invisible hand to promote an end which was not part of his intention." (Smith 1981, IV.ii.9, p. 456). This very passage became the *locus classicus* for all neoliberal theories to come – the tenet that reducing or better curtailing state intervention would "unleash" the invisible forces of the market to create national wealth. By contrast, a different interpretation by those warning about the neoliberal appropriation of Adam Smith tends to point out the critical stance of the moral philosopher Smith and to stress Smith's skepticism regarding "[...] the clamour and sophistry of merchants and manufacturers [who] easily persuade them ["the populace"] that the private interest of a part, and of a subordinate part of society, is the general interest of the whole" (Smith 1981: I.x.c.25, p.144). Accordingly, a certain strand of research on Smith has underlined the profound and serious discussions of social and moral issues in his oeuvre (see Kirchgässner 1991; Volkmann 2003, for surveys). For this school of thought, the Scottish philosopher's thinking is deeply marked by a most ambivalent attitude towards economic life. On the one hand he expressed an ingrained disdain for conspicuous consumption and ostentatious display of wealth. On the other he delivered the blueprint for an economic system based on private ownership and self-interest.

This Adam-Smith-Problem (Oncken 1898) marks an ambivalent, even self-contradictory attitude towards economic life and its agents. It can be explored in a multi-facetted manner if one turns, as I will do in this contribution, to the historical context of English or rather British history. The historical trajectory of this debate can be traced back to the Middle Ages – revealing that the debate circles around merchants and society, trade and economy, but also in a broader sense deals with the relationship of the individual and society. This contribution aims to describe the traces of this debate about the merchant and his position in society in English literature from the Middle Ages to the eighteenth century. Starting with the genesis of the *homo oeconomicus*, this short literary survey will end with the establishment of a new paradigm in the age of the Enlightenment.

As to a theoretical foundation of such an overview, a bevy of recent theoretical concepts need to be taken into account. Any historical approach informed by recent theories needs to be highly skeptical regarding the temptation to tell a "grand narrative," one which retells a teleological development of historical concepts. Rather, in the tradition of anthropologist's Clifford Geertz' "thick description," focal points need to be worked out and embedded in a diachronic presentation. Theories such as race, class and gender studies or the New Historicism have stressed the necessity to avoid a sweeping "history of mentalities" and rather focus on nodal points, interpreting concrete sources or texts in the context of how they interrelate to previous and other texts of their age. In addition to this concept of texts as highly influenced by other texts – in the sense of "intertextuality" – the understanding of fictional texts as interactively engaging in a dialogue with the "real world out there" seems to be of paramount importance. As has been pointed out frequently, literary texts do not offer a one-to-one representation of their age or their geographical or historical contexts or of particular epistemes. Rather, according to the specific mode of their genre, their literary devices and style, they offer representations of "reality." This is an invitation to the critic to analyse and interpret a text's meanings in a process of negotiation with the critic's own world view (for critical approaches see Veeser 1994; Watts 2003; Mein and Schößler 2005; Hempel and Künzel 2009).

As highly complex and semantically dense representations of reality especially canonized literary texts pose an open invitation to gain access to historical phenomena. Non-canonical texts, though, can also serve as additional, supplementary or contradictory perspectives to the issue under observation. It is by means of a focus on this "textual interplay" that a complex and multifaceted history of the evolution of *homo oeconomicus* in literature from the Middle Ages to the eighteenth century and beyond can be traced (for a more elaborate and lengthy study see Volkmann 2003).

6.2 Rejection of Commercial Life in the Middle Ages

Trading and the mercantile life as well as concerns about profit were clearly rejected and socially stigmatized throughout most of the European Middle Ages (see Kohl 1986). This negative sentiment remained intact up to the end of the Middle Ages in England and Scotland, partly as a result of the slow evolution of commercial activities within the feudal system of the British isles. A slow rise of commercial life commenced in the tenth and eleventh centuries under the protection of the crown. However, the reputation of commercial activities remained one of a potentially socially corrosive and destructive force. Traders and merchants were seen as following their individual interests and these socially dangerous activities needed to be harnessed and contained by integrating them into the medieval system of order. The profession of the merchant was seen as inherently tending to greed and avarice, to illicit and prohibited practices of usury, even to malpractice and cheating. This, in turn, meant that the merchant was inclined to jeopardize his own spiritual salvation. The merchant, as public opinion tended to have it, tended to undermine and destabilize the common weal by furthering the socially unacceptable desire for luxurious goods and a disrespected life of dissipation. The merchant was blamed for being responsible for spreading expensive, morally disreputable luxury goods and socially dubious practices. These were all the more anathema as they were marked as stemming from abroad and thus were consumed at the expense of furthering basic domestic goods. Mercantile activities, as Thomas of Aquinus already had it, were only deemed respectable if they reduced the lack of basic goods, if they followed the principle of the "just price" and if profits gained from individual enterprise were returned to the community of the merchant.

In a broad corpus of literature from the Middle Ages, ranging from descriptions of livery companies to homilies, a conventionalized disdain for commercial thought and profit-making is expressed. A first nodal point of this text tradition comprises the allegorical verse poem *Piers Plowman* (c. 1362-93) by the son of a peasant, William Langland. The book lambasts social injustice caused by the devastating plagues around 1348. They had exacerbated social conditions in England, had generated social unrest and finally led to peasants' revolts. Langland contrasts in his long poem the exploitation and suppression of depraved itinerary workers with the luxurious life style and sinful extravagancies of the aristocracy and religious orders. He utters scathing remarks about greedy peddlers of religious indulgence, gluttonous monks, corrupt vicars and the social devastations wroughed by the luxurious excesses of the female sex. With the latter accusation he perpetuated a well-established cliché about female materialism and wastefulness. For Langland, the growing social disease of hankering after earthly matters and property is embodied in the profession of the merchant, whom he derides in the literary tradition of the vituperation of social ranks ("Ständeschälte").

> For thyse men don most harm to þe mene peple,
> Rychen thorw regraterye and rentes hem beggeth
> With that þe pore peple sholde potte in here wombe.

For tok thei on trewely they tymbred nat so heye,
Ne bouhte none burgages, be þe ful sertayn.
(Langland 1994, III: 81–85)

For these men do the greatest harm to the common people
They enrich themselves through trade and buy goods with things
Which should be used to fill the stomachs of the poor.
For if they traded honestly, they would not have come so high.
And would not have bought property, there is no doubt about that.
(My translation, LV)

Langland's *tour d'horizon* of social and moral shortcomings of his age culminate in a radical rejection of all earthly matters: Only through the pursuit of poverty can the desire for material goods be overcome, and only poverty can save from worldly temptations. Wealth, conversely, is considered to be the root evil of all human existence.

Allas! þat rychesse shal reue and robbe mannes soule
Fro þe loue of oure lord at his laste ende.
(Langland, XVI: 1f.)

Yes, wealth shall be detrimental to them and when they die,
Wealth will tear their soul from the love of our Lord.
(my transl, LV)

It is interesting to observe how influential theological and spiritual vituperations and condemnations in the line of Langland's attack proved to be on a high number of expository texts produced by merchants of that age. They provide insights into mechanisms of self-marginalization and how a socially dominant ideology shaped the profession's self-image. Particularly, a multitude of testaments by merchants reveal a rather apologetic sentiment with merchants trying to make amends for their "sinful lives" by donating to charity in order to save their souls. This was seen as a last, desperate act to redress the balance in favour of making good for allegedly pernicious profit-making (see Kohl 1986). Similar, though less radical dispositions than Langland's regarding profitmaking can be found in many literary texts of the late Middle Ages. William Chaucer's *Canterbury Tales* (c. 1400), the most important literary work of this age, at least makes an effort to defend economic thinking by lending a voice to traders and merchants. In Thomas More's radical social criticism, the genre defining narrative *Utopia* (1516), we find a literary reaction to the social upheavals of the late Middle Ages. According to the dictum *sheep eat men*, they were defined by extensive sheep farming accompanied by severe processes of expulsion, migration from the land and pauperization. Here, arguably for the first time in literary history, we encounter a conspiracy theory. Morus insinuates that a few rich people deliberately aim at making the poor bleed with the intention to destroy the social order. Existing asymmetries and exploitative structures are juxtaposed with a positive fictional example of equal social distribution organized in a communist island community, where commercial thought is strictly marginalized.

There is one literary text, however, which elevated the discussion about *homo oeconomicus* at the end of the Middle Ages. It is a propaganda poem of sorts, ominous in its tone and rhetoric. Around 1437 the booklet about the English art of policy, *The Libelle of Englyshe Polycye*, was published. Its unknown author, hailing from a mercantile community, argued in favour of a strong bond between crown and trade. Only if the higher aristocracy and the merchants worked together would the common weal, the common wealth of the English maritime nation, prosper. The key argument brought forward is a defensive one. It is the fear of the French maritime threat, which would have to be countered through supporting the maritime expansion of Britain. In an ominous argumentative link the author establishes a new idea. He combines the conventional thought of using foreign trade as a means of evenly spreading God's goods across the planet with a praise of the patriotic task of maritime traders. They support and further national wealth trough exporting British goods like wool.

> For yef marchaundes were cherysshede to here spede,
> We were not lykelye to fayle in ony nede;
> Yff they bee riche, thane in prosperite.
> Schalbe oure londe, lordes and comonte.
> (*The Libelle of Englyshe Polycye* 1926, 482–485)

> If you support the merchant, I do not fear
> That the power will leave us in case of a crisis,
> For if he is rich, so will our country be
> Prosperous, the aristocracy as well as the common people.
> (My transl.,LV)

6.3 The Merchant in the Elizabethan Age (c. 1600): Elevating a Still Ambivalent Character

In the Elizabethan Age (1558–1603) commercial activities were bolstered up by the argument that they embodied the mutually beneficial connection between crown and merchant class. This was deemed as instrumental to raising national wealth. Traditionally, the reign of Queen Elizabeth I of the House of Tudor is regarded as a period of transition between feudalism and early modern capitalism (vgl. Southall 1973; Hirschman 1977; Breuer 1979). It was the age of early capitalist forms of production, trade and consumption, emanating from the food, wool and clothes trade. The core of a rapidly growing commercial centre grew increasingly, with an urban market gravitating from London. After the defeat of the Spanish Armada (1588) semi state-run merchant companies like the East India Company (founded in 1600) explored new oversea territories. Growing national and international markets fostered commercial trends in thought and action. They also furthered the social intersecting of new and old wealth, aristocratic and bourgeoise circles. A new type of merchant seaman or global tradesman evolved. In fictional narratives and dramas of the age we find attempts to hedge in the socially corruptive threats and tendencies towards extreme materialism and egoism by means of references to the so-called Elizabethan World Picture (see Southall 1973).

The concept of a world view shared by all contemporaries of Shakespeare was first introduced by the literary historian M. W. Tillyard in his seminal study of 1943, *The Elizabethan World Picture*. Recent research has questioned the idea of a unified, homogenous world view of the age and pointed out the conservative, authoritarian elements in such a hypothesis (Veeser 1994). Rather, the "world view," or way of experiencing their world, of the Elizabethans must be regarded as a mental frame, in which the individual may have different and conflicting opinions and beliefs, which could be analysed with reference to the frame (Suerbaum 1996: 85). At the core of the Elizabethan world view remains the medieval belief in a structured universe, mirrored in the categories of *order* and *degree*. As part of human society the individual has to serve their community, and any individual initiative, dynamism and social energy has to be made subservient to the common goal. Fundamentally, a plethora of texts from the age give evidence to the belief that economic thinking as a self-centred disposition must be combined with moral and social perspectives. Increasingly, though, we find images of the merchant as a patriotic servant of the English or Scottish community, particularly when opposing or countering Spanish expansionism. Literary and non-literary texts alike create an aura of heroism around sea farers and pirates serving the national cause, with Sir Walter Raleigh and John Hawkins attaining the status of national icons in spite of their ruthless actions on the seas, far away from social norms and society. They were revered for character traits and deeds which would have exploded all social ties at home. By the same token, there remained a stong distrust of ostentatious display of wealth, which turned into disdain and hatred if luxury was openly displayed by the *nouveaux riche.*

The conflicting trends of the Elisabethan age were still contained through the elasticity of the Elizabethan World View. The ambiguous views on commercial life can be exemplified through a much commented soliloquy by the protagonist of William Shakespeare's tragedy *Timon of Athens* (1607–1608) on the significance of gold:

> Gold! yellow, glittering, precious gold! No gods,
> I am no idle votarist. Roots, you clear heavens!
> Thus much of this will make black white, foul fair,
> Wrong right, base noble, old young, coward valiant.
> Ha! you gods, why this? What this, you gods? Why this
> Will lug your priests and servants from your sides,
> Pluck stout men's pillows from below their head:
> This yellow slave
> Will knit and break religions; bless the accurs'd […].
> Thou common whore of mankind, that putt'st odds
> Among the rout of nations, I will make thee
> Do thy right nature.
> (Shakespeare 1949: IV.iii.26–34, IV.iii.42–44)

The passage does not lack the usual reference to the socially problem of riches, the frowned upon elements of gold and with it all material possessions. It was Friedrich Engels who pointed out another aspect of gold as a "visible deity" ("sichtbare Gottheit"), as the great leveler of traditional social hierarchies, guilds and ranks. Gold, in Engel's interpretation of this Shakespearean passage, does not only aim at resolving all social ranks, but also turns humans into "alienated, disenfranchised and self-objectifying beings" ("entfremdeten, entäußernden und sich veräußernden Gattungswesen," quoted in Volkmann 2003: 165). Yet another propensity of gold as foregrounded in Timon's ruminations remains unmentioned by Engels. It is the historically new concept of gold or money as a source of personal empowerment, as an instrument which can be utilized by all human agents striving for individual success. This new view implied a radical change, as can also be perceived in the permutation which Lady Fortune (Fortuna) underwent during the Renaissance. As fickle "lady luck" this allegory of fortune was deemed to be untamable throughout the Middle Ages. Iconically she was represented as the lady in charge of the "wheel of fortune," which simultaneously represented the unstoppable passing of time and the uncontrollable nature of femininity. Lady Fortune reigned over the ups and downs of individuals or groups. The new reading of Lady Fortune now suggested that the powers of chance and luck could be made subservient to one's own interests if dealt with cogently and wisely (see Reichert 1985).

6.4 Individualism vs. the Common Good in Elizabethan Drama

Among the Elizabethan playwrights it was prominently Christopher Marlowe who enjoyed irritating his contemporaries and probing the boundaries of religious and social norms and taboos. His iridescent writing can be interpreted as the raging reaction of Renaissance man battling with the newly opening freedom gained by the loss of medieval order and degree. His protagonists rebel forcefully and restlessly in tragedies like *Tamburlaine, I & II* (1590) und *Doctor Faustus* (1601/04). As so-called over-reachers (in today's parlance they might be called super-entrepreneurs) they struggle to break the boundaries created by the Elizabethan cosmos, and they fail tragically. In their differently expressed drive for knowledge, expansion and enrichment they reflect the unshackled dynamism of the economic forces which were paradigmatic of the "modern world of growth and competition" (Breuer 1979: 116), and which was marked in Marlowe's plays by an early colonial desire. As with his other protagonists, the unbound promethean force of restless longing was represented by Marlowe's most ambivalent hero, Barabas in *The Jew of Malta* (c. 1592/1633) – inexorably moving from destruction to self-destruction. His megalomaniacal self-fashioning as the mover and shaker of all world trade represents a composite of various stereotypes of the Middle Ages. Barabas seems like an avatar of the allegorical figure of *avaritia* und is simultaneously a diabolical reflection of Christian hatred of Jews and money-lenders. Such an ambivalent presentation must be seen against its historical background, which is that Jews were expelled from England in 1291 and were a socially marginalized minority in Marlowe's age; lending money against interest, forbidden as usury in the Middle Ages, was permitted at a rate of 10%, yet remained socially tabooed. As a monstrous incarnation of *homo oeconomicus* Barabas gets more and more entangled in his ludonic tactics, in his strategy of playing with all things, including humans and their feelings and loyalties. The grandmaster of the brave new world of commerce finally gets caught up in his own web of machinations – falling prey to his unbound hubris.

As opposed to Marlowe's plays, Shakespeare's dramas are marked by an attempt to integrate commercial life into the meaning creating framework of the Elizabethan World View. Thus, even in his "dark" comedy *The Merchant of Venice* (c. 1600) the dangerous wheeling and dealing of Shylock the Jew can be contained. The money lender, without whom the business world of Venice cannot exist, is relegated to the margins of society and branded as an outsider. He is a trouble maker among the male bonding of Venetian merchants, whose spokesman is the honest and noble oversea merchant Antonio. Fashioned as a true altruist when it comes to his social group, he begs Shylock to lend him 3000 ducats for supporting the courting of a rich foreign princess, Antonia, by his somehow too risk-friendly close friend Bassanio. When Bassanio cannot return the bond on time, a moment of severe crisis is created. Sylock insists on the terms of the lending contract, which is "one pound of flesh" to be cut out of the Christian's chest in case of failure to pay back punctually. At court, only the appeal to Christian "mercy" and a legal trick can deter Shylock and thwart his evil ambitions (which can be interpreted as the irrational reactions of a completely discriminated against social outsider). The legal method of solving economic issues may, incidentally, hint towards future ways of handling such matters. Futurity is also demonstrated by Antonio's favoured method of doing business, which is diversification. Different form medieval practices of investing in immobile possessions, he engages in global expansionism, investing in trading ships on all seas. Yet all his wealth cannot keep him from a melancholic disposition, which has sometimes been interpreted as the melancholy of Renaissance man, sometimes as the melancholy of merchants who secretly suffer from the verbal abuse heaped upon them in medieval texts:

> My ventures are not in one bottom trusted,
> Nor to one place; nor is my whole estate
> Upon the fortune of this present year:
> Therefore, my merchandise makes me not sad.
> (Shakespeare 1949: I.i.42–45)

Thus Shakespeare, on the one hand, created in Shylock a racial and cultural stereotype steeped in medieval traditions – which is often problematized in recent productions. On the other, he wrote the first realistic portrayal of a merchant in English literature with his character Antonio. This realistic image, though, was to remain the exception in English literature from the Renaissance to the Age of Enlightenment, up to Daniel Defoe's portrayals of trading protagonists. Another contemporary of Shakespeare, the playwright Ben Jonson, for example, again used vitriolic satire to fashion merchants as prototypes of a society exploding through monetary excess. In Marlowe's grotesque drama *The Jew of Malta* Jonson found the blueprint of an economic nightmare which he sketched out with the acidic pen of a satirist: In Jonson's dramas the destructive forces of money sever all social cohesion and loyalties. In them he vivisects a world of corruption, hypocrisy and pretense. The money-grabbing egomaniac Volpone in the eponymous tragic comedy (1606) as well as the protagonist with the telling name Sir Epicure Mammon in *The Alchemist* (1610) come across as satirical deformations of *homo oeconomicus*. They display the terrors of economic thinking as the root of all evil and, like Barabas, bring about their own downfall through their hubristic longings for more and more material wealth. Jonson remains highly indebted to medieval morality plays, though unable or unwilling to point to a Christian alternative.

6.5 Different Perspectives of the Seventeenth Century

In the early seventeenth century reactions to commercial life in early capitalism followed two opposing directions, with little common ground shared by them (McVeagh 1981; Nicholson 1994). Following the tradition established by dramatist Ben Jonson, representatives of the so-called *citizen comedy* depicted merchants and tradesmen as the main culprits of a toxic social atmosphere, a miasma of greed, ambition and money-grabbing. This was staged in plays like Thomas Middleton's *Michaelmas Term* (1607) or Philip Massinger's *A New Way to Pay Old Debts* (1633) before the Puritans closed all playhouses in 1642. In them the practice of gentrification was displayed as the magic formula used by social upstarts to cleanse themselves from the stigma of low birth and to gain access to the upper echelons of society. These, however, continued to be taken by the aristocratic establishment. Without any qualms and full of treachery, the upstart protagonists hankered after the status symbols of the gentry. This they aimed at through getting married into the aristocracy and through taking over the greatest status symbol of the age, a country estate. However, in the citizen comedies such appropriation turned out to be disastrous for the *arrivistes*. Lacking in education and etiquette, without any sense of social decorum and ignorant regarding the unwritten rules of sophisticated interaction, the *new men* proved to be quite "out of place" and also unable to hide their lack of social concern. Their crude behaviour was exposed against the norms and values of the Gentry, on stage displayed through their verbal blunders or breach of etiquette. This turned them into the butt of harsh social ridicule. Ultimately, their destructive egoism was unveiled, in the tradition of medieval and Renaissance drama. It is surprising to find that more than a generation later, in restauration comedies after 1660 such as in Edward Ravenscroft's *The London Cuckolds* (1681), this tradition of putting merchants and tradesmen up to ridicule is seamlessly upheld, even with greater hyperbolic effect.

A different, opposing line of tradition is simultaneously established at the beginning of the seventeenth century. A group of early bourgeois dramatists such as Richard Johnson, Thomas Dekker and Thomas Heywood as well as the prose writer Thomas Deloney worked as the literary mouthpiece for the evolving social class of commerce and trade. Dekker's witty comedy *The Shoemaker's Holiday* (1599) is still a recommendable read. While contemporary audiences reveled in the slapsticklike, colourful humour of the play and enjoyed the optimistic popular comedy, recent criticism has drawn attention to the mechanisms of exclusion at work in this play, which claims to present the inner perspective of a newly evolving social class of traders and merchants. This is done at the expense of suppressing aspects of fraudulent business practices and actual conflicts of the age. On the contrary, bourgeois existence and the trading profession are glorified as morally exemplary and worth imitating. Seen from today's critical perspective, such openly displayed ideological stances of the bourgeois comedy may appear as the collective self-praise of content philistines. Based on a true story, the protagonist of *The Shoemaker's Holiday* – a simple, honest and yet ambitious master craftsman – succeeds in climbing the social ladder to the very top by finally becoming Lord Mayor of London. This happens much to the benefit both of his profession and his country. Resorting to old-fashioned values of charity and social responsibility, master Simon Eyre clearly shows that the newly established cloth manufactures of the age, which actually posed an enormous threat to social peace, could prove to be positive for the common weal and that social tensions could be contained – at least in this affirmative piece of literature.

With the rise of the merchant class a new genre of tragedy evolved, the *domestic tragedy.* Famously, in George Lillo's *The London Merchant* (1731) the merchant was celebrated as the prototype of his bourgeois class, which hitherto had not been deemed worthy of being represented in great tragedy. While the drama in a unique and new manner foregrounds the private sphere of its social setting, it simultaneously focuses its plot on the actions of a bourgeois moral and ethical paragon, the righteous and esteemed merchant with the telling name Thorowgood. The model merchant is given several opportunities in the drama to express in long, declamatory speeches his glorious achievements as a national and international benefactor. In the tradition of the moral essays by Joseph Addison and Richard Steele he ennobles the profession of the trading merchant and elevates him to the lofty status of a true state-carrying patriot. Here is a short excerpt from Thorowgood's deliberations about trade and business, in which he declares them to be a sort of science:

> 'Twill be well worth your pains to study it as a science, see how it is founded in reason and the nature of things, how it has promoted humanity as it has opened and yet keeps up an intercourse between nations far remote from one another in situation, customs, and religion; promoting arts, industry, peace, and plenty; by mutual benefits diffusing mutual love from pole to pole. (Lillo 1965, III.1.3–9)

It is interesting to note that this idealizing and partly sermonizing description of mercantile life, together with a rather far-fetched plot and the stock characters of the play resonated well with the urban audiences of the age. Melodramatic plot turns as well as the sentimental look at a bourgeois fate and the failings of Thorowgood's apprentice were all presented on stage in a manner which created a striking exemplum of warning. During Lillo's life time the tragedy was staged for many seasons and continued as a repertoire piece, which was performed publicly around Christmas and Easter. It is said that mercantile circles supported the staging with the aim of furthering the moral instruction of young apprentices.

6.6 The Paradoxical Nature of Puritanism as a Driving Force Behind Commercial Life

The rise of the English or rather British bourgeoisie is traditionally closely linked to the influence of Puritanism or Protestantism. Max Weber und R. H. Tawney propounded the wide-spread thesis of the birth of capitalism out of the spirit of the Puritan or Protestant work ethic (for a short introduction, see Guttandin 1998). And indeed, Puritanism had a formative influence through its emphasis on the stressful uncertainty about life after death, its redefinition of the value of hard work, and mostly, through the valorization of material success as a sign of "being chosen." In its increasingly secularized form it served as the "fuel" ("Brennstoff", Max Weber) for establishing the world view of the *homo oeconomicus* and the concomitant ideology of the pursuit of commercial profit. However, already Weber and Tawney pointed out the obvious paradoxes inherent in the origins of Puritan and Protestant thought, detecting anti-capitalist sentiments in its early proponents. Many religious thinkers and churchmen raised their voices to warn of the unshackled enrichment of individuals and extolled their followers not to pursue the path of money and money making. The two most-acclaimed Puritan authors of seventeenth century Britain, John Milton and John Bunyan, were also rather skeptical regarding the commercial tendencies of their epoch. It is no small wonder, then, that the counterpart to Bunyan's type of the righteous believer, the protagonist Christian in *The Pilgrim's Progress* (1st part around 1667), is a tradesman by profession and typically called Mr. Badman. He cheats and outsmarts his customers and leads a life of dissipation and debauchery. And, of course, he has to pay the price of eternal damnation in the end. Exemplary of Bunyan's stance on the world of commerce and trade is a well-known passage from his allegorical narrative *The Pilgrim's Progess.* Set in a city called Vanity, resembling London, a fair called Vanity Fair is described in this scene. Everything is for sale, all sorts of merchandise, and among the goods, peddled by Beelzebub himself, one can even purchase "Truth," that is, a warped form of spiritual guidance.

Such obvious criticism of commercial life appears as one of the core paradoxes of Puritanism. It is the unleashing effect of this faith which is reflected in the inner turmoil and restlessness of the protagonists of Bunyan's and Milton's works, as is the case with Satan in Milton's *Paradise Lost*, 1667. Self-discipline as an answer to a hostile world, contradictory forces working within the individual – these are the tensions which hint at the dynamics of the Puritan world view, which in turn has been seen as one of the essential driving forces behind early capitalism and the genesis of *homo oeconomicus.*

6.7 The Rise of the Merchant after the Glorious Revolution

With the Glorious Revolution of 1688/1689 the true rise of the merchant as a literary character commences (on this period, see Riedel 1990; Prinz 2003). In the commercial sector, the financial revolution paved the way for a sustained but not completely untroubled period of growth. The foundation of the Bank of England in 1694 was instrumental in providing a stable and reliable basis for the financial sector of Britain. Simultaneously, state-run or -supported monopoly companies enjoyed a success boom, also in the area of slave trade. The restored Stock Exchange proved helpful for the economy as well. An economic shock was caused by the first financial crash of modern times, the South Sea Bubble, which was the culmination point of months of mindless investment in a dubious, partly state-run enterprise.

There were dramatists who expressed support for commercial change, such as Richard Steele or George Lillo. The authors of classicism, though, responded to the age of the financial revolution with well-established images of horror. Supporters of the so-called Bolingbroke circle such as Jonathan Swift, Alexander Pope and John Gay, but also the painter and caricaturist William Hogarth, developed a two-pronged strategy of criticism: On the one hand, they praised traditional principles of serving the common goal and painted idealized images of a simple and patriarchial society, modelled after idyllic rural retreats. On the other, they lambasted urban decay and the life of dissipation and egoism as prevalent in the metropolis.

Daniel Defoe's reaction to the uncertainties and changes of his age were completely different. Deemed by some a hack writer, the extremely prolific author – at least 375 texts were officially penned by him – actively took part in the newly evolving market of literature and publications. Like him, his protagonists had to battle with falling and rising life lines. Both Robinson Crusoe and Moll Flanders, to point out two characters from eponymous novels, are driven by inner uncertainties and try again and again to gain a sense of stability and security in their lives shaped by trade and exchange. Constantly, they face loss and strokes of fate, though in different geographical areas. While the heroine of *Moll Flanders* (1722) weaves her way through life as a trickster and a part-time prostitute and narrates more than two-hundred episodes taking place in London but also in the American colonies, Robinson Crusoe (in the novel from 1719) creates a microcosm of civilization from scratch, through his own will and force. Frequently, he has been interpreted as a true *homo oeconomicus*, only interested in rational approaches to nature, time and humans. He appears to be lacking all sense of the aesthetic and seems disinterested in the Other, be it the indigenous people he encouters, be it the females that appear in his life. He reacts to both with a feelings of fear, restraint and indifference or calculating how to make use of them as his inferiors.

It was the Dutch born London physician Bernard Mandeville who sketched out the most cynical world view of his age, in the satirical doggerel poem "The Grumbling Hive: or, Knaves Turn'd Honest." First sold by street vendors in 1705, the poem was later rewritten and augmented by various essays, to be published as a somehow coherent theory of modern society with the title *The Fable of the Bees* (1714, 1723–1725). Mandeville's claim to fame still rests in what became to be known as the "Mandevillian paradox," the formula of "private vices, publick benefits." The author's view of individuals and society is illustrated throught his fable of the bees. While in the hive of the poem greed, dissipation and fraud reign high and all the bees only seek their own advantage, the whole population prospers and grows nicely. It is even envied by all the other hives or nations.

[...] Luxury
Employ'd a Million of the Poor,
And odious Pride a Million more:
Envy it self, and Vanity,
Were Ministers of Industry
[...]
Thus Vice nurs'd Ingenuity,
Which join'd with Time and Industry,
Had carry'd Life's Conveniences,
Its real Pleasures, Comforts, Ease,
To such a Height, the very Poor
Liv'd better than the Rich before,
And nothing could be added more. (Mandeville 1988, I.25f.)

This budding bee nation is severly disturbed, however, when moral philosophers intervene and indignantly decry the moral decay in the busy hive. As a result, moral order is estblished. This, however, happens to the detriment of the hive – work ethic deteriorates and the bees become so lazy that they fall easy prey to their rivals and are on the verge of extinction. The moral of the fable is expressed triumphantly:

Fraud, Luxury and Pride must live,
While we the Benefits receive.
(ibid., 36)

In his essays, Mandeville cynically elaborates on his provocative ideas: Not only brothels, but moreover famines, great fires and all sorts of crime sprees prove to be benefical for the common good, if viewed from a broader, macroeconomic perspective. These tenets turned Mandeville into a philosopher of neoliberalism *avant la lettre* – in his hyperbolic belittling of the fate of individuals and his praise of the self-regulatory forces of the market as the end all of all human exchanges. Thus Mandeville offers an early caricature of *homo oeconomicus* as a representative of what critics later dubbed "the terror of economics," presenting an utterly objectifying and reifying view of humans. Mandeville's ideas reverberated in theories of Utilitarianism and *laissez-faire* or Manchester liberalism of the nineteenth century. And it is small wonder that Bernard Mandeville's deliberations found a most controversial response again at the end of the twentieth and the beginning of the twenty-first century in the age of neoliberal thought (see Volkmann 2007; Beckert 2011; Pires and Braga 2015).

Primary Literature

George Lillo. 1965. *The London Merchant*, ed. William H. McBurney. London: Edward Arnold.
George Warner, ed. 1926. *The Libelle of Englyshe Polycye: A poem on the use of sea-power*. [ca. 1436]. Oxford: Clarendon Press.
Langland, William. 1994. *Piers Plowman: The C-text*. [ca. 1362–1393], ed. Derek Pearsall. Exeter: University of Exeter Press.
Mandeville, Bernard. 1988. *The Fable of the bees or private vices, publick benefits* [1705/1714]. 2 vols, ed. F.B. Kaye. Indianapolis: Liberty Press.

Shakespeare, William. 1949. *The complete works of William Shakespeare*, ed. W.J. Craig. London: Oxford University Press.
Smith, Adam. 1981. *An inquiry into the nature and causes of the wealth of nations*, 2 vols, ed. R.H. Campbell, A.S. Skinner; textual ed. W.B. Todd. Indianapolis: Liberty Fund.
———. 1984. *The theory of moral sentiments,* ed. D.D. Raphael and A.L. Macfie. Indianapolis: Liberty Fund.

Secondary Literature

Beckert, Jens. 2011. The transcending power of goods: Imaginative value in the economy. In *The worth of goods. Valuation & pricing in the economy*, ed. Beckert Jens and Patrik Aspers, 106–130. Oxford: Oxford University Press.
Benson, John, and Laura Ugolini, eds. 2003. *A nation of shopkeepers: Five centuries of British retailing*. London: Tauris.
Breuer, Horst. 1979. *Vorgeschichte des Fortschritts: Studien zur Historizität und Aktualität des Dramas der Shakespearezeit: Marlowe – Shakespeare – Jonson*. München: Wilhelm Fink.
Guttandin, Friedhelm. 1998. *Einführung in die Protestantische Ethik Max Webers*. Opladen/Westfalen: Westdeutscher Verlag.
Hempel, Dirk, and Christine Künzel, eds. 2009. *"Denn wovon lebt der Mensch?" Literatur und Wirtschaft*. Frankfurt a. M: Peter Lang.
Hirschman, Albert O. 1977. *The passions and the interest: Political arguments for capitalism before its triumph*. Princeton: Princeton UP.
Kirchgässner, Gebhard. 1991. *Homo oeconomicus: Das ökonomische Modell individuellen Verhaltens und seine Anwendung in den Wirtschafts- und Sozialwissenschaften*. Tübingen: Mohr.
Kohl, Stephan. 1986. *Das englische Spätmittelalter: Kulturelle Normen, Lebenspraxis, Texte*. Tübingen: Max Niemeyer Verlag.
McVeagh, John. 1981. *Tradefull merchants: The portrayal of the capitalist in literature*. London: Routledge & Kegan Paul.
Mein, Georg, and Franziska Schößler. 2005. *Tauschprozesse. Kulturwissenschaftliche Verhandlungen des Ökonomischen*. Bielefeld: Transcript.
Nicholson, Colin. 1994. *Writing and the rise of finance: Capital satires of the early eighteenth century*. Cambridge: Cambridge University Press.
Oncken, August. 1898. Das Adam Smith-problem. *Zeitschrift für Socialwissenschaft* 1: 25–33, 101–108, 276–287.
Pires, Edmundo Balsemão, and Joaquim Braga, eds. 2015. *Bernard de Mandeville's tropology of paradoxes. Morals, politics, economics, and therapy*. London: Springer.
Prinz, Michael. 2003. Aufbruch in den Überfluss? Die englische 'Konsumrevolution' des 18. Jahrhunderts im Lichte der neueren Forschung. In *Der lange Weg in den Überfluss. Anfänge und Entwicklung der Konsumgesellschaft seit der Vormoderne*, ed. Michael Prinz, 191–217. Paderborn: Ferdinand Schöningh.
Reichert, Klaus. 1985. *Fortuna oder die Beständigkeit des Wechsels*. Frankfurt a. M: Suhrkamp.
Riedel, Wolfgang. 1990. *'Die unsichtbare Hand': Ökonomie, Sittlichkeit und Kultur der englischen Mittelklasse (1650–1850)*. Tübingen: Narr.
Southall, Raymond. 1973. *Literature and the rise of capitalism: Critical essays mainly on the sixteenth and seventeenth centuries*. London: Lawrence & Wishart.
Suerbaum, Ulrich. 1996. *Shakespeares Dramen*. Tübingen/Basel: Francke.
Tillyard, E.M.W. 1963 [1943]. *The Elizabethan world picture*. Harmondsworth: Penguin.
Veeser, H. Aram, ed. 1994. *The new historicism reader*. New York/London: Routledge.

Volkmann, Laurenz. 2001. Mandeville's beehive and Smith's invisible hand: Conflicting voices of ethics and economics in early industrialism. In *Talking forward, talking back: Critical dialogues with the enlightenment*, ed. Kevin Cope and Rüdiger Ahrens, 13–42. New York: AMS Press.

———. 2003. *Homo oeconomicus: Studien zur Modellierung eines neuen Menschenbilds in der englischen Literatur vom Mittelalter bis zum 18. Jahrhundert*. Heidelberg: C. Winter.

———. 2007. Back with a vengeance: The return of Bernard Mandeville. In *Anglistentag 2006 Halle. Proceedings*, ed. Sabine Volk-Birke and Julia Lippert, 45–52. Trier: WVT.

Watts, Michael, ed. 2003. *The literary book of economics: Including readings from literature and drama on economic concepts, issues, and themes*. Wilmington: ISI-Books.

Part III
The Image of the Merchant in Europe from Early Modern Times Until Nineteenth Century

Chapter 7
The Long Journey from "Deceiver and Conman" to "Honorable Merchant." The Image of the Merchant in Spanish Literature and Its Contexts from the Sixteenth to the End of the Eighteenth Century

Manfred Tietz

Abstract The image of the merchant in the sixteenth, seventeenth and eighteenth centuries is one of the less studied objects of Spanish literature, cultural and economic history. The starting point of this contribution is the negative image of the merchant as a 'deceiver and conman' in Spain in the late Middle Ages and the early modern period. This image changes in the course of the sixteenth century in a positive way due to the economic rise of Spain in the Siglo de Oro. The theologians of the important school of Salamanca ideologically legitimized this change – with great moral scruples. The eighteenth century, with its profound secularization and professionalization of the merchant class, completed the process of its recognition as 'honorable man and benefactor' in a modern society.

> En France est marquis qui veut; et quiconque arrive a Paris du fond d'une province avec de l'argent à dépenser [...] peut mépriser souverainement un négociant; le négociant entend lui-même parler si souvent avec mépris de sa profession, qu'il est assez sot pour en rougir. Je ne sais pourtant lequel est plus utile à un Etat, ou un seigneur bien poudré qui sait précisément à quelle heure le Roi se lève, à quelle heure il se couche, et qui se donne des airs de grandeur en jouant le rôle d'esclave dans l'antichambre d'un ministre, ou un négociant qui enrichit son pays, donne de son cabinet des ordres à Surate et au Caire, et contribue au bonheur du monde. Voltaire: *Lettres philosophiques* (X), 1734.

M. Tietz (✉)
University of Bochum, Bochum, Germany
e-mail: Manfred.Tietz@rub.de

C. Lütge, C. Strosetzki (eds.), *The Honorable Merchant – Between Modesty and Risk-Taking*, Ethical Economy 56, https://doi.org/10.1007/978-3-030-04351-3_7

7.1 Preliminary Thoughts on the Negative Image of the Merchant in the Spanish Literature and the Mindset of El Siglo de Oro

Unlike the image of peasants and farmers (*campesino/villano*) or beggars and tramps (*mendigos/Picaros*) during the Renaissance and the Baroque of the Spanish world at that time,[1] studies on the image of the merchant in contemporary Hispanic literature are few and far between. This is not all that surprising, however. Collectively, the entire rather heterogeneous so-called "middle class" (the *clases medias* or *medianía*) and the gradually forming "bourgeois groups" – lawyers, scholars, doctors, court and city officials, but also the merchants[2] – were hardly an object of the literary imagination.[3] The recent essay from Germán Torres published before the recent collection of essays Temas del comercio y la economía en la narrativa hispana (2008), which he co-edited, represents an exception, albeit one that requires supplementing. In his very general overview article entitled "La figura del hombre de negocios en la literatura hispana,"[4] the author outlines how the image of the merchant in Spain and Latin America has changed from the Middle Ages to the present day in Spanish-language literature in Spain and Latin America. According to the author, this – to a large extent topical – image fundamentally vacillates across time between two extremes. On the one hand, the merchant is a kind of eternally human character, which – like the figure of Shylock in Shakespeare's Merchant of Venice (1596/1998) – is problematically driven by greed and opportunism. On the other hand, at the latest with the onset of modernity, the merchant appears in the guise of the new rich and social upstart, who questions the existing social order. He is consequently viewed negatively, mocked, and socially devalued by those whose privileges he disputes – the representatives of this (largely feudal) order, the nobility, and the clergy. Germán Torres sees this certainly not unproblematic view – which precisely conceals the figure of the positive, "honorable merchant" – confirmed in his brief overview of merchant figures in medieval and early modern Spanish literature. Here, Torres sketches works from the early *Poema de mío Cid* from the middle of the twelfth century to the *Libro de Buen Amor* from the middle of the fourteenth

[1] With regard to the rural population, cf. the still relevant standard work of Noël Salomon (1965, 1985), which looks simultaneously at social history and literature. The same applies to the study of Michel Cavillac (1983) on the so-called "picaresque novel, which is selective, but offers a detailed consideration of the economic-ideological environment. On the other hand, the discussion devoted to merchants covers only a small part of the analysis. Among the figures of "Literatur in Bewegung" examined by Hanno Ehrlicher (2010), the "long-distance traveling merchant"– in contrast to the "pilgrim" and the "pícaro" – was not been taken into account.

[2] From the simple tradesman to the big businessman, they were little differentiated by their contemporaries as *mercaderes*, *comerciantes* or *hombres de negocios*. These terms are also used in the following text to a large extent synonymously for the designation of the merchant phenotype.

[3] Maravall (1979, p. 274).

[4] Torres (2008, pp. 1–33).

century[5] and Mateo Alemán's *Guzmán Alfarache*, a picaresque novel from the turn of the sixteenth and seventeenth century, all the way to the literary work of Francisco de Quevedo, the powerfully eloquent defender of the traditional, conservative-Catholic Spain, who died in 1645 and principally saw in the merchant's actions an accumulation of earthly riches without any moral and professional honor due to its lack of reference to the afterlife.

To be sure, Germán Torres points out that in the wake of the Renaissance and a new social relevance of commerce and merchants in the sixteenth century, there are occasionally positive images of the merchant in Spanish literary texts. One of these is the figure of rich *pleberio* in Fernando de Rojas' *Celestina* (1499), a pioneering and widely read work during this time. Social historian José Antonio Maravall (1911–1986) also observes that this literary figure, whose first successful "mercantilistic and honorable life plan" completely fails due to the suicide of his daughter, could be evidence that the view emerged around 1500 in Spain, as in Italy, that "wholesale trade, which moves a considerable amount of goods, is quite honorable and thus became a source of social respectability [*honra*] and wealth."[6] By and large, however, in the Spanish *El Siglo de Oro* – especially in its second half (the Baroque) and the Counter-Reformation, which profoundly impacted all areas of life – the idealized images of the dominant feudal groups of the nobility and the clergy in the late Middle Ages emerge (the heroic soldier and conqueror, on the one hand, as well as the saint and missionary, on the other). By the contrast, the idealized image of the rich merchant attributable to the bourgeoisie at that time does not appear to have gained acceptance. Indeed, in the years from the failure of the "liberal revolution" of the *Comunidades de Castilla* (1521) until well into the eighteenth century, the middle class had tenuous standing from a mentality-historical, real-social and political perspective. In the ideological context of the Counter-Reformation, whose preeminent saints Juan de Dios (1495–1150) and Teresa de Ávila (1515–1582) followed the religious ideal of freely chosen poverty, the individual wealth characteristic of the (large) merchants obviously had a negative connotation.[7] The merchants were therefore repeatedly confronted with the charge that they were

[5] With regard to the medieval texts, however, Torres overlooks the fact that the narrative texts, which originate from Arab-Jewish tradition such as the *Disciplina clericalis* (around 1115) by Petrus Alfonsi and the Arabic-oriental wisdom literature do indeed have figures of worldly-wise rich merchants.

[6] Quoted from Germán Torres (2008, p. 26, n. 4): "the comercio en grande, y que mueve considerables riquezas, it honorable y como tal se converte en fuente de honra y enriquecimiento."

For the basic economic ideas, which manifest themselves in Rojas' text and determine the action of the persons, which is completely guided by selfishness and self-interest, cf. the analysis of Maravall (1964). On the ambivalent image of the merchant in Mateo Alemán and his "novela picaresca" *Guzmán de Alfarache,* see the social and mentality history of Cavillac (1983, 2001, 2013, 2014)

[7] Tellingly, today's patron saints of Catholic merchants (with the exception of the Archangel Michael and King Louis IX of France) are usually saints who have abandoned their status as successful merchants and spent the rest of their lives in absolute poverty: Francis of Assisi (1181/2–1226), Guido of Anderlecht (d. 1012) Homobonus of Cremona (1150–1197), Mauritius (d. 290), Nicholas of Myra (270/86–326/45/51/65 and Romanus of Rouen (d. 640).

exposed to certain "pecados profesionales," i.e. to implicit and therefore unavoidable sins – especially the mortal sin of greed (*avaritia*). They *ipso facto* must be bad Christians. It is telling, therefore, that in Calderón de la Barca's (1600–1681) most famous play – the Corpus Christi play *El gran teatro del Mundo*, which reflects the social structure of counter-reformatory Spain in a normative way – only one figure is condemned directly to eternal hell: the rich man. Whereas he is blatantly presented as unrepentant, the poor man, in the guise of the beggar, is allowed to enter directly into the kingdom of heaven. Thus, in the social reality of Spain at that time, the "comerciantes" were excluded (despite their wealth) from the particularly "honorable" (knights) orders,[8] as were all those who practiced a "common, low or craft profession."[9] The vocation of merchant was in any case not an option for representatives of the "clases dirigentes" such as the aristocracy, who spurned the merchant's occupation and status (unlike in Italy, especially in Genoa and Venice, where the [prosperous] merchant enjoyed the highest social prestige). This phenomenon was undoubtedly due to the fact that (large and long-distance) trade in Spain was often not only in the hands of unpopular foreigners, especially Italians, Flemings, and Germans, but also the Jews. Having been officially expelled from Spain since 1492, the Jews were greatly despised because of their "impure blood," as were their descendants, who had allegedly converted only for the sake of appearances (*conversos* or "new Christians"). The Spanish "Old Christians," who were particularly concerned about their "blood purity" (*limpieza de sangre*), distinguished themselves by shunning specifically Jewish professions – such as that of a merchant or financier – to avoid a reputation of ethnically and racially habituated dishonor.[10] Unsurprisingly, as a quote from a relevant text from the early seventeenth century text demonstrates, it was not just the simple merchant, but every merchant as such had the reputation "to steal, to practice usury, to not maintain the fair and inalienable price, and to continue to write debts on his books, which have probably already been paid three times over."[11] While this text is satirical, it certainly reflects the widespread views on commerce and businessmen at the time. The *Diccionario de Autoridades* – the dictionary which presents the language of *El Siglo de Oro* (though it was not published

[8] Cavillac (2014, pp. 41–42).

[9] Cruickshank (2011, p. 293): "oficio vil, bajo o mecánico."

[10] As regards the social relevance of "blood purity," Juan Ignacio Gutiérrez Nieto (1996, p. 385) rightly states: "For the period from about 1575 to 1650, not keeping an eye on the obsession [sc. of the Spaniards] with regard to blood purity, means that one does not succeed in penetrating into the deeper layers of the social reality of that specific period of time, a period which has not been repeated in Spanish history and cannot be repeated." ("No tener en cuenta la obsesión por la limpieza en el período comprendido entre 1575 y 1650, como fechas aproximadas, es no saber penetrar en planos profundos de la realidad social de esa coyuntura concreta, irrepetida e irrepetible en la historia de España"). See also the most recent relevant study on the subject of Jesús Hernández Franco (2011). It is no coincidence that the grandfather of St. Teresa of Ávila, who was of Jewish descent and a merchant, had retreated to the remote town of Ávila with his family from Toledo, the Spanish commercial center at that time, in order to conceal these two "blemishes."

[11] Carlos Garcia: Desordenada codicia de los bienes ajenos (1619), here quoted from Torres (2008, p. 6): "[que] hurta, dando a usura, pasando el justo y riguroso prescio y asentando en su libro la deuda que ventura estará tres veces pagada."

until 1726–1736) – provides an example sentence under the keyword "mercader": "There is no merchant who would not try to cheat those who trust him the most with honey-sweet rhetoric, seeking to give his wares a quality that they do not have with a myriad of fake assurances."[12] Such an equation of the merchant with the dishonorable conman and deceiver was not uncommon at this time.

The texts of the Bible, which were authoritative and normative for the Spaniards, especially contributed to a negative view of merchants. Also influential was the dogmatic theology, which took all matters of worldly life under its purview, and, particularly, the theology of the sixteenth century of much-quoted scholastic Thomas Aquinas (1225–1274). The expulsion of the traders and buyers from the temple reported in *Mt.* 21:12 ("vendents et ementes") supported the moral and social diminishment of the merchant, as did the relevant statements in Thomas' *Summa Theologiae* II-II, q. 77. Here, the necessity and usefulness of the merchant's status is generally acknowledged. It is further observed, however, that buying and selling (which was always connected with Church proscribed interest taking) invariably leads to the suspicion of dishonesty – "quaedam turpitudo," II-II q. 77, a. 4, a. 4 – especially as the boundary to usury, which Thomas (*De peccato usurae*, II-II q. 78) unambiguously classifies as a sin, is rather fluid.[13] In addition, the Spanish merchants themselves – and especially those from the upper class – did not contribute to a positive class consciousness. From the middle of the seventeenth century, at the latest, they seem to have been increasingly interested in their social advancement, specifically the acquisition of aristocratic titles, as well as in their own financial security through the purchase and exploitation of property. Of less interest was innovative, necessarily risky trade,[14] which the country would have urgently needed for its prosperity – a view that was even shared by the Spanish politicians of the time.

[12] Vol. IV, p. 548 a.: "No hai *mercader* que con palabrillas melifluas, no procure clavar al que mas se fía dél, tratando de hacer creer, con mil juramentos fingidos, la bondad de que carece su mercaduria."

In France, Jacques Savary had already fought in 1675 in his programmatic work on the "parfait négociant" against such a negative view of the merchant, which originated from the perspective of the "upper classes" (aristocrats, clergy) and had developed his own professional norm (writing, arithmetic, modern foreign languages; no humanistic education, i.e. neither Latin nor philosophy or theology) for the training and professional practice of an honorable merchant. See Julia (1995, pp. 215–256).

[13] At the same time, though, *moral theology* did remain silent: Fray Antonio de la Vega thus complains: "These people are so busy with their business and trade that they don't even have time to remember God at all." ("Anda esta gente tan enfrascada en sus negocios y tratos que aun para acordarse de Dios no tienen lugar.") Quoted from Rivero (2005, p. 6). This statement can already be found in Thomas (II-II, q. 77, a. 4 ad tertium), which turns on *Tim* II, 2, 4 invokes: "Nemo militans Deo implicat se negotiis saecularibus."

[14] Vila Vilar (2001, p. 93), shows how in the first decades of the seventeenth century the merchants in Seville began to invest their assets not so much for commercial investments as for purely representative purposes (sumptuous silverware, ecclesiastical foundations etc.) and invest their profits not in the form of risk capital, but in trouble-free "government bonds" (juros) in order to secure their main objective of ascending the social hierarchy ("ir subiendo peldaños en la escala social").

These preliminary remarks may suggest that the concept of the "honor or dishonor" of the merchant is neither manifested in historical reality nor in the various discourses of the time (especially in literary and theological discourse), nor, for that matter, can it be meaningfully defined in an abstract and universally valid way. To better understand the phenomenon of the "honorable merchant" in the Spanish *El Siglo de Oro* and the following epoch, several exemplary merchant resumes from the sixteenth to the eighteenth century will be outlined in their historical reality. In particular, they will be set in relation to the period's theological discourse – or, as will be seen, theological discourses – on the various historical phenotypes of the merchant.

7.2 The Historical Dignification and Theological Legitimation of the Merchant in the Reality of the Spanish Sixteenth Century

The negative, less honorable image of the merchant, which had resulted from some literary and normative theological sources, must not obscure the fact that at least the rich merchant in the historical social reality in the Spain of the sixteenth century could also be quite a positive figure endowed with signs of respectability and who played a socially relevant role. From a German perspective, it is worth paying special attention to the Fuggers. They had a close network of relations across extensive parts of Europe, in particular European Spain, the Spanish Netherlands, the Spanish zones of influence in Italy and, ultimately, also the Spanish Americas. Without their trade and financing activities, the Spain of Charles V and Philip II is hardly conceivable, and not just from a financial point of view.[15] The truth of this statement is supported by the fact that their trading company, which also conducted vast banking transactions (as was customary at the time), had an extra-territorial status in Andalusian Almagro.[16] Also worth mentioning in this context is Anton Meuting (1524–1591), a Bavarian merchant closely associated with the Fuggers. Mark Häberlein and Magdalena Bayreuther (2013) recently conducted intensive research on him as a highly active merchant between Upper Germany and Spain. A look at Meuting's remarkably varied activities shows that the merchant's (albeit here difficult to define) honor consisted in the fact that – in the sense of Bourdieu – he not only possessed *economic capital* and was able to use it in accordance with established rules and customs. He also possessed *cultural capital*: an excellent knowledge of foreign languages,[17] national and cultural understanding due to a

[15] See Hermann Kellenbenz (1970).

[16] It should be recalled that the Fuggers sought to clarify the "honor" of their actions as merchants and bankers through religiously founded social foundations. For example, Jakob Fugger (1459–1525), the head of the large-scale enterprise, founded the Augsburg "Fuggerei" in 1521, an extensive residential complex for needy (Catholic) residents of the city.

[17] Häberlein (2010, pp. 23–45).

considerable geographical mobility, an ability to gain access to the highest spheres of the courts, and, finally, an artistic understanding in the broadest sense of the word for also recognizing, above all, the luxury needs of his rich clientele of nobility and clergy and thus creating and satisfying demand. Meuting's life shows "that the boundaries between trade and diplomacy were fluid in the 16th century and that there were dynamic developments and shifts between the roles of merchant, princely agent, and diplomat."

Showing how far the prince's recognition of the merchant and thus the manifestation of his "honor" might go, Ulrich Ehinger (1485–1537), who worked for the Augsburg Welser Society in Spain, was conferred the honor of a Santiago knight, which was typically reserved for the Spanish nobility. As José Antonio Maravall has demonstrated, wealthy merchants in the sixteenth and the first decades of the seventeenth century generally rose socially and attained "social honor." Along with the jurists (*letrados*), they were deliberately accepted by the royalty into the power elites as "middle class" (*medianía*). For merchants, though, this seems to have only been done to a limited extent. The mobility of society at the time of the Renaissance, including the merchant class, came again to a standstill when the re-feudalization of Spanish society took place in the seventeenth century. This brought about renewed esteem for the nobility and its privileged use in civil service, the rejection of work (not just manual work) and the general disdain for active involvement in trade and industry.

Despite these curtailments, however, these examples show more than the socially significant role and the actual recognition of the "honor" of wealthy merchants in Spain. They also explain why – despite the general theological reservations about the status of merchants – in Spain during the sixteenth century a whole philosophical-theological school dealt with this vocation and – in addition to traditional scholasticism – looked for its possible theological, especially moral-theological, legitimacy. Specifically, the Neo-Scholastics of the so-called "School of Salamanca" did not abandon the fundamental theological guidelines of scholastic theology. Rather, under the influence of discovery, colonization and missionary work as well as the economic exploitation of America (which upset many conventional patterns of thought), they rethought a large number of legal and economic questions, including those of (wholesale) trade. Apart from the visionary of this entire school, the astute theologian and founder of modern natural law Francisco de Vitoria (1483–1546), Juan de Medina (1490–1547), Martín de Azpilcueta (1492–1586), Tomás de Mercado (1523/30–1575) and Luis de Molina (1535–1600) deserve special mention here in the field of economics. As authors, they should all be regarded as pioneers of a thoroughly modern theory of commerce and economy, who contributed in contemporary practice to overcoming the traditional qualification of interest taking (one of the central complexes of commercial activity) as a sin. Following Eberhard Geisler,[18] I will now outline some trains of thought and evaluations of the merchant

[18]The above-mentioned book is now available in Spanish translation: *El dinero en la obra de Quevedo. La crisis de identidad en la sociedad feudal española a principios del siglo XVII*. Kassel: Reichenberger 2013. On the economic thinking of Mercado, cf. also the review article by Manuel J. Lagares Calvo (2013, pp. 71–95).

written by the Dominican monk Tomás de Mercado. His relevant major work is titled *Tratos y contratos de mercaderes y tratantes* [Trade and Contracts of Merchants and Traders] (Seville 1569; a heavily supplemented edition was published with the title *Suma de tratos y contratos* [Manual for Trade and Contracts], Seville 1571). As he explains in the foreword, he wrote the work at the insistence of the Sevillian merchant and banker Angelo Brunengo to help Brunengo from a position of a confessor with his moral dilemma. Mercado is not only concerned – as a follower of Thomas Aquinas and ultimately of Aristotle – with "the legitimation of trade" and of the merchant class, which to him (reformulating Aristotle's theses theologically) arises from "the neediness of a fallen world."[19] Rather, his aim is to "portray commerce as an inherently valuable and ennobling activity," i.e. as the field of activity of the "honorable merchant" phenotype which is of great benefit to the community at large. He does not doubt the existence of this phenotype, despite Thomas von Aquinas suspicion of *turpitudo*, and, with his treatise, he wants to give it moral-theological orientation. To ground this fundamental revaluation of the merchant, the theologian Mercado does not fall back on the Bible, but on the ancient pagan authorities Solon, Hesiod, and Plutarch. In their time, they were of the opinion

> that no form of life pursued by the individual, nor any activity with which he/she is engaged, nor any trade or business he/she could practice was valued and promoted by the people as much as the activity of the merchant. The prosperity and benefit that it brings in its entirety both for those directly involved in the trade itself and for the republic (sc. the community) was obvious.[20]

According to Mercado, merchants not only provide people with a multitude of useful or even indispensable things for life, such as clothing. In addition to such purely physical items, they also meet the spiritual needs of their fellow citizens (in line with Bourdieu's idea of cultural capital mentioned above), for

> if they talk to very different people, visit different kingdoms, have dealings with many peoples, experience habits and customs that are different from their own, and if they are finally concern themselves intellectually with the different forms of government and state regulations of other peoples, then they [sc. the merchants] will become "universal people," with the experience and skill to carry out any kind of business that may be offered to them. In this way, they acquire and promote a great deal of sophistication and experience in dealing with and behaving in both the individual and public spheres.[21]

---

[19] Geisler (1981, p. 46).

[20] Mercado (1975, unpag.): "que en aquellos tiempos ningún género de vida que el hombre siguiese, ni ejercicio ninguno en que se ocupase, ni trato ni oficio en que se ejercitase, era tan estimado y tenido entre las gentes como la mercancía, por la gran comodidad y provecho que causa, así en los tratantes como en todo el cuerpo de la república."

[21] Ibid.: "porque, conversando con muchas gentes, estando en distintos reinos, tratando con varias naciones, experimentando diferentes costumbres, considerando el diverso gobierno y policía de los pueblos, se hacen hombres universales, cursados y ladinos para cualesquiera negocios que se les ofrezcan. Adquieren y aumentan una gran prudencia y experiencia para guiar y regirse, así en los sucesos particulares como generales."

Even though Mercado's qualification of merchants as "outstanding men ("varones excelentes") refers to merchants of classical antiquity, he does not hesitate to attribute to the merchants of his time the highest qualities of knowledge of the world and the ability to solve every problem. As Eberhard Geisler points out, the theologian Mercado does not criticize merchants for their – theologically always negatively connoted – material earthly wealth, but understands it as a fair reward for restoring "the satisfaction of paradisiacal needs" after the original sin," albeit only approximately. This means that the merchants are not only exemplary individuals; they also fulfil a role in the history of salvation. From Geisler's point of view, it is thus possible to support the thesis that man "fulfills God's commandment precisely as a citizen who engages in commerce." Mercado therefore does not hesitate to recommend this "honorable merchant"[22] as "the ideal politician" and thus to set him alongside the nobility, who in Spanish feudal society at that time regarded this leadership role as its very own, God-given privilege.[23]

The theologian Mercado nevertheless sees this merchant, effectively raised to the level of nobility and honor, exposed to great moral dangers. Thus, his writing is by no means simply a textbook of (theologically permissible) actions as a merchant and interest-taking financier, but at the same time a guide to the pious life. In the fourth and fifth chapter of the first book of his treatise "On the purpose and intention that the merchant should have in his duties" ("Del fin e intenci6n que debe tener el mercader en sus tareas") and "On some useful and necessary regulations" ("De algunos documentos útiles y necesarios"), Mercado therefore drew up an inventory of specific qualities which the individual must possess to be able to satisfy the ideal type of the "honorable merchant." To begin with, there are two general basic attitudes ("intenciones") in all commercial activities:

1. The primary objective of the merchant's commercial activities must never be his own (in principle justifiable) modest profit or individual wealth, but always to "provide the community with the food, clothing, and other commodities it lacks."
2. The aim of every trade must also be to generate a surplus ("profit"/*lucro*), which should not, however, be given to the merchant himself, but always to others, especially the poor, as alms ("limosna") – today we would consider this a kind of social-security contribution. These two general demands give rise to a clear sequence: first of all, the common good must have priority for the merchant, then the support of the poor, and, only thirdly, his own profit.

[22]Geisler (1981, p. 49–50).

[23]The extent to which this positive view of the merchant is removed from the topically traditional ecclesiastical view, may be shown once again by a reference to Agrippa von Nettesheim (1486–1535). In his first published work from 1530 *On the uncertainty and vanity of all arts and sciences*, 72nd chapter (De mercatura or On the merchant class) concludes the following in evoking two of the most important church fathers (Chrysostom and Augustine): "Mercator Deo placere non potest. A merchant cannot please God. For this reason, a Christian certainly should not be a merchant, or, if he wants to become one, he should be kicked out of the churches. Augustine declares: a merchant and a soldier, he cannot do genuine repentance" (2013), p. 203.

Hence, in the practical implementation of these general objectives, the merchants have to account for additional specific points where their respectability (though no longer fundamentally questioned) manifests itself. Mercado cites no less than seven points:

1. The wealth acquired through trade should not be discredited by an imposing house or an elaborate way of life, for excessive luxury arouses the suspicion that the commercial activities on which the wealth is based might have been fraudulent.
2. The amount of words used when conducting business should be kept to a minimum, for otherwise the suspicion of deception and coaxing could arise.
3. During the sales negotiation, it is not necessary to constantly refer back to the vow as an authentication gesture, which in any case loses its persuasiveness due to its frequent usage and, on the other hand, contains the constant danger of (also unwanted) perjury (and thus of a grave sin).
4. The merchant should be charitable and socially engaged, or – in the theological language of the time – give alms ("ser muy limosnero"), whereby the economic needs of the poor are not cited as justification. Instead, he speaks (citing *Lk* 11.41: "But give alms of what is there, behold, everything is pure in you."[24]) from the perspective of the merciful alms-givers and the purifying power of almsgiving.[25] This purification of sins, in turn, is necessary because the merchant inevitably, even if unintentionally, succumbs to misjudgments in the constantly unavoidable determination of the respective "justo precio" (fair price). He thus sins here and, in turn, runs the risk of endangering his soul's salvation.
5. The merchant should read a lot, but implicitly not occupational or even entertaining literature, as became available to a growing extent with the genre of novella or novel on the cusp of modernity, rather "good books" ("buenos libros"). Against the backdrop of the prohibition of vernacular Bible reading in Catholic Spain, this refers to rapidly growing market for pious or devotional literature. The aim was to embed the believer in his religious practice intellectually and emotionally and to direct his attention – beyond all earthly professional activities – to the kingdom of God as the actual goal of a good life. Mercado thus argues with reference to the apocalyptic visions of *Apoc.* 18:9–19 that there will come a time when the world of merchants and their wealth will fade away and only efforts on behalf of their salvation will endure. Consequently, the merchant "must spend more time and effort on acquiring virtues, not money."
6. Moreover, the daily attendance of mass and the reception of the Eucharist are imperative.

[24] "Dad limosna y seros han todas las cosas limpias."

[25] In the numerous debates on mendicants and almsgiving of the sixteenth century, the theological viewpoint was repeatedly advanced – in the sense of a theodicy – that God created the poor, or allowed them to exist, so that the rich through almsgiving had the opportunity to "purify" their sinful status. This was argued despite the clear biblical saying that it is easier for a camel to go through the eye of a needle than for a rich person to enter the kingdom of God and obtain eternal life (M*k* 10:20, *Lk* 18:25, *Mt* 29:24).

7. Finally, the merchant, whose profession constantly exposes him to the danger of grave and the most severe sins, must seek a confessor who is able to guide his conscience in a world of buying and selling that is constantly exposed to sin. As Mercado describes in great detail, however, this must be a wise, not overly scrupulous man who is fundamentally familiar with the world of merchants – a man who is content to present his theological view of things to the merchant, but who in the end is also prepared to leave the merchant (in the context of morally theological probabilism) with a great deal of freedom of choice.

The following becomes clear in summarizing these remarks of one of the keenest minds of the Salamanca philosophical-theological school, who is also the most knowledgeable in economic questions: Unlike in the medieval tradition, but also as in contemporary so-called belles-lettres, the merchant does not appear here as a permanent occupationally-related deceiver and cheater, but rather as a representative of an honorable status. On the other hand, the merchant is still regarded as the social phenotype, which, more than any other profession, is exposed to the danger of social and moral theological sinfulness. He is thus also at risk of falling into the dishonor of a society still thoroughly shaped by (Catholic) Christianity, even if the possibility of making oneself "honorable" exists under strict religious conditions. The "honorable" merchant is, in the view of the Salamanca school, a "homo religiosus" – a pious, Catholic merchant. But Mercado concedes to him a considerable amount of autonomy, both as concerns the complex question of the choice of the confessor and with regard to the area of "freedom of conscience," which is restricted specifically to commercial activities.[26] At the same time, however, Mercado and his view of the "honorable" merchant are still entirely determined by a worldview in which theology claims a monopoly on the world and its interpretation and jurisdiction over the realm of the profane world of economics. In this world, with its "très forte interpénétration entre 'culture' marchande et culture juridico-théologique," as Rodolfo Savelli put it,[27] the honor of the merchant is still at the service of his own salvation. In the enlightened and secularly organized society and economy of the eighteenth century, which follows its own immanent (market) laws, honor (in the sense of Kant's "disinterestedness") will ultimately consist in guaranteeing the functioning of this mundane system. This is to be done even if the system is tied (as it were for the external representation and legitimacy of the pursuit of profit) with the lofty social values of individual and entirely secular virtue, the pursuit of happiness for all people, and the promotion of the fatherland. From this "enlightened" secular perspective, Mercado's merchant is not yet really "honorable." For him, the self-centered aspiration to otherworldly salvation is still very much in the foreground and not a mundane, altruistic and – in the sense of Kant – "disinterested" ethical duty.

[26] See Pilar Rivero Gracia (2005) and Rodrigo Muñoz (2003, pp. 359–372). See also fn 13 of this work. A quick overview of these various theological perspectives of the merchant, including the world of Protestantism, is provided by Michel Morineau (1995, pp. 421–438).

[27] Savelli (1995, p. 406). Nevertheless, Savelli states that we are at the same time "face à l'émergence d'une morale économique ,laïque' par rapport à la tradition aussi bien juridique que théologique" (p. 410), which helped solve the theologically problematic interest problem and freed it from its connection with the phenomenon of usury.

7.3 The Long Journey to the Secularization of the Image of the Honorable Merchant from the Seventeenth to the Eighteenth Century

For the most part, however, merchants in the historical reality of later sixteenth and seventeenth century Spain, a period characterized by the most severe economic crises and national bankruptcies, were not able to put in to practice the ideal *external image* that Mercado conceived for them around the middle of the sixteenth century. One reason was the fact that the productive Spanish economy largely came to a standstill under the impact of huge quantities of precious metals from the Spanish Americas – with high inflation, an enormous increase in imported luxury for the upper class, and the simultaneous impoverishment of the lower classes. In this downturn, Spanish merchants were marginalized and "dishonored" by their powerful competitors, who were increasingly less concerned with trading in commodities (*negocio de cosas*) than with speculative financial transactions that came quite close to usury.[28] In general, Spain lost its independent, active merchants (including in its Italian possessions such as Naples[29]). This prompted the Conde de Olivares (1587–1645) – the all-powerful minister of Philip III, who was fully aware of Spain's economic decline between 1623 and 1643 – to express the desire that the Spaniards should reclaim the lost merchant spirit ("reducir los españoles a mercaderes").[30] In fact, this change to an "image ennoblissante du commerce,"[31] which was also repeatedly demanded by the so-called *arbitristas*, would not take place until the European Enlightenment. Spain took part in this epoch despite its supposedly completely otherworldly Catholicism, although certainly not in its most radical form. The reflection on and the actual renewal of the Spanish trade started already at the end of the seventeenth century under King Charles II. Then, in the 1740s, trade was implemented in line with mercantilism by a series of economically (theoretically and practically) knowledgeable politicians and ministers such as José Patiño y Morales (1666–1736), Gerónimo de Uztáriz (1670–1732), José del Campillo de Cossío (1693–1743), along with the outstanding enlightened ministers Campomanes (1732–1803) and Floridablanca (1728–1808). Each contributed to profoundly changing the overall framework of trade in Spain. They abolished the monopoly of the port of Cádiz in American trade, made a general commitment to free trade (*comercio libre*) and to extensively changing its practical implementation from 1778, and significantly

[28] On this complex economic situation and its reflection in the *novela picaresca*, whose protagonist comes from the impoverished classes, as well as the debates on these economic questions and proposals for solutions among the *arbitristas*, see Cavillac (1983, p. 449).

[29] See Musi (1995, pp. 77–95). The antithesis of the "honorable merchant" emerged in the then Spanish Naples from 1630s and 1640s, (pp. 86–88) in the form of Bartolomeo d'Aquino and other Neapolitans, who had become wealthy in trade. His social recognition rested exclusively on his – dubiously acquired and conspicuously displayed – wealth.

[30] Cavillac (1983, pp. 251–313). Cavillac (ibid., p. 296) rightly referred to Olivares as the "champion du lobby marchand."

[31] Ibid., p. 279.

revived commerce.[32] The activities of the numerous *Sociedades económicas de amigos del país* further contributed to this development. Like the rapidly expanding press sector in the second half of the eighteenth century,[33] they not only spread economic knowledge in Spain at the very top of the government, but also in the middle strata of the population. This process was tied to a broader reception of European thought about economic interdependencies and the function and character of the merchant, even though relevant literature such as the works of the German Paul Jakob Marperger (1656–1730) or the Frenchman Jacques Savary (1657–1716) were not translated into Spanish. The culmination of this development was certainly the establishment of the first Spanish Chair of Economics and Commerce (*cátedra de economía y comercio*) in Zaragoza in 1785. It was characteristic for the situation in Spain, however, that the subject of economics and commerce, conceived according to rationalist-laical criteria, immediately came into conflict with the Inquisition. It was thus very quickly banned again at the latter's instigation, for a rational understanding and planning of the economic processes was incompatible with the idea of an all-encompassing divine providence.[34] A characteristic feature of this situation – which deviated from the European standard at the time and can be described as markedly backward – may be the reference to the library holdings of the very wealthy wool merchant Pedro Miguel de Lingués (1811) from the commercial elite of Northern Spain: Of the 158 books in his estate, 106 are religious works (whose reading Mercado had strongly recommended to his merchant)[35];of the remaining inventory, only two are specifically related to trade issues.[36]

[32] On the success of this trade reform policy, cf. the relevant study by Niels Wiecker (2012) on the Iberian Atlantic trade between 1700 and 1800. On the beginnings of mentality history in trade with the Iberian peninsula, cf. the general observations of Jorun Poettering (2013) on the relationship between trade, nation, and religion. In all these business dealings, however, the Spanish merchants were often only the straw men of their foreign business partners, to whom independent trade in Spain and in Spanish America was officially banned.

[33] Horst Pietschmann's survey article (1992), pp. 151–167, on these enlightened societies which aimed to promote economic activity in Spain still serves as a good point of departure

[34] See Guillermo García Pérez (1974). According to Javier San Julián (2011), Adam Smith's seminal work for the economic thinking of the Late Enlightenment, in which questions of economics are treated in purely mundane (and moral-philosophical, but not theological) terms, met a similar fate (see Peña López and Sánchez Santos 2007). Indeed, the *Inquiry into the Nature and Causes of the Wealth of Nations,* which appeared in 1776, was translated into Spanish in 1777 at the suggestion of the enlightened Minister Campomanes, a promoter of (free) trade; this translation remained fragmentary, however, and was never published. In 1792, the Spanish Inquisition put Smith's work on its index, but this did not prevent a Spanish translation and the publication of the complete edition in 1794. The undertaking, though, was probably initiated by another powerful minister – Manuel de Godoy (1767–1851). Nevertheless, the translator – Josef Alonso Ortiz – hastened to announce in his preface that he expurgated everything anti-Spanish and anti-Catholic in the *Inquiry* from his version. See Javier San Julián (2011).

[35] Fernando Mikelarena Peña (2005, pp. 63–87). The religious books concern mainly hagiographies and classical Spanish piety literature, such as the writings of Juan Nieremberg, Luis de Granada, Diego de Estella, Teresa de Ávila or the Spanish translation of Imitatio Christi by Thomas a Kempis (pp. 72–75).

[36] The two relevant commercial texts are already somewhat older works: the *Arithmetic demostrada theórico-práctica para lo mathemático y mercantil* (1699, 1719) by the Valencian mathematics

There was a new rationalist conception of economy and trade in the Spanish eighteenth century, which is quite consistent with the point of view of things in the article *Commerce of the Encyclopédie* von d' Alembert and Diderot (vol. 3, p.). 690–699). There is also a well-documented professionalization of the Spanish merchant apprenticeship in the phase of the Enlightenment.[37]Against this background, and despite rejection of these developments by the conservative forces of the country (in particular by the reactionary part of the clergy), the question to be briefly dealt now is whether and to what extent this historical situation brought with it a new, possibly secularized image of the merchant.

Unfortunately, a comprehensive body of texts for the normative as well as the purely descriptive (self-) representation of the "Spanish merchant" phenotype in the eighteenth century stills appears to be missing. Therefore, recourse will be taken to one descriptive and two short (broadly understood) autobiographical texts to examine the question of the self-image that was being developed at this time of the "honorable merchant."

7.4 Case Studies on External and Self-Portrayals of the Merchant in the Age of Spanish Enlightenment: From the Theoretician Valentín de Foronda and the Practitioners Juan de Eguino and Isidoro de la Fuente Pérez

The descriptive text is a eulogy on trade held at the general assembly of members of the *Basque Society of Friends of the Country* by the just 28 year old Valentín de Foronda (1751–1821) in 1778. He can be attributed to the more radical or at least more resolute members of the Spanish Enlightenment. The title alone emphasizes that the speaker regards the work of merchants to be "honorable": *Treatise on how honorable the profession of merchant is [...].* Only 6 years after the incompatibility of nobility and the merchant profession had been nullified, and 3 years before *La*

professor Juan Bautista Corachán (1661–1741) and an unidentifiable book on the "comercio libre de Yndias" (p. 86, n. 138).

[37] Roberto Fernández Díaz and Carlos Martínez Shaw (1995, pp. 309–319). The four main areas of vocational training for the merchant were "la comptabilité, la géographie, les conditions générales sur le plan économique et politiques des marches sur lesquels ils [sc. the merchants] devaient opérer et les langues"(p. 310). These are four clearly secular fields in which religion, so strongly emphasized by the School of Salamanca, is no longer mentioned. This is also reflected in the commercial correspondence, in which, over time, religious salutations such as *Dios le guarde muchos años* ("God keep you safe for many years (sc. give you a long life") fell more and more out of use (pp. 316–317).

noblesse commerçante of Abbé Coyer appeared in Spanish translation,[38] Foronda polemicized forcefully against an idle yet highly status-conscious nobility. His remarks, though, were more rhetorical than historical or empirical in nature. This same applies to his unconditional praise of commerce (comercio), in which – without any detailed reference to theological argumentation patterns as in Mercado[39] – he sees the absolute primary source of all prosperity of the individual and of the community. At the same time, he attributes to it enlightened knowledge and the humanization of mankind. The merchant and his profession are thus not only "honorable" in his view, but also (even if this phrase is not explicitly used) the highest form of a human being and citizen.

In his still foundational study *The Origin of the Bourgeois World and Philosophy of Life in France* (1927 and 1930), Bernhard Groethuysen shows in great detail (on the basis of extensive theological literature on the complexes of merchant, trade, interest taking and usury) how merchants freed themselves over the course of the eighteenth century and especially the Enlightenment from a comprehensive theological interpretation of their actions as sin. Groethuysen also demonstrates that they no longer saw their honor as lying in being a "good Christian," as the neo-scholastic Mercado had conceded to them under various provisos. On the one hand, for the merchant of the Enlightenment, honor – this "legitimization category [sc. of the merchant], which is attributed externally" – results rather from his professional activities, which also includes his personal enrichment and interest taking. On the other hand, however, honor arises in particular from the fact that he does not raise any doubts about his "credit" – this central value, which is entirely immanent to the mundane system. And, finally, honor results from a philanthropy which is

[38] *La nobleza comerciante Traducción del tratado que escribió en francés el Abate Coyer, hecha para la utilidad de la Real Sociedad Económica de los Amigos del País de Mallorca, con un discurso preliminar y varias notas/por Don Jacobo María de Spinosa y Cantabrana* [...]. Madrid: Ibarra 1781. The lengthy preface (pp. XXXI–LXXXV) of the anonymous translator not only tries to persuade the Spanish nobility to become active as (wholesale) merchants, but it also contains a detailed eulogy on trade (*comercio*) as the source of all the wealth of a nation. The *arbitrista* Martín González de Cellorigo (Cavillac 1983, pp. 272–278) made a very similar demand around 1600, albeit without finding the same resonance: "Trade is the spirit that gives life and breath to human invention, industry, and the arts: It is the impetus that creates a productive force out of the wealth and power of the state. Without it, agriculture and the arts would not produce anything new; without it, the fine arts would perish, as would the sciences and good taste, the well-being of citizens, the survival of humanity, the power of the nation and the survival of the state, which is clearly dependent on trade."("El Comercio es el espíritu que da vida, y aliento al ingenio, á la industria y á las Artes: es el resorte maestro, que da fuerza productriz de las riquezas, y del poder del Estado: sin él serán lánguidas la Agricultura, y las Artes: perecerían las bellas artes, las Ciencias, y el buen gusto, la comodidad de los Vasallos, la subsistencia de los hombres, el poder de la Nacion, y la conservacion del Estado, que depende precisamente del Comercio"). (pp. XXXIII–XXXIV).

[39] Foronda refers in his text only once to the biblical figures Cain and Abel, who are said to have been "the first humans, and also the first merchants who, between themselves, exchanged a handful of grains for a drink of milk." ("foron los primeros hombres, y también los primeros comerciantes, entre ellos se cangeaba un puñado de granos por un trago de leche"). (1984, pp. 601–602).

understood morally and philosophically and no longer theologically as Christian charity (*caritas*) and the meritorious pursuit of virtue. Instead, it is construed as uninterested benevolence.

I will now briefly examine the two autobiographical texts that two Spanish merchants handed down to us from the time shortly before and after 1800. They represent what was at the time probably what most advanced self-conception of the merchant.

The first case is that of Juan de Eguino, a wealthy and experienced merchant based in Cadiz, who was active in the American trade in the decades before 1800, especially with and in Lima. The following discussion is based on a contribution by the Basque economic historian Xabier Lamikiz, who examined a previously little-known collection of documents, thus supplementing the rather sporadic sources on the personal statements of Spanish merchants about their profession. Specifically, at issue is the correspondence (about 2000 letters) of Spanish merchants that was confiscated in the eighteenth century[40] by English warships on the high seas. The letters, which were thus spared the usual annihilation the Spaniards practiced themselves, continue to be largely ignored in English archives to this day. In this context, Eguino sailed by ship in 1779 to Callao, the center of the Spanish Pacific trade. He undertook the trip at 60 years of age, and despite all the risks, because he suspected that his business partner (*corresponsal*) in Lima was cheating him. Indeed, the suspicion was soon borne out. Eguino, however, skillfully managed to ensure that there was not an open and ruinous scandal, the loss of the "credit." The whole issue remained nothing more than a tedious but successfully dispelled rumor that damaged but did not cause to fail the vast business in question, which was of a size of 800,000 pesos (eight times more than a "normal business"). For historian Lamikiz, the "Eguino case" is highly illustrative of the self-conception of the merchant in the Spanish late eighteenth century and thus the idea of honor. This self-conception is determined by three principles, resting on the axiomatic idea of self-interest (*interés propio*)[41]: (1) the principle of "confidentiality" (*confidencialidad*) or trade secrets (*secreto*), "lo sagrado de sus libros,"[42] which the Spanish merchants successfully defended throughout the eighteenth century against the state, which wanted to enforce the inspection of businesses and accounting; (2) the principle of "good repute" (*reputación*) within the community of merchants, and (3) the principle of "trust" (*confianza*).[43] These three principles can clearly be summed up under the common French term "credit." These are obviously secular principles resulting

[40] Lamikiz (2007, pp. 113–142).

[41] See Vollhardt (2001, pp. 219–242). See also Hirschman (1987), who shows how these theologically objectionable passions turn into virtues under the pressure of economic and professional needs in the early modern period, particularly the idea of self-interest and interest. In the context of the legitimization of wholesale trade, it should be noted that in Romance languages the word "interest" is also the term for monetary interest (intérêts/interessi/intereses).

[42] Lamikiz (2007, p. 119).

[43] Lamikiz sees parallels to the great handbook of secular merchants in the eighteenth century, Wyndham Beawes' *Lex Mercatoria Rediviva or The Merchant's Directory. Being a complete guide of all Man in Business* (1752), 922 S.

from the merchant's own, and the ever-increasing de facto, "laïcisation de la vie économique"[44] from the eighteenth century onward. They are alone sufficient, without any theological justification, to characterize the phenotype of the "honorable merchant." Those who do not follow the principles of this self-regulating, autonomous economic system are doomed to failure as merchants, regardless of their personal religious beliefs. Thus, the "honorable merchant" is also exempted from the guidance of theology in the course of the Spanish Enlightenment and is far removed from the thought process of the neo-scholastic School of Salamanca. This does not in any way imply, however, a separation of economics and ethics, as is doubtless often wrongly assumed about Adam Smith.[45] Despite the enlightened "secular option,"[46] Eguino considers this ethical aspect in the historical reality of the eighteenth century Spain to still be rooted for the private citizen in conventional Christianity. This merchant was thus until the end of his life an avid member of the "Brotherhood of the Most Holy Christ of Humility and Patience," founded by Basque merchants in Cádiz, Andalusia.

On the other hand, Isidoro de la Fuente Pérez conveys a completely different image of the "respectable merchant," which is shaped by a thoroughly religious self-conception. A typical merchant from the Basque north of Spain, Pérez was born in 1754 in very modest circumstances and emigrated to Spain at the age of only 17 years, or more precisely to today's Mexico. There, he succeeded in acquiring enormous prosperity as a single-minded trader, rising from a simple shop assistant to a respected wholesale merchant. He also married well, which proved helpful. From 1810, he came under the most extreme pressure as a conservative Spaniard due to the turmoil of the Latin American independence struggles. In 1816, he returned to his Spanish homeland as an independently wealthy "Indiano," at peace with himself, with God, and the world. In the last years of his life – in any case before 1822, as evidenced by a date in the manuscript – he then wrote a description of his life. The text, in any event, comprises a little more than 40 printed pages and was published only recently (2007) for the first time.[47]

While the author does not make any direct statements about the intention of his text, there is no doubt that this is not the confession of a sinner. Instead, despite the rather neutral self-description as a "report" (*relación*), it is in a certain sense a modern autobiography of a self-confident individual in which the author presents himself in the first person as a model example of an "honorable merchant." Nonetheless, this image of an "honorable merchant" is *sui generis*, for it was a product of the social-historical as well as the mentality-historical and religious situation in the Spanish world at that time. The text's editor, the Mexican ethno-historian Tomás

[44] Savelli (1995, p. 420).

[45] See Peña López and Sánchez Santos (2007, p. 82).

[46] On this conception and its demarcation from "secularization," which was long understood as a radical and inevitable break, cf. the detailed observations from Charles Taylor (2012).

[47] Tomás Pérez Vejo (2007, pp. 193–262); the imprint of the vita (*Relación verídica que con el fin, de renovar beneficios recibidos, y repetir gracias al cielos: voy a hacer de algunos de los acontecimientos que he experimentado durante mi trágica y larga vida*) includes pages 219–262.

Pérez Vejo, sees the life of the merchant Isidoro de la Fuente Pérez as being determined by two basic trends that are difficult to reconcile. On the one hand, there is a kind of Protestant work ethic in the sense of Max Weber,[48] which can be attributed to modernity, and, on the other, there is a "squandering of funds for mere ostentation and for pious institutions," which is still entirely consistent with the Baroque period.[49] In fact, Isidoro de la Fuente Pérez learned the merchant vocation from the bottom up, first as a largely unpaid commercial employee and salesman for many years, before he gradually achieved considerable wealth as a hard-working self-employed individual retailer[50] and later as a wholesaler.[51] At the same time, de la Fuente is not in any way burdened by the ethical and religious problems that the moral theologian Mercado recognized in this activity. On the contrary, in retrospect, he is of the opinion that he always acted as a "decent and honorable person"[52] and, as far as his personal spending was concerned, as an extremely frugal man.[53] He thus reports that he always went to confession as a good Catholic. There is no evidence in his autobiographical reflections of the urgency that Mercado so emphatically speaks in view of the fundamental or at least potential sinfulness of all commercial activity and regarding exercising the utmost care when searching for a suitably experienced confessor. This is undoubtedly an indication of a secularization of the ideal of the "honorable merchant," which was not yet observable in Mercado. De la Fuente here also makes use of the "secular option," which was becoming increasingly evident in the wake of the Enlightenment and increasingly obvious in professional life.[54] It is therefore telling that Isidoro de la Fuente Pérez repeatedly cites the topos of the coexistence of "lo divino" and "lo humano," of the religious and secular world. Thus it is not a problem for him if, on the one hand, he pays intensive visits to church in the morning and, on the other, cultivates[55] his social contacts (*paseo*) in

[48] Ibid., P. 204: "una especie de ética protestante del trabajo." He also stresses that he never indulged in the card game that was so widespread among the Spaniards in America at the time or other forms of idleness (256).

[49] Ibid., p. 208: "despilfarro en gastos suntuarios y obras pías."

[50] Ibid., p. 250: "trabajaba sumamente."

[51] Ibid., p. 231: "gané más que medianamente." He thus confesses openly to unambiguous profit maximization and self-interest: "From the beginning, I have made every effort to make money, but always with honor and decency." ("Desde el principio anhelé como el que más por el afán y el ansia de tener dinero, aunque siempre con honradez y decoro, sin usar de mecánicas y bajezas, [...].) "(p. 256).

[52] Ibid., p. 256: "hombre de bien y honor."

[53] Ibid., p. 261.

[54] Groethuysen formulated this fact and mentality change as follows for the more advanced French sector: The citizen – in the exemplary figure of the merchant – lives "outside of the Christian-Catholic sphere of ideas; [...]. Citizens no longer need the Church's conceptual world; they find in their own views and values, and only in them, that which they need in order to regulate social and economic life and to assert their claims." (1978), 2, pp. 209–210.

[55] On the (moral) theological assessment of sociability in the Spanish Baroque, cf. the volume edited by Mechthild Albert *Sociabilidad y literatura en el Siglo de Oro* and in particular the article by Vf.s (2013, pp. 93–113): Indeseada sociabilidad': concepto y crítica de la sociabilidad en los contextos teológicos.

the afternoon and goes to bullfights and, in the evening, even visits the theater[56] – which is always suspicious from a theological point of view. In doing so, he combines two areas that moral theologians considered to be largely incompatible, not only in the Baroque period. On the other hand, however, he establishes clear hierarchy for both areas, with stronger emphasis than the above-mentioned merchant Eguino. De la Fuente stresses his deep-rooted piety, which manifests itself, among other things, in his membership of the Third Order of the Franciscans, in his concern for a religiously appropriate treatment of his wife's corpse (which is not decomposed and therefore transported into the realm of the sacred), in his daily visit to mass, and in an impressive willingness to give alms and donations. For example, he had at least two churches and a monastery built largely at his own expense, furnished them with pictures, expensive dining utensils, and luxurious chasubles, and finally had hundreds of masses read, which, of course, had to be paid for as well. Nevertheless, it is a rather commercial and secular sign that, on the one hand, he remembers very[57] precisely the considerable sums of money spent in each case and, on the other, does not address the question of an otherworldly reward for all his good deeds for the poor. This is also true of his "providential discourse." Consistently presenting himself as a self-made man,[58] he also repeatedly emphasizes his business success as well as the overcoming of the bitter misfortunes of divine providence (*providencia*). At the same time, he underlines how well he – in a thoroughly bourgeois sense of self-care – invested his money in lands and property in order to secure his own livelihood. At the end of his autobiography, he thus creates the image of himself as a devoted merchant who understands how to combine self-interestedness and charity, who is respected by all, who is engaged in reading and writing, and who, in short, is a – in the terminology of the German Enlightenment – a "happy" patriarch highly satisfied with his life's work. He resembles an (albeit Catholic and pious) Johann Buddenbrook, who is above all suspicion of both secular dishonor and religious "pecados profesionales," which, in the opinion of neo-scholastic philosophers and theologians, is inherent to the merchant class.

---

[56] In 1802, during a stay in Mexico City with his wife, he and his wife enjoyed "everything that was offered in the religious and secular sphere; morning sermons and other extraordinary religious festivities; afternoon strolls and evening theater visits. We also visited the merriments in the surrounding villages as well as the bullfights, if there were any." ("de cuanto se proporcionaba en lo Divino y en lo humano, logrando por la mañana de Sermones y funciones muy solemnes, del paseo por la tarde y comedia por la noche, sin omitir de ir a las diversiones de los pueblos inmediatos ni a los Toros cuando los había") Pérez Vejo (2007, p. 236).

[57] One, for instance, therefore reads: "[...] I have equipped the parish church of Caloca [sc. his home village] with silver altars, as they are needed for the mass; for this purpose, I spent about 14,000 *reales* and the same amount again for a picture of the crucified and another picture of the Sorrowful Mother of God [...]." ("[...] surtí a la Parroquia de Caloca de los Vasos Sagrados de plata necesarios para celebrar los Divinos Misterios, en que gasté como catorce mil reales, y otros tantos en una Imagen de Jesucristo Crucificado y otra de Nuestra Señora de los Dolores [...]."). Pérez Vejo (2007, p. 262).

[58] "[...] I trained myself with the greatest efficiency and love in commerce, quickly learning what was necessary for my future [...]." ("[...] me instruía con la mayor eficacia y amor en el comercio, en el que en poco tiempo aprendí lo necesario para lo futuro [...]. ") Pérez Vejo (2007, p. 228).

Still, this positive image of the merchant, who appears to reconcile the religious and secular options in a specifically Spanish way, did not develop into a social ideal in the Hispanic world in the years that followed. By contrast, the historical reality of the merchant may have had the last word. Of increasing concern were the massive circumvention of state trade rules, multiple corruption and the equally widespread smuggling practices in American trade.[59] Also speaking against the presumption of a social implementation of this idealized image of the honorable merchant is the persistent theological criticism of the practice of deceptive bankruptcies, shameless luxury, and a lack of charitable behavior of at least of some merchants. A sermon that was held in 1789 in Cádiz, the most important Spanish trading hub of the eighteenth century, confirms this criticism. Before judges of a high court, *the Real Audiencia de la Casa de Contratación,* the preacher castigated merchants as morally depraved for (apparently not uncommon) feigned bankruptcies and characterized them as deserving the most severe punishment.[60] Final proof that the image of the "honorable merchant" was not inscribed in the Spanish collective memory is found in the fact that the liberal intellectual and author Manuel José Quintana (1772–1857) only invokes representatives of the aristocracy, military leaders, conquistadors and even a missionary in his series of historical-pedagogical essays for youth of exemplary Spaniards ("españoles célebres." 3 vols., 1807–1832–1833). By contrast, no one is included in the essays who might have been attributed to one of the varieties of the "honorable merchant" category outlined here.[61]

References

Alloza Aparicio, Ángel, and Beatriz Cárceles de Gea. 2009. *Comercio y riqueza en el siglo XVII. Estudios sobre cultura, política y pensamiento económico*. Madrid: Consejo Superior de Investigación Científica.

Braudel, Fernand. 1990. *Sozialgeschichte des 15.-18. Jahrhunderts. Vol. II. Der Handel*. München: Kindler.

[59] See the summary of the development in the eighteenth century by Malagón Pinzón (2001, pp. 51–74).

[60] *Discurso moral que en el dia primero de abril de 1789 [...] predicó a la Real Audiencia de Contratación á Yndias, y Real Tribunal del Consulado en la M.N. y L. ciudad de Cádiz el M.R. P. Fray Augustin de Espinosa. Lector de Sagrada Teología en su Convento de RR. PP. Franciscanos Observantes [...]. Dáse á la estampa á expensas de varios zelosos, y nobles individuos del Comercio, apasionados del Orador.* Con licencia. Cádiz. En la imprenta de M. Manuel Rodríguez Flores [...]. [1789], 49 pp., especially pp. 40–48. Text available in UB Sevilla (fondosdigitales.us.es)

[61] Quintana describes the lives of the following nine "famous Spaniards": the medieval national hero El Cid; Guzmán el Bueno; Roger de Lauria; the Prince of Viana; the Gran Capitán; Vasco Núñez de Balboa; Francisco Pizarro; Álvaro de Luna, and Fray Bartolomé de las Casas. For a more detailed characterization of these idealized images, cf. the essay of Vf.s (1991, pp. 319–345).

As Jochen Hook (1995, pp. 49–60), has shown, in German culture at this time, for example in Goethe *Wilhelm Meister* and in Novalis, there is a positive image of the merchant, who is also intended as a social role model.

Castaño, Javier. 2011. Flüchtige Schimären der Convivencia: die Juden in Kastilien und ihre Eliten (1418–1454). In *Integration – Segregation – Vertreibung. Religiöse Minderheiten und Randgruppen auf der Iberischen Halbinsel (7. bis 17. Jahrhundert)*, ed. Klaus Herbers and Nikolas Jaspert, 179–212. Berlin: LIT.

Cavillac, Michel. 1983. *Gueux et marchands dans le Guzmán de Alfarache (1599–1604). Roman picaresque et mentalité bourgeoise dans l'Espagne du Siècle d'Or*. Bordeaux: Institut d'Études ibériques et ibéro-américaines de l'Université de Bordeaux.

———. 2001. La figura del mercader en el 'Guzmán de Alfarache'. *Edad de Oro* 20: 69–84.

———. 2013. San Agustín en el gran debate sobre los pobres: 1545–1599 (de Domingo de Soto y Juan de Robles hasta Pérez de Herrera y Mateo Alemán). *Criticón* 118: 45–56. Online-Ausgabe: http://criticonrevues.orgues/301. Accessed 23 Sept 2015.

———. 2014. El discurso del mercader y sus incidencias literarias. *Criticón* 120 (121): 41–56.

Coria-Sánchez, Carlos Mateo, and Germán Torres, eds. 2008. *Temas del comercio y la economía en la narrativa hispana*. New Haven et al.: Yale University Press.

Cruickshank, Don W. 2011. *Calderón de la Barca. Su carrera secular*. Madrid: Gredos.

Dubet, Anne. 2003. Los arbitristas entre discurso y acción política. Propuesta para un análisis de la negociación política. *Tiempos Moderno* 4 (9): 14 S.

Ehrlicher, Hanno. 2010. *Zwischen Karneval und Konversion. Pilger und Pícaros in der spanischen Literatur der frühen Neuzeit*. München: Fink.

Fernández Díaz, Roberto, and Carlos Martínez Shaw. 1995. L'apprentissage de la correspondance par les commerçants espagnols au 18e siècle. In *Cultures et formations négociantes dans l'Europe moderne*, ed. Franco Angiolini and Daniel Roche, 309–319. Paris: Edition de l'École des Hautes Études en Sciences Sociales.

Foronda, Valentín de. 1984. Disertación sobre lo honrosa que es la profesión del comercio, leída en las juntas generales que celebró la sociedad bascongada en Vilbao en año de 1778. In Foronda, Valentín de: *Los suenõs de la razón*, ed. M. Benavides, and C. Rollán, 587–602. Madrid: Editora Nacional.

García Pérez, Guillermo. 1974. *La economía y los reaccionarios. La Inquisición y los economistas al surgir la España Contemporánea. Prólogo de Enrique Tierno Galván*. Madrid: EDICUSA.

Geisler, Eberhard. 1981. *Geld bei Quevedo. Zur Identitätskrise der spanischen Feudalgesellschaft im frühen 17. Jahrhundert*. Frankfurt am Main et al.: Lang.

———. 2013. *El dinero en la obra de Quevedo. La crisis de identidad en la sociedad feudal española a principios del siglo XVII*. Kassel: Reichenberger.

Groethuysen, Bernhard. 1978. *Die Entstehung der bürgerlichen Welt- und Lebensanschauung in Frankreich. Vol. 1. Das Bürgertum und die katholische Weltanschauung. Vol. 2. Die Soziallehren der katholischen Kirche und das Bürgertum*. Frankfurt am Main: Suhrkamp.

Gutiérrez Nieto, Juan Ignacio. 1996. El pensamiento económico, político y social de los arbitristas. In *El Siglo del Quijote 1580–1680. Religión, Filosofía, Ciencia*, ed. Ramón Menéndez Pidal, 329–465. Madrid: Espasa-Calpe.

Häberlein, Mark. 2010. Fremdsprachen in den Netzwerken Augsburger Handelsgesellschaften des 16. und frühen 17. Jahrhunderts. In *Fremde Sprachen in frühneuzeitlichen Städten. Lernende, Lehrende und Lehrwerke*, ed. Mark Häberlein and Christian Kuhn, 23–45. Wiesbaden: Harrassowitz.

Häberlein, Mark, and Magdalena Bayreuther. 2013. *Agent und Ambassador. Der Kaufmann Anton Meuting als Vermittler zwischen Bayern und Spanien im Zeitalter Philipps II*. Augsburg: Wißner.

Hernandez Franco, Jesus. 2011. *Sangre limpia, sangre española. El debate de los estatutos de limpieza (siglos XV–XVII)*. Madrid: Cátedra.

Hook, Jochen. 1995. Le marchand dans la société allemande à l'époque moderne. In *Cultures et formations négociantes dans l'Europe moderne*, ed. Franco Angiolini and Daniel Roche, 49–60. Paris: Editions de l'École des hautes études en sciences sociales.

Hirschman, Albert O. 1987. *Leidenschaften und Interessen. Politische Begründungen des Kapitalismus vor seinem Sieg*. Frankfurt am Main: Suhrkamp.

Julia, Dominique. 1995. L'éducation des négociants français au 18e siècle. In *Cultures et formations négociantes dans l'Europe moderne*, ed. Franco Angiolini and Daniel Roche, 215–256. Paris: Editions de l'École des hautes études en sciences sociales.

Kellenbenz, Hermann, ed. 1970. *Fremde Kaufleute auf der Iberischen Halbinsel*. Köln et al.: Böhlau.

Kessler, Andreas. 1999. *Reichtumskritik und Pelagianismus. Die pelagianische Diatribe de divitiis: Situierung, Lesetext, Übersetzung, Kommentar*. Freiburg: Universitätsverlag.

Lagares Calvo, Manuel J. 2013. Tomás de Mercado. In *Economía y Economistas andaluces (Siglos XVI al XX)*, ed. Rocío Sánchez Lissén, 71–95. Madrid: Ecobook.

Lamikiz, Xabier. 2007. Un 'cuento ruidoso': condifencialidad, reputación y confianza en el comercio del siglo XVIII. *Obradoiro de Historia Moderna* 16: 113–142.

Malagón Pinzón, Miguel. 2001. El Consulado de Comercio de Cartagena. *Revista Estudios Socio-Jurídicos* 3: 51–74.

Maravall, José Antonio. 1964. *El mundo social de "La Celestina"*. Madrid: Gredos.

———. 1979. *Poder, honor y élites en el siglo XVII*. México et al.: Siglo Veintiuno.

Mercado, Tomás de. 1975. *Suma de tratos y contratos. Edición y estudio introductorio de Restituto Sierra Bravo*. Madrid: Editoria Nacional. Hier zitiert nach der Ausgabe von Nicolás Sánchez-Albornoz. http://www.hacer.org/pdf/Tratos.pdf. Accessed 20 Oct 2015.

Mikelarena Peña, Fernando. 2005. La Biblioteca de Pedro Miguel de Ligués, comerciante de lanas de Cintruénigo. *Sancho el Sabio. Revista de cultura e Investigación vasca* 23: 63–87.

Morineau, Michel. 1995. Entre usurier et 'philistin': le 'bon marchand' et le 'négociant éclairé'. In *Cultures et formations négociantes dans l'Europe moderne*, ed. Franco Angiolini and Daniel Roche, 421–438. Paris: Edition de l'École des Hautes Études en Sciences Sociales.

Muñoz, Rodrigo. 2003. Comerciantes y teólogos en el Siglo de Oro español. Claves de la libertad en el ámbito económico. *Revista Empresa y Humanismo* VI (2): 359–372.

Musi, Aurelio. 1995. Marchands et culture à Naples à l'époque espagnole. In *Cultures et formations négociantes dans l'Europe moderne*, ed. Franco Angiolini and Daniel Roche, 77–95. Paris: Editions de l'École des hautes études en sciences sociales.

Oermann, Nils Ole. 2015. *Wirtschaftsethik. Vom freien Markt bis zur Share Economy*. München: C.H. Beck.

Pelorson, Jean-Marc. 1980. *Los letrados, juristes castillans sous Philippe III. Recherches sur leur place dans la société, la culture et l'état*. Poitiers: Université de Poitiers.

Peña López, José Atilano, and José Manuel Sánchez Santos. 2007. El problema de Smith y la relación entre moral y economía. *Isegoría. Revista de Filosofía Moral y Política* 36: 81–103.

Pérez Vejo, Tomás. 2007. La vida como estereotipo: memorias de un comerciante montañés en la Nueva España del siglo XVIII. *Historia Méxicana* 57: 193–262.

Pietschmann, Horst. 1992. Die 'Sociedades Económicas de Amigos del País' und die Verbreitung der 'nützlichen Wissenschaften' in Spanien und Hispanoamerika im Zeitalter der Aufklärung. In *La secularización de la cultura española en el Siglo de las Luces*, ed. Manfred Tietz and Dietrich Briesemeister, 151–167. Wiesbaden: Harrassowitz.

Poettering, Jorun. 2013. *Handel, Nation und Religion. Kaufleute zwischen Hamburg und Portugal im 17. Jahrhundert*. Göttingen: Vandenhoeck & Ruprecht.

Rivero Gracia, Pilar. 2005. Mercaderes y finanzas en la Europa del siglo XVI: material teórico para elaborar una unidad didáctica. *clio. History and History Teaching* 31: 1–53. http://clio.rediris.es. Accessed 10 Nov 2015.

Salomon, Noël. 1965. *Recherches sur le thème paysan dans la "comedia" au temps de Lope de Vega*. Bordeaux: Institut d'Études ibériques et ibéro-américaines de l'Université de Bordeaux.

———. 1985. *Lo villano en el teatro del Siglo de Oro*. Madrid: Castalia.

San Julián, Javier. 2011. *Los avatares de la primera traducción de la Riqueza de las Naciones al español (The adventures of the first translation of Adam Smith's Wealth of Nations into Spanish)*. http://eet.pixelonline.org/files/research_papers/SP/Translation%20Wealth%20of%20Nations%20into%20Spanish.pdf. Accessed 10 Nov 2015.

Savelli, Rodolfo. 1995. Modèles juridiques et culture marchande entre 16e et 17e siècles. *Cultures et formations négociantes dans l'Europe moderne*. Franco Angiolini, Daniel Roche, 403–420. Paris: Editions de l'École des hautes études en sciences sociales.

Taylor, Charles. 2012. *Ein säkulares Zeitalter*. Frankfurt am Main: Suhrkamp.

Thomas von Aquin. 1961–1965. *Summa theologiae [...]*. Madrid: T. I-V. Biblioteca de Autores Cristianos.

Tietz, Manfred. 1991. Quintanas *Vidas de españoles célebres*. Zur Frage der nationalen Identität in der spanischen Spätaufklärung. In *Akten des internationalen Kolloquiums Spanien und Europa im Zeichen der Aufklärung (Duisburg 1986)*, ed. Siegfried Jüttner, 319–345. Frankfurt am Main: Lang.

———. 2013. 'Indeseada sociabilidad': concepto y crítica de la sociabilidad en los contextos teológicos del Siglo de Oro. In *Sociabilidad y literatura en el Siglo de Oro*, ed. Mechthild Albert, 93–113. Madrid/Frankfurt am Main: Iberoamericana/Vervuert.

Torres, Germán. 2008. La figura del hombre de negocios en la literatura hispana. In *Temas del comercio y la economía en la narrativa hispana*, ed. Carlos Mateo Coria-Sánchez and Germán Torres, 1–33. New Haven: Yale University Press.

Vilar Berrogain, Jean. 1973. *Literatura y economía: la figura satírica del arbitrista en el Siglo de Oro*. Madrid: Revista de Occidente.

VilaVilar, Enriqueta. 2001. Los mercaderes sevillanos y el destino de la plata de India. *Boletín de la Real Academia Sevillana de Buenas Letras* 29: 85–101.

Vollhardt, Friedrich. 2001. Eigennutz – Selbstliebe – individuelles Glück. In *Entdeckung des Ich. Die Geschichte der Individualisierung vom Mittelalter bis zur Gegenwart*, ed. Richard Dülmen, 219–242. Darmstadt: Wissenschaftliche Buchgesellschaft.

von Nettesheim, Agrippa. 2013. *Ungewißheit und Eitelkeit aller Künste und Wissenschaften*, ed. Karl María Guth. Berlin: Hoffenburg.

Wiecker, Niels. 2012. *Der iberische Atlantikhandel. Schiffsverkehr zwischen Spanien, Portugal und Iberoamerika 1700–1800*. Stuttgart: Steiner.

Chapter 8
The Figures of the Honorable Merchant and the Philanthropic Entrepreneur-Paternalist in Eighteenth Century Spanish Sentimental Comedies

Beatrice Schuchardt

Abstract The present article puts the genre of the sentimental Spanish comedy of the eighteenth century under closer scrutiny, a genre with a moral as well as educational remit. The portrayal of the merchant and entrepreneur on stage as paternalistic characters, attributed with fulfilling an exemplary role mindful of their responsibility towards society, are the subject of this analysis. Both stock characters serve the purpose to bring into the awareness of a predominantly bourgeois audience, to what extent economically profitable – and at the same time socially responsible – actions within one's own microcosm can exert a positive influence on the macrocosm of the entire Spanish nation. Over the course of the theatrical, enlightened reform discourse, the sentimental comedy strikes a balance between the mutual feeling of friendship and economic *ratio*. Concisely, this feeling is just another form of patriotism, conceived by Spanish eighteenth century economists, e.g. Francisco de Cabarrús, as a strong bond among the members of the Spanish society. While taking a closer look at the sentimental comedies *El hombre agradecido* (1796) by Luciano Comella and *La industriosa madrileña y El fabricante de Olot* (1789) by Francisco Durán, this paper aims to illustrate the significance of both the honorary merchant as well as the benevolent entrepreneur by taking into account the following aspects: the crucial importance of the time lag for the trade industry of the eighteenth century; the role of transatlantic trade chains as an upcoming form of 'social network'; the correlation between economically moderate and socially responsible actions; and, last but not least, the portrayal of a sound work ethos as a new virtue of the flourishing bourgeoisie.

Translated by Ivana Pavlovic.

B. Schuchardt (✉)
University of Siegen, Siegen, Germany
e-mail: schuchardt@romanistik.uni-siegen.de

C. Lütge, C. Strosetzki (eds.), *The Honorable Merchant – Between Modesty and Risk-Taking*, Ethical Economy 56, https://doi.org/10.1007/978-3-030-04351-3_8

8.1 The Merchant and the Sentimental Comedy: Reception Processes from England to France, and Then to Spain

In the history of theater of Western Europe, the character of the merchant has always been closely linked to the so-called "*género sentimental*"[1]: with *The London Merchant, or the History of George Barnwell* (1731), George Lillo composed "a bourgeois tragedy",[2] in which the theme of the merchant has been incorporated in manifold adaptations on the multiple stages throughout Europe, and in France and Spain in particular. Deirdre McCloskey bestows great importance to this play by claiming that 25 years after its initial publishing, Lillo's *London Merchant* served as a blueprint for the German bourgeois tragedy (*bürgerliches Trauerspiel*) and the French *drame bourgeois*.[3] However, as the studies conducted by Yvonne Fuentes (1999) and María García Garrosa (1990) have shown, the various reception processes among England, France, Germany, and Spain seem to be of great diversity and complexity.[4] The European reception process of the *London Merchant* sets out in France, where the first translations are published in the middle of the eighteenth century.[5] Among its adaptations are *Jenneval, ou le Barnevelt Français* (1769) by Louis Sébastien Mercier, *Les deux amis, ou le négociant de Lyon* (1770) by Pierre Augustin Caron de Beaumarchais, and *Le Fabricant de Londres* (1771) by Charles-Georges Fenouillot de Falbaire de Quingey.[6] As to the reception processes from England to France, and Spain, Yvonne Fuentes in her study coins the term *triángulo sentimental*, and identifies *Le Marchand de Londres, ou l'Histoire de George Barnwell* (1751) by Pierre Clément de Genève to be a direct translation from Lillo's original. The French version includes two further scenes at the gallows, and – contrary to the original – bears no references to the queen of England and religion.[7]

According to Ivy McClelland, the fact that social and economic issues increasingly figure on eighteenth century stages in Spain, and mostly in neoclassic and sentimental plays, is on the one hand due to a proclamation by Carlos the Third, stating the inherent sense of honor in business of trade, and due to the influence of the press on the other hand.[8] In the face of a large number of economic treatises on the importance of trade and the merchant for the Spanish national economy, furthermore a plethora of various texts on the economic reform discourse of the enlightened

[1] This hypernym for various sub-genres of the sentimental theater can be found in García Garrosa (1990, p. 45) and García Garrosa (1991, pp. 85seqq).

[2] McCloskey (2016, p. 267).

[3] See ibidem.

[4] See García Garrosa (1990) and Fuentes (1999).

[5] See McClelland (2009, p. 175).

[6] See ibidem.

[7] See Fuentes (1999, p. 225).

[8] See McClelland (2009, p. 175). The authors do not specify which proclamation they refer to.

absolutism by economists such as Jovellanos[9] and Foronda[10] can be considered to have contributed to the emergence of the merchant on Spanish stages. Economic treatises written e.g. by Gaspar Melchor de Jovellanos and Valentín de Foronda at the end of the eighteenth century increasingly focus on the role of the merchant and his overall contributions to the common good when discussing issues such as industry, trade, business, and business ethics. This should be taken into account given the surging popularity of protagonists from the economic walk of life.[11] In the end, it is due to a myriad of interdisciplinary discourses which emphasize the role and influence of the Spanish crown on neoclassic theater plays especially, that the character of the merchant, as described in aforementioned writings, finds its way onto the theater stage.

Hence, numerous Spanish adaptions of the prominent figure of the merchant can be found from the times of Shakespeare on already, and even before Lillo's text was published. McClelland regards the following plays to be inspired by French adaptations of the *London Merchant* by Lillo: *Las ceguedades del vicio y peligros del rigor [. El joven Carlos]*[12] (1776) by Manuel de Ascagorta, and the comedies *Los perfectos comerciantes* (1782) and *El fabricante de paños o el comerciante inglés* (1783) by Antonio Valladares de Sotomayor.[13] However the latter as well as the anonymous and undated *El comerciante de Burdeos* are considered to be based on the version by Falbaire de Quingey.[14] Moreover, McClelland discerns José Concha's *El buen criado* (1775) and Gaspar Zavala y Zamora's *El triunfo del amor y la amistad, Jenwal y Faustina* to be Spanish adaptations inspired by the *London Merchant* and its French versions.[15] *El triunfo del amor y la amistad*, the play most closely linked to the Spanish versions of Lillo's original, is based on *Jenneval* by Mercier. Parallels can be drawn between the *London Merchant* by Lillo and the Spanish *Jenwal* with regard to the key role of friendship between the apprentices George Barnwell and Trueman (Lillo), and Jenwal und Smirn (Zavala y Zamora). Furthermore, both plays

[9] Concerning Jovellanos' perspective on the merchant, see Witthaus (2017, pp. 166seqq) and Möller (2018).

[10] As to Foronda's perspective on commerce and the merchant, see Tietz (2017, pp. 115seqq).

[11] See Foronda (1984, pp. 587seqq), cited in Tietz (2017, p. 115sq). and Jovellanos (1998), cited in Witthaus (2017) and Möller (2018).

[12] This play's caption is *El joven Carlos*. On this subject, see Fuentes (1999, p. 228). McClelland, however, refers to *El joven Carlos* as an independent play. In this particular case, it shall be agreed with Fuentes, who has proven at the hand of annotations in *Diario de Madrid* that the play premiered three times successively in 1803 at the *Teatro de los Caños*.

[13] *El comerciante inglés* was dated back to 1778 by García Garrosa (1991), p. 86 by references to a corresponding performance in Barcelona. In her study, Fuentes (1999, p. 212) points to the respective review of the *Comerciante inglés* in the Madrilenian *Memorial Literario* from the year 1785, but she presumes that the performance from 1785 is based on an anonymously published text. As far as García Garrosa's comparing analysis of Valladares' Spanish adaption of the merchant theme and the anonymously published texts is concerned, it can be said that the author of Quingey's *Le Fabricant de Londres* constitutes the basis for the Spanish versions. Garrosa herself does not elaborate on Lillo's *London Merchant* as a common source for the French and Spanish versions.

[14] E.g. García Garrosa shares this point of view, see (1991, p. 86).

[15] See McClelland (2009, pp. 176sq).

revolve around the construed plot of love among the following characters: the wealthy merchant, his (destitute) employee, and the daughter of the merchant. The merchant as the main protagonist is the sole common denominator of the aforementioned Spanish adaptions, seizing the merchant theme, and the English blueprint.

Among all existing subgenres of comedy, it is the sentimental comedy in particular which appears to have a close affinity to portraying the merchant's universe. The inherent moral and social obligation of this subgenre to educate the people[16] renders a possible explanation for this phenomenon. The inherent role can be traced back to the Restauration period in England and the play *Love's Last Shift* (1696) by Colley Cibber, who wrote the preface of Lillo's *London Merchant*.[17] In France during the age of the Enlightenment, the *drame bourgeois* is intricately related to philosophers like Denis Diderot or Phillippe Néricault Destouches, as well as Pierre-Claude Nivelle de la Chaussée for the *comédie larmoyante*.[18] The system of values as well as the concept of family of the bourgeoisie – the new social motor – manifest in the moral lessons of the rather tragic, and far less comedic, sentimental comedies.[19] Thus, it is hardly surprising that the protagonists from the business sector, including the merchant, play a significant role in the Spanish theater, too, since they represent the role models for economically and socially responsible actions. In this era, Antonio Maravall declares there to be a new moral, rather secular gauge,[20] clearly differing from the previous traditional, religious, and social values. This change is quite explicitly reflected upon in the concept of the business ethos and family values of the *hombre de negocios*.[21]

With the advent of the sentimental comedy – first in England and France, then in Spain – several changes in social structures come about in the affected countries. This genre is accountable to a quite bourgeois audience, yearning to see its very own dire straits from their professional and family life on stage.[22] From the seventeenth century in England and the late eighteenth century in Spain, a shift can be discerned

[16] See also Llanos Mardones (1989).

[17] See Fuentes (1999, p. 29).

[18] See eadem (1999, pp. 58sseq) and García Garrosa (1990, pp. 15sseq). Lagarde and Michard further differentiate the genre by making a distinction between *comédie de caractères* and *comédie attendrissante et moralisante*. See Lagarde/Michard (2003, pp. 32seqq). The *comédie attendrissante et moralisante* has also been as referred to as a *comédie sérieuse* in Stackelberg (1992, pp. 43seqq).

[19] With regard to Spain, see Antonio Maravall (1991, pp. 113seqq. and pp. 245seqq.) as well as Rommel (2006, p. 8) with regard to England: "The *merchant* as [...] entrepreneur dissociated himself from the other nobility and, at the same time, he was striving towards bringing about a change in values as well as a social change", translated by Ivana Pavlovic (I.P.). The term 'change in values' refers to a framework within which "the ideas of self-interest – usually used as a synonym for egoism – smoothly turned into an economically and morally legitimized, natural, and henceforth positive pursuit, promoting the well-being of society". Rommel (2006, p. 14), translated by I.P. In his study, Rommel dedicates different economic, philosophical, political, and literary texts from England to addressed change in values.

[20] See Maravall (1979, p. 302) with reference to E.G. Barber (1975, pp. 19seqq).

[21] See ibidem.

[22] See Angulo Egea (2006, p. 328).

from a replica in verse to a replica in prose.[23] Joan Pataky-Kosove[24] noted this very shift in *El viejo y la niña* (1786) by Moratín, which by secondary literature was declared to belong to the genre of "comedia lacrimosa"[25] or "comedia de costumbres".[26] Among researchers, though, the authors Moratín and Comella are quite often juxtaposed as rivals,[27] since the first represented a rather neoclassical notion of theater, influenced by the court, and the latter advocated a more popular theater style that was closer to the concerns of the lower classes of society.[28] Nevertheless, both take a common stand on the fact that their plays reflect the mindset and ideas of the age of Enlightenment.[29] According to Angulo Egea, the difference between the authors lies in the respective target audience of their plays: Moratín's audience is rather mercantile-bourgeois, Comella aims at appealing to the 'working masses'.[30]

It is of great interest that both authors attribute great importance to emotion. Maravall considers sentimentality as quite characteristic for the 'bourgeois mentality'[31] during the times of Enlightenment in Spain.[32] It also exerts influence on other plays, whose main protagonist, the entrepreneur, is from the mercantile walk of life, as is the case for example in *La señorita malcriada* (1788) by Tomás de Iriarte or in *La industriosa madrileña y El fabricante de Olot* (1789) by Francisco Durán. Economically inspired comedies, in which merchants, entrepreneurs, craftsmen, or workers are portrayed as protagonists on the one hand, and lavish *petimetres*[33] and

---

[23] See Fuentes (1999, p. 37): "El uso de la prosa será una constante en los dramas sentimentales ingleses, pues entienden que, si para llegar al público es menester representar las penas de personajes de su misma clase social, éstos han de hablar el mismo lenguaje y en la misma forma. Comprendieron los dramaturgos sentimentales [ingleses] que no se puede conmover a un comerciante mostrando las penas de un rey lejano [...]."

[24] See Pataky-Kosove (1979, p. 379).

[25] See Dowling, p. 67.

[26] See ibidem.

[27] This is also due to a published and devastating critique of Moratín' s play *El viejo y la niña* by Comella – he published the text under a pseudonym – after which they literally ensued in a *Quérelle*. See Angulo Egea (2006, p. 67).

[28] In this respect, Angulo Egea (2006, p. 68) speaks of a "reiterada separación dramática del siglo XVIII entre 'populares' y 'neoclásicos'". The difference between both is given insofar, as that "[que] [l]os populares entendían el teatro como espectáculo, mientras que los neoclásicos lo concebían más como una manifestación literaria centrada en el texto, la palabra."

[29] See Angulo Egea (2006, p. 67).

[30] See Angulo Egea (2006, p. 64), translated by the author. The original speaks of Comella's audience as a "masa laboriosa".

[31] See Maravall (1979, p. 299). Maravall considers the bourgeoisie rather to be a 'group of citizens' with a common mentality, than a social 'class' with its own 'class awareness'. Translated by I.P.

[32] Maravall (1979, p. 269seqq).

[33] For introductory references on the character of *petimetre*, see Joaquín Álvarez Barrientos (2005, pp. 235seqq) as well as the studies by Rebecca Haidt (2003), (1999), (1998) and Ana Hontanilla (2008) for further reference. For particular reference to the drama plays from the age of Enlightenment in Spain, see Schuchardt (2014).

greedy imposters[34] as antagonists on the other hand, induce a shift of focus to the professional sphere of the bourgeois class, while the sentimental dimension of the comedies deals with private issues. The sentimental comedies *El hombre agradecido* (1796) by Luciano Comella and *La industriosa madrileña* by Durán, which will be analyzed on the following pages, serve to outline how Spanish sentimental comedies of the late eighteenth century conceive both the entrepreneur and the merchant as characters that are to be considered as exemplary on a moral, social and economic level.

8.2 *El hombre agradecido* (1796) by Luciano Comella: The Merchant, the Time Lag, and the Trusted Chain of Correspondents

By referring to Shakespeare's *Merchant of Venice* (1600), Daniel Fulda elaborates on the growing importance of the so-called "time lag" in the trade business in the seventeenth century in Europe, which goes hand in hand with the advent of a new type of merchant.[35]The *Merchant Adventurer*, who personally oversaw the transport of his goods to his clients, is superseded by the merchant, who is waiting in his counting house for the arrival of his goods.[36] The time lag – whose importance Gervais also emphasizes[37] – leads to the fact that the merchant is no longer able to meet unexpected dangers.[38] The significance of this time lag for the mercantile everyday life becomes ultimately obvious when taking a closer look at Comella's sentimental comedy *El hombre agradecido*: The stage directions also remark on the fact that a clock has to be placed on the merchant's work desk, a device which then actually 'sets off' the storyline:

> *La escena es en Madrid en la sala de una casa perfectamente puesta. El Teatro representa una pieza de una alhajada con sus espejos de vestir naturales, y sus mesas, cornucopias, arañas de cristal en medio, taburetes decentes, mesa á [sic] un lado con su recado de escribir y una papelera. En el fondo de la pieza habrá una puerta, que introduce á [sic] un quarto decente. Encima de la mesa habrá un relox. Sale afanada Doña Antonia, y mira que hora es.*[39]

[34] See the author's habilitation dissertation in progress: *Economy in Spanish Comedies at the End of the Eighteenth Century: Discourses – Protagonists – Spaces* (*Ökonomie in spanischen Komödien des ausgehenden 18. Jahrhunderts: Diskurse – Akteure – Räume*), University of Siegen (2017).

[35] See Fulda (2005, p. 82).

[36] According to North (2008, p. 28), the shift from the *Merchant adventurer* to the new type of merchant already takes place in the thirteenth century in Italy: "It was no longer necessary for the overseas merchant to accompany his goods per trade caravan or ship to his fairs, but he would rather orchestrate the entire business process of his enterprise directly from his counting house in Genoa, Florence, or Pisa," translated by I.P. I owe this hint to Isenmann (2017).

[37] Gervais (2008, p. 467) literally refers to a "time lag".

[38] Fulda (2005, p. 82).

[39] Comella, Luciano Francisco (1796, p. 1). The spelling used in the citations is that of the eighteenth century. Therefore, it differs from modern Spanish orthography.

The clock's fairly central position in the room indicates that the main protagonist, the merchant named Don[40] Lorenzo, represents a kind of merchant matching the 'new type' sketched by Fulda. Furthermore, the pretentious décor of the room with its chandeliers, illuminated mirrors, and dressing tables opposite to the marginalized position of the work desk as well as the file cabinet sheds a light on the core dilemma, which advances the plot: The income of the resident merchant is to an extraordinary extent disproportionate to his expenses, the private and professional household is in an imbalanced state, while debit presides over credit. This disproportion becomes already evident in the first scene on stage, when Doña Antonia,[41] Lorenzo's sister, takes a look at the clock. In the following replica, she comments the late arrival of the landlady in the face of the dire situation of the family, which threatens the very existence of the mercantile household and requires imminent action; hence, also the presence of the landlady. The subsequent dialogue reveals that the landlord Lorenzo is in prison because of the business' pending bankruptcy and the therein involved debts, while the landlady – Doña Blasa,[42] who has a quite telling name – is enjoying herself at a ball, and deliberately procrastinates her return despite her knowledge of the matter at hand.[43] The reason for which this is indeed a remarkable fact is that she is the one responsible for the family's precarious situation: coming from a poor background herself as the daughter of impoverished nobility, she spent a horrendous amount of money at the cobbler's, the French mercer's, the jeweler's, and while gambling.[44] Blasa does not contribute in any respect to the

---

[40]After introducing the main characters of the play, I will refrain from explicitly mentioning the titles "Don" or "Doña".

[41]The resemblance in names of Antonia and Antonio, Shakespeare's eponymous merchant from *The Merchant of Venice* (1600), is no coincidence at all, as just like Antonio, Antonia embodies all mercantile virtues: She acts reasonably and is in accordance with the dramatis personae introduced as the "joven juiciosa", see Comella (1796), p. 1. In the spirit of her role, she knows her rights as a citizen and thusly puts an arrogant court clerk in his place. She appreciates the virtue of moderate behavior and action, and reprimands the clerk and her sister-in-law in this respect. She steps up for a more respectful interaction with one's supervisor and upbraids the rude servant to show more respect towards her landlady. Furthermore, she tries to call upon Lorenzo's modesty, although this attempt is rather futile. See for all act I. Accordingly, she criticizes her brother for marrying a woman of noble upbringing, which is deemed inappropriate for a merchant: "[...] Que. estos/ sonrojos [de espejos de vestir con sus adornos de talla dorados] al Comerciante malgastador é indiscreto/no corrijan? Ay hermano!/tu condescente genio con tu muger, en qué abismo/te ha anegado de tormentos?/Por su vanidad y luxo/te vés en la cárcel preso, /sin amigos, sin apoyo, /sin caudales ni conceptos: /los desiguales enlaces/jamas acertados fueron/en el Comerciante." Comella (1796), p. 2.

[42]The name "Blasa" derives from the Spanish term "blasón" (English: "charge", but also "fame" or "honor") and means the 'bloated one' or the 'pretentious one'. It points at the same time to her traits of character and her social status as an aristocrat.

[43]As we get to know from the first polylogue, Antonia had send Blasa many different messages in this regard.

[44]Over the course of the play, we find out what Blasa spends her money so lavishly for. First of all, she is not willing to sacrifice her numerous dresses and jewels in order to bail her husband out of prison. See Comella (1796), p. 3. When she unexpectedly comes into some money intended for

household.[45] Because of the very fact that she of all people, who as the merchant's wife is usually considered to be the pillar of the mercantile household, to be in charge of the servants – hence a precious 'commodity'[46] –, is the one to arrive too late, and, by doing so, causes greater damage, she is serving the purpose of a symbolical 'wildcard', denoting the time lag.

The constellation of characters at hand together with the plot gist exemplify the typical pattern of action common to Spanish plays of the eighteenth century that focus on economic subjects: A bourgeois household – including the mercantile business – is in a state of chaos. This was brought about by economically irrational behavior, i.e. lavish, egocentric, and irresponsible, of a prominent character type, typical for this age, the *petimetre*[47] or *petimetra*, epitomized in this case by Blasa.[48] The character of the landlord, by contrast, is either powerless or completely absent when confronted with the situation, as he either previously passed away or because he is absent for other reasons, be it physically or mentally; thus, he represents a landlord who, by ignoring his due obligations, turns into a "blank character in the order system". In this situation of powerlessness and chaos, a savior creating order comes to rescue. This character is able to fill the void and is himself a known authority, such as an uncle or an experienced rich friend of the family. Moreover, the latter assumes the role of a matchmaker, reprimands the landlord to resume his due

restoring the mercantile household, she spends it immediately: "Mil reales al Zapatero. *Separa dinero.* /Quatro mil a la Francesa/de las gasas. Otros quatro/para el que baylar me enseña/y para una relox [sic] de moda/doce onzas. Aun me queda/mucho dinero, bien puedo/echarme en la faldriqueta. [...] para el juego de esta noche/otras diez [...]." Comella (1796), p 5sq.

[45] Blasa herself justifies this with her aristocratic heritage, which reinforces and underpins the critique of the nobility being a useless class: "[...] de las tertulias, compuestas/todas de mugeres y hombres, /que en nada jamas se emplean, /porque son nobles [...]." See Comella (1796), p. 13. On the criticism on the nobility in the eighteenth century in Spain see also well Krauss (1973, pp. 87seqq): "Criticising the nobility is part of the everyday life", translated by I.P. Krauss refers to the letters of Conde de Cabarrús and Cañuelo's contributions in the journal *El Censor*, among others, as prominent examples of widespread criticism of the nobility, denouncing their indolence and uselessness.

[46] In Comella's play, the social function of the merchant's wife is being referred to as someone able to enrich the family, and who the household can benefit from. This becomes obvious in one of Bruno's replicas, where he speaks on the yet unused potential of Blasa as a profitable wife: "[...] Tu muger, /que será esta segun creo, /si como tiene donayre [sic], /tiene discurso y talento, /te puede ser para todo/de utilidad y provecho, /[...]." Comella (1796, p. 10).

[47] In the following, the masculine form shall be understood as including both genders.

[48] Blasa has the prototypical characteristics of a *petimetra*, as we have seen it as well at the example of Jéronima in Nicolás Fernández de Moratín's *La petimetra* and Mariano from Tomás de Iriarte's *El señorito mimado o la mala educación* (1787). On this subject, see Schuchardt (2014). Blasa is egocentric, vain, i.e. she values to keep up appearances, which results in her not only deceiving others, but also overestimating her very own value. See Comella (1796, p. 13), where Blasa retrospectively demands a compensation (Spanish: "recompensa") for having married Lorenzo, and thus a member of the bourgeoisie. Moreover, she spends money lavishly on French luxury goods, wrongly rating their value as well as her own, and calls herself an "ecónoma perfecta". Comella (1796, p. 16). In total, she is a burden to the household, and her inclinations are rather vicious, as she indulges in gambling. This trait of characters of hers resembles Mariano from Iriarte's *El señorito mimado.*

obligations and/or takes his role by inducing the *petimetre's* change of heart, or by excluding him from the household.[49] The order-maker assists one further member of the household, who act economically and sound and is hence virtuous by nature[50] – this pivotal role is usually represented by a diligent, hard-working bachelor (or bachelorette) standing in stark contrast to the *petimetre* –, to get a spouse, a previously vain endeavor due to the financial distress of the family. This savior is a "good catch" because he lifts up the morale next to improving the family's financial situation. As shown in the play by Comella, the good catch can be both: the financial savior and the order-maker. In Comella's play, it is the character of Bruno who takes up the role of the order-maker. He is an honorable member of society with a great sense of responsibility, and a quite successful merchant in overseas trade. This fact constitutes the decisive analogy to the character Thorowgood from *London Merchant* by George Lillo,[51] where the image of a merchant beyond any doubt is created on stage.[52] Similar to captain Lievens, a character penned by Comella in *El hombre singular o Isabel Primera de Rusia* (1795), Bruno represents the archetypical financially sound-acting benefactor and sophisticated philanthropist.[53] Since he acquired great wealth in Jamaica[54] and is pretty familiar with the English's business practices due to the time he spent there,[55] Bruno as a prosperous merchant successful in foreign trade is predestined to be the order-maker. Therefore, Bruno is able to restore Lorenzo's insolvent business, and by giving generous sums to the indebted couple, he ultimately succeeds to bring about a change of heart of the *petimetra* Blasa, who was previously unwilling to face reality. Over the course of the comedy's plot evolvement and the necessary solemnization of marriage, Bruno is capable to successfully court and marry Lorenzo's prudent sister Antonia, who acts both economically responsible and according to bourgeois values, and displays sound actions. With the fact that both complement each other ideally and are thusly able to amplify their moral and financial capital – this aspect is a recurring plot motif of business-related neoclassical Spanish comedies in the eighteenth century as well[56] – Comella

[49] This could come about by either legal consequences – such as incarceration of exile – or by the *petimetre* being forced to enter a disadvantageous marriage. In this regard, see as well Schuchardt (2014), p. 280.

[50] Based on Aristotle's doctrine of *mesotes*, Wegmann et al. (2009, p. 13sq) define virtuous actions to be moderate in the spirit of "a balanced mean between to non-virtues, one too deficient, the other too abundant, and both circumstances shall be avoided."

[51] See Rommel (2006, p. 184): "George Lillo's *The London Merchant, or The History of George Barnwell* of 1731 brings the entrepreneur, acting responsibly on a social level, to the fore, embodied by the character of the merchant Thorowgood", translated by I.P.

[52] See Rommel (2006, p. 22).

[53] See Huerta (1991, p. 187). The ascribed roles to Don Lievens by Fernando Huerta in the Spanish original are "bienhechor, […] enemigo del lujo" as well as "verdadero modelo de humanitarismo ilustrado".

[54] In the play, Bruno indicates, "que en quince años poco ménos [sic]/he adquirido saneados/quatro milliones de pesos". Comella (1796, p. 6).

[55] See ibidem.

[56] See Schuchardt (2014) and eadem (2017).

presents the prospect that witty Antonia values Bruno's business acumen, which she calls a "sabia economía".[57] Thus, Bruno's mercantile ethos is characterized to be cautious and moderate,[58] sound and ultimately honorable. Therefore, it is amongst his basic business principles to swiftly pay his debts, to uphold honest business transaction, to not fall prey to frauds,[59] and to undertake solely profitable investments.[60]

After Blasa had spent all the money given to her by Bruno in her typically lavish manner, Antonia, urged by Lorenzo, takes it upon herself to once again ask Bruno for help. He in turn points to the moral 'loss-making business' incurred, as the money gifted was intended for restoring the order of the unraveled mercantile household:

> Yo lo [el dinero] dí baxo el supuesto,
> de que el dinero que daba
> había de ser el móvil
> de la dicha de esta casa;
> y así, puesto que otra ruina
> mi dinero le prepara,
> no quiero darlo.[61]

As his adviser and order-maker, Bruno recommends Lorenzo to adjust his business strategy by putting his focus on a rather active instead of passive business. In this context, Comella includes in his play a differentiation within an economic concept, which prevailed in Spain in the eighteenth century and which was included in José de Carvajal y Lancaster's *Testamento político* (1745), that is the difference between "comercio activo" and "comercio pasivo".[62] Bruno's suggestion refers to a kind of trade, which – in the words of Carvajal – deals with "passive material", i.e. commodities such as wool, iron, and silk, but is distributed "actively", when transport costs are financed out of one's own resources.[63] Bruno's recommended change of

---

[57] See Comella (1796, p. 24).

[58] Thus, Bruno enjoins Lorenzo to caution with regard to his wife ("precaución") and to moderation considering her passion for grandeur. See Comella (1796), p. 11. His call for Blasa to moderate her behavior was previously voiced by Antonia, who urged Blasa to "[…] modera el porte y el fausto, /vive conforme al empleo/o destino de mi hermano", Comella (1796), p. 5.

[59] See Comella (1796), p. 18: "El bribón del Mayoral/me engañaba en dos pesetas; /pero le cogí, y le eché una valiente pendencia: [...]"

[60] Accordingly, Wegmann et al. (2009, p. 13) also define the honorable merchant as somebody, who "is unfailingly considering through all of his actions to find the right balance, whereas honesty, trust, diligence, consideration, and credibility are not opposed to a pursuit of profit", translated by I.P. This means, that with all due respect to his honesty, a merchant has to keep his profit in mind, which requires the necessary amount of caution and suspicion, as we have seen it at the example of Bruno.

[61] See the following replica rendered by Bruno in Comella (1796, p. 24).

[62] See Artola (1969, p. 68).

[63] Ibidem, translated by I.P. According to Artola, the differentiation between passive and active trade shows Carvajal's deep interest to promote Spanish sea trade, since goods from the Spanish

business focus actually points out the damage Lorenzo's passive trade inflicted on the Spanish economy:

> [...] Vosotros,
> por falta de inteligencia,
> con el comercio pasivo
> os contentais, cuya senda
> os conduce al monopolio,
> á la ruindad y baxeza,
> por no daros las ganancias
> suficientes; y quisiera
> que tú y otros adopterais
> el activo, y refundierais
> en favor de la nacion [sic]
> lo que gana la Francesa.
> Las gasas, plumas, reloxes,
> cintas y medias de seda,
> que nos trueca por dinero,
> si el comercio activo hicierais,
> las trocariais por lana,
> por lino, por hierro y seda,
> y se quedara en España
> el dinero que se llevan
> los Franceses [...].[64]

The quoted replica illustrates that the household is stricken by financial difficulties due to the *petimetre* and his longing for foreign luxury good is the epitome of the national economic situation in Spain. The discourse on the *petimetre* is intricately intertwined with the spirit of reform of the Spanish Enlightenment, with the objective to boost the national economy.[65] Furthermore, the aforementioned replica emphasizes the importance of having a sound business strategy at hand in order to successfully engage in trade. With regard to the trade network of the eighteenth century, Pierre Gervais highlighted in his study on transatlantic trade relations of this era, how vital such strategies were to safeguard your business' success: "[...] these networks were highly dependent on professional strategies, and narrowly constrained by the necessities entailed by the maintenance of those strategies."[66] The fundamental functioning of those networks is based on rational strategies as well as on its members pursuing a responsible and honest way of life. In accordance with this, Bruno proclaims the importance of honorable behavior, which ennobles a person to larger extent than the bought aristocratic title which Lorenzo so desperately aspires at the instigation of his noble wife: "La verdadera/nobleza es la honradez."[67]

---

overseas colonies as well as from other countries, e.g. the Asian region, should mainly be transported by Spanish ships in order to offset the Spanish trade balance. See Artola (1969, p. 69).

[64] Comella (1796, p. 12).

[65] On the importance of the endangered private household by the *petimetre* as a *pars pro toto* of the Spanish nation, see Haidt (2003, pp. 151seqq) and Hontanilla (2008, pp. 52seqq).

[66] Gervais (2008, p. 471).

[67] Comella (1796, p. 11). Here it becomes evident, that the term *honor* as a key term of the Spanish Golden drama, is now, in the eighteenth century, being replaced by the term *honradez*, central to

The respectability of a merchant, which Bruno regards to be his obligation in private as well as professional life,[68] defines the basic nature of eighteenth century trade relations. Pierre Gervais described these relations as a "trusted chain of correspondents",[69] where reliable – in other words, trustworthy – merchants, counting on each other, constitute the links. This very chain based on the trust and experience of the trade partners conversant in their respective business field renders it possible for each merchant to "outsource" expertise in the face of a vast variety of trade goods.[70] Moreover, each merchant is capable of bridging the time gap between order receipt, delivery, and payment receipt, as most trading activities are not settled by cash payment, but in terms of liabilities and invoices.[71] The typical business practices of transatlantic trade in the eighteenth century resulted in the emergence of a chain and social fabric[72] of trade partners, interconnected by services to be rendered and by already concluded transactions. After discussing the binary concepts of a 'service rendered' and 'consideration', we will now put under closer scrutiny the concept of 'gift' and 'gift in return' as portrayed in Comella's play. Within the mercantile framework, his notion abandons the suggested aneconomic aspect of handing out a gift as an 'action without any required exchange',[73] but rather embeds it within an economic context.

the theater plays of the Enlightenment and of vital bourgeois value. The latter is directly linked to the bourgeois notion of virtuousness (*virtud*). According to Angulo Egea, the complementary terms *honor* and *virtud* underpin the dichotomy of two models of society: the "new" bourgeois and the "old" feudal order, in which the topic of the 'two Spains' is already insinuated: "Dos palabras claves enfrentan dos formas diferentes de entender el mundo: honor y virtud. Los modernos principios ilustrados, tratando de dignificar la posición y los trabajos de las nuevas clases acomodadas, de la clase media adinerada, dedicada a los negocios, la industria y el comercio, difundieron ideas que establecían la calidad y la posición de los hombres acuerdo a su conducta, no a los títulos heredados de sus antepasados. La virtud de los individuos era determinante, y no el honor hereditario." Angulo Egea (2006, p. 118). Angulo Egea refers in this respect also to a speech excerpt from Comella's play *El pueblo feliz* (1789), p. 3.

[68] See the following speech excerpt from Bruno in the third act of the comedy, where he acquiesces to take charge of Lorenzo's business upon being urged to do so by Lorenzo's wife after she finally saw reason: "[...] de gobernar se encarga/mi honradez vuestro comercio". Comella (1796, p. 31).

[69] Gervais (2008, p. 265).

[70] Gervais (2008, p. 264).

[71] At the example of the merchant from Boston, Mr. Green, and his trade partner from London, Mr. Lane, Gervais illustrates, "[that] little cash changed hands": "Green, for instance, almost never sent any cash to Lane, but 'remitted' his debts by sending 'bills'." Gervais (2008, p. 468).

[72] In his study, Gervais (2008, p. 466) also speaks of networks, but then argues the case to choose the chain as a more adequate metaphor, tailored to the needs of a mercantile reality. In this regard, he also refers to the importance of rather familial and cordial relations, e.g. the trust one sets in trade partner one's father already did business with, as well as to the importance of one's reputation: "[...] reputation was a decisive element, and it included non-economic ties." Gervais (2008, p. 468).

[73] See Stamer (2010) referring to Derrida (1991).

8.3 The Blurring of Lines Between Gift and Investment in *El hombre agradecido*

The fact that within the scope of the *trusted chain of correspondents* as depicted by Gervais, the service rendered and consideration lay the groundwork for functioning trade activities. Moreover, both aspects are indispensable to a morally stable society, as already indicated in the title of Comella's sentimental comedy *El hombre agradecido*. The title announces the subject matter of the "grateful man", hence the topoi of the dichotomy 'gift' and 'gift in return' is stated.[74] Nevertheless, it necessary to stress that in Comella's sentimental comedy the dividing lines between 'gift' and 'gift in return' on the one hand and 'investment' and 'barter' on the other hand are blurred. In the very first line of the play, namely the title, it is indicated that if there is a grateful person, there must be somebody he owes his thanks to. Therefore, it should it in the first place be pondered on the question, who might represent the savior or philanthropist in this specific context. There are two possible ways of answering the question who the person is, which the 'grateful man' mentioned by the title of the play is indebted to.

Option 1

Taking a closer look at the last replica read out by the choir,[75] it becomes evident that Bruno is the philanthropist in question. Not once or twice, but thrice[76] has he given money as a gift to Lorenzo, as it is stressed multiple times,[77] without expecting any consideration in return – an action, which at first glance fulfills all prerequisites to be deemed a gift: According to Fulda and his assumptions based in the theory of Derrida,[78] a gift is detached from any notion of investment or returns[79]:

> A gift is characterized by the dissolution of any reciprocity at the given moment, which is particular to barter. In stark opposition to any kind of barter or exchange, it constitutes an action without any intentions or strings attached, from which the individual wants to free itself after being shackled by modern calculus not only in economic sphere, but also in different areas of life.[80]

---

[74] On the importance of gift, gift in return, and economy in the Spanish theater of the *Siglo de Oro* see Geisler (2014, pp. 59seqq).

[75] Comella (1796, p. 32): "Viendo al hombre agradecido/como el beneficio paga."

[76] This gift is made up of three components: first, a certain amount of money to bail Lorenzo out of jail, see Comella (1796, p. 8sq), second, the handing over of a purse, whose content is imminently lavishly spent by Blasa, see Comella (1796), 11sq., and third, by a payment of 4000 Pesos for Lorenzo to set up his business anew, see Comella (1796, p. 28).

[77] Many a different replica refer to Bruno foregoing any kind of service in return. By putting the foregoing as such, it becomes a stylistic device itself as a *geminatio*, emphasizing the nature of Bruno's action. See Comella (1796), p. 9: "[...] Vuelvo á decir, /que de esta casa no quiero/*nada, nada*", Comella (1796), p. 20: „[...] haciendo lo que yo hago, /*sin ninguna* recompense" und Comella (1796: 19): "[...] aquí estoy yo, que ahora mismo/*sin* exigir *recompensa*, /daré el dinero que baste/para que á comerciar vuelva [su hermano]", italics mine.

[78] See Derrida (1991).

[79] Fulda (2005, p. 89), translated by I.P.

[80] Ibidem, translated by I.P.

Even though Bruno already emphasized that he forgoes any kind of repayment when handing over his gift, upon observing more closely, the lines between what constitutes a gift, a trade, or barter becomes swiftly blurred, as soon as it is evident that Bruno's gift has indeed a desired purpose – consequently, it cannot be considered a gift any longer. His actions aim to achieve a moral reformation of the married couple gone astray.[81] Hence, Bruno's gift is basically an investment, the expected returns of which would restore a functioning mercantile household on a social and business level. At the end, it turns out that the money gifted was a profitable investment for Bruno and it served the purpose to attain his desired objective; it is profitable to an extent even beyond his initial expectations: Apart from restoring the social balance of Lorenzo's household, Bruno is permitted to marry Lorenzo's prudent sister Antonia, who according to mercantile ratio displays true wit and acts as appropriate. Together with his new wife, Bruno will be able to accumulate greater moral as well as financial capital, hence literally illustrating the useful 'enriching' benefits of a wife to her husband (see above). The 'restoration' of the mercantile household thanks to the 'injections of capital' proves to be an action guided by reason, since, at the end of the play, it induces the intended change of heart in the misguided characters of the traditional sentimental comedy, accompanied by many tears and an abundance of respectful gestures.[82] As the key actions by the savior are guided by reason, apart from being based on calculated trade principles, he also holds up the core values of the enlightened utilitarian principle developed by Jeremy Bentham in *Introduction to the Principles of Morals and Legislation* (1789).

Option 2

However, if Bruno's gift is to be considered from the play's holistic point of view, it is revealed that the only reason why Bruno was able to gather his wealth is that he was taken in by Lorenzo's father Anselmo as an orphan, who provided him with the necessary education and basic capital to start his business. In this respect, it becomes clear that the money Bruno handed to Lorenzo was in fact a gift in return, a due debt since he paid for a gift he once received.[83] As Fulda underlines: a

---

[81] I refer to the above-mentioned replica from Comella (1796, p. 23).

[82] Over the course of his repentant change of heart, Lorenzo falls down on his knees before Bruno, see Comella (1796, p. 29). Plenty of and sighs are uttered at the end of the play. See Comella (1796, p. 30). Nevertheless, in comparison to the French sentimental comedy with instructions of an abundance of emotional gestures, the Spanish and English maintain a rather low profile, as noted by Fuentes (1999: 229). As already mentioned at the outset, tragic gestures and exclamations are specific characteristics of sentimental comedies. They constitute the main components in Denis Diderot's conception of the *drame bourgeois*, as applied in his plays *Le fils naturel* (1757) and *Le père de famille* (1758), and theoretically reflected upon in the corresponding epilogues. See the treatises "Entretiens sur le fils naturel" (1757) and "Des genres dramatiques" (1758). On Diderot's theoretical conception of the *drame bourgeois*, see Diderot, Denis (2005b [1758]), pp. 139seqq. as well as Hale (1988, p. 193seqq) and Pappas (1981, pp. 225seqq)

[83] This becomes clear with Bruno pointing to an outstanding old debt on his part. See Comella (1796), p. 11: "[...] aunque estoy rico, y tú [Lorenzo] pobre, /me hallo en la precisa deuda de servirte [...]." See as well Comella (1796), p. 28: "[...] que tengo /en mas estima la fama/del hijo [Lorenzo] de un bienhechor [Anselmo], /que todo el oro y la plata, que la codicia desea, /y consume la arrogancia".

gift cannot do without a gift in return.[84] In addition, both actions are separated by a longer period of time,[85] which is also given in Comella's play. As a consequence, a second possible answer to the question, who is the one the eponymous grateful man owes his thanks to, would be Anselmo, the previous benefactor of the now rich and successful Bruno. By establishing the principle of gift and gift in return, Comella strikes a balance between ideal (i.e. morally upright) and economic (i.e. economically profitable) actions. Therefore, the underlying message would be: Morally upright actions are profitable on a social scale, i.e. useful, as they improve society's morale and standards, and are henceforth worthwhile. The lesson to be learnt is explicitly voiced by Bruno towards the end of the comedy, when referring directly to the Spanish king as the imminent benefactor of virtual and useful conduct:

> [...]
> pero para uno que trata
> en hacerse útil al Reyno
> no le es esto [el Arbol Genealógico] de importancia.
> Del mérito y la virtud
> es la nobleza la paga;
> sé útil, sé virtuoso,
> y te premiara el Monarca
> con un premio que valdrá
> mas que las pompas pintadas,
> supuestas la mayor parte
> para engañar la ignorancia.[86]

Typical for plays dated from the age of Spanish Enlightenment, the moral lesson at the end of the play reflects the educational task of the theater,[87] a task directly associated with the core principles of this time: *utilidad* and *felicidad.*[88] Maravall clarifies to what extent the term usefulness (*utilidad*) goes hand in hand with the notion of inherent "goodness" (*bien*) in the eighteenth century. To be more precise, they were even considered as synonyms.[89] In this process, the concept of inherent "goodness" abandons the economic context and becomes part of the moral context or, as Maravall put it aptly, reflecting Gusdorf[90]: "El orden de la moral invididual se disuelve en el orden de la utilidad social."[91] In Cabarrús' words: the "fin individual" and the "fin común" become one and the same goal to attain. Ultimately, this results in the prevailing notion that the efforts of an individual contribute to the common

---

[84] See Fulda (2005, p. 89): "Without being eligible to a legal, externalized claim, a gift implies to expect a gift in return."

[85] See Fulda (2005, p. 90) with reference to Bourdieu (1998, p. 163).

[86] Comella (1996, p. 32).

[87] See Maravall (1991, pp. 382seqq).

[88] See Maravall (1991, pp. 161seqq).

[89] See ídem, p. 251: "Las nociones de utilidad y bien se encuentran equiparadas."

[90] See Gusdorf (1972, p. 453).

[91] See Maravall (1991, p. 251).

good, i.e. the society's national harmony, and the prospect of each member of the society.[92] Accordingly, it can be assumed that Bruno's gift to Lorenzo is at the same time a patriotic investment in the overall good of Spain; only through this action, Bruno can attain his personal benefit, as inherent to the play's morale.

8.3.1 The Role of Friendship as an Allegory for Spanish Economic Reform Discourse

When talking about patriotism, one cannot neglect the significance of friendship in Comella's play. Friendship[93] as an ideal value itself and its direct connection to camaraderie and the social environment within the framework of an enlightened, rather moralizing discourse and a key theme is not only confined to *El hombre agradecido*, but it is referenced to in a myriad of plays of the Spanish era of Enlightenment. The most prominent ones – which also include the topoi in the title – are *La escuela de la amistad o El filósofo enamorado* (1796) by Juan Pablo Forner,[94] as well as *El delincuente honrado* (1774) by Gaspar Melchor Jovellanos[95] and the aforementioned *El triunfo del amor y la amistad o Jenwal y Faustina* (1793). Another scholar of the eighteenth century in Spain who emphasizes the vital role of friendship is María Angulo Egea: Pursuant to her, the latter was equaled to virtue and goodness.[96] This view serves as an explanation to account why a business-related topic was embedded in the genre of the sentimental comedy. The character exhibiting the particular traits of economically exemplary behavior and action is the friendship-cherishing merchant. The importance of friendship in the economic discourse in enlightened Spain explains why in this particular play the lines between the complementary pairs of gift and gift in return as well as barter and trade dissolve gradually: If friendly actions contributing to the greater social good are deemed to be a necessary virtue of an ideal merchant, then, in theory, he is unfailingly bound to live up to his social obligation. Thus, trade – in the spirit of enlightened utilitarian thinking – should be guided by *sensibilidad* and *amistad*. This notion closes the loop to Gervais' model of the *trusted chain of correspondents* as a social network: Anselmo, Bruno, and Lorenzo precisely illustrate the make-up of such a chain on an economic

[92] See idem, p. 261, translated by I.P. The Spanish original indicates an "armonía del todo".

[93] Agnieszka Komorowska conducts a systematic analysis of friendship at the Spanish theater of the seventeenth and eighteenth century in her habilitation dissertation. See the panel discussion *Male or Female Friends? Writing and Staging Friendship in 17th and 18th Century Spanish Literature*, Harvard, 17.-20.03.2016 lead by Claudia Gronemann and Agnieszka Komorowska on the issue of friendship in the seventeenth and eighteenth century in Spain within the scope of the *Annual Meetings* der *American Comparative Literature Association*.

[94] See Gies (1998, pp. 449seqq).

[95] On the role of friendship *El delincuente honrado* and *El señorito mimado*, Pérez Magallon (2001, pp. 185seqq).

[96] See Angulo Egea (2006, p. 132) with reference to Gies (1998, pp. 449seqq).

as well as on a moral level. This is the case, because Anselmo awarded a commodity to his former apprentice Bruno in the form of profound education and training as well as basic capital, and this commodity is ultimately returned to his son Lorenzo in the shape of material commodities: the clearance of is debt, the provision of a basis to restore his insolvent business, and a moral lesson. Hence, the once given gift is imminently returned to the initial benefactor. By doing so, Comella's play strikes a balance between the model of Gervais' trade chain, which was initially only applicable to trade transactions, and Spanish enlightened economic and moral discourses.

8.4 Durán's *La industriosa madrileña, y El fabricante de Olot*: The Character of Esteban as a Philanthropic Entrepreneur-Paternalist and the Value of Work

The equivalent to Comella's honorable merchant is Esteban, the honorable entrepreneur in Francisco Durán's in *La industriosa madrileña, y El fabricante de Olot.* Durán was not the only one to stage and draw attention to the exemplary and honorable entrepreneur, but the same approach can be found e.g. in Iriarte's portrayal of the Catalan textile manufacturer Eugenio in *La señorita malcriada* (1788),[97] or Lillo's *London Merchant* converted into an entrepreneur in Valladares de Sotomayors *El fabricante de paños* (1784).[98] This fact suggests the assumption that Durán, Iriarte, and Valladares de Sotomayor chose exactly this new kind of stock character who has exemplary traits, because it conveys values immanent to the age of Enlightenment such as *utilidad, felicidad*, and *bien común,*[99] just like the merchant. Both dramatic characters, the merchant Bruno and the textile manufacturer Esteban, are on-stage-representatives of the Spanish economic trade and industry sectors, which according to the economic reformers of the late eighteenth century were in great need of expansion and further promotion for the sake of the nation. Lorenzo Normante y Carcavilla, for example, attributes the flourishing of nation-states to their economic advances in agriculture and trade, and the industrial sector in particular.[100] Similar ideas on the key role of trade and industry can be discovered in the economic writings of Jovellanos.[101] As similar as the mercantile virtues of moderation and humility are at the center of Comella's plays, the household of the Catalan textile manufacturer Esteban exhibits moderate features in Durán's play. There, we

[97] See Schuchardt (in print).

[98] On this play, see the analysis of García Garrosa (1991) and Guinard (1984).

[99] A similar thought can be found in the writings of English and French Enlightenment philosophers, in particular with Shaftesbury und Diderot. See Maravall (1991, p. 261sq).

[100] See Normante y Carcavilla (1784, p. 15), quoted in Maravall (1991, p. 255).

[101] See Maravall (1991, p. 255) with regard to Jovellanos (1952b, p. 38) as well as Möller (2018).

come across instructions of stage design like "sillas y un vestido decente",[102] and there is barely any furniture in the room apart from the working desk, which furnishes evidence for the entrepreneur's diligence and zeal. It is repeatedly underlined in Duran's play to what extent the manufacturer's highly acclaimed work ethics spurns and promotes the prosperity of the entire region of Olot. It is extremely intriguing and interesting to discern a content-related congruence of the replicas of Bruno the merchant and Esteban the manufacturer. To adduce an instance: the dialogue between Esteban and Silvestre, his antagonist and half-brother. The latter is a representative of the conception of early mercantilism – considered outdated in the late eighteenth century –, i.e. that a state's wealth shall only be measured in its stock of precious metals, a fact which thusly renders it possible for the gentry to display their status by wearing jewelry of foreign provenance.[103] Hence, Silvestre sets little store by the "industria",[104] an ambiguous term for Esteban's manufacture *and* his workers' diligence, to what Esteban ripostes:

> Y que en un capricho de esos
> disipen todas las rentas,
> que les rinden los afanes
> de una poblacion entera,
> para que el jugo espanol
> vaya a manos extrangeras.[105]

Esteban the entrepreneur takes the stand of a patriotic enlightener, when pointing out that an entire nation's wealth was squandered in order to keep up appearances, a gambit which played the domestic capital into the hands of other foreign countries, and into the hands of France in particular as one of Spain's principal industrial competitors in the textile sector. This notion is taken up by the image of the "manos extrangeras". Through the words of the patriotic manufacturer the play condemns the 'wrong' system of values of the antagonist Silvestre, as he bets on the wrong consumer strategy. Consequently, he is bound to fail which he ultimately does as a deceiving, lavish but lazy character, resembling the *petimetre*.[106] The aforementioned dialogue between Esteban and Silvestre can be regarded as an analogy to Bruno's urge upon Lorenzo to his "comercio pasivo", which inflicts damage on the

---

[102] Durán (n.d.: 1).

[103] See Durán (n.d.: 7).

[104] See Maravall (1991, pp. 139seqq), who explains the etymology of the term "industria" and its semantic change in Spain in the eighteenth century. The modern meaning of *industria* "para designar a las empresas e instalaciones en que una labor [...] se desenvuelve", hence in the sense of industrial facility, is only established in the last quarter of the eighteenth century. Maravall (1991, p. 151). Prior to this time, the meaning of "actividad económica transformadora" prevailed, in other words the "work process", i.e. it carried the notion of "confirmation" or "making an effort". Maravall (1991, p. 149). Jovellanos defines *industria* to be as follows: "Toda operación dirigida a mejorar las producciones de la tierra se puede llamar industria, aunque comúnmente se toma esta voz en un sentido menos vago y general..." Jovellanos (1952a, p. 448), quoted in Maravall (1991, p. 156).

[105] Durán (n.d.: 7).

[106] See the author's analysis in Schuchardt (2015, p. 119).

national economy. Embodied by the popular figure of Esteban, Durán's comedy brings up the 'new' social virtues and an economic reform discourse inspired largely by Adam Smith, therefore making the value of work and its contribution to the common good one of his play's main subjects, which also applies to the writings of Campomanes, Jovellanos, and Ramos. The following is stated in the *Discurso sobre economía política* (1769), published by Ramos under his pseudonym Antonio Muñoz:

> Las cosas y sus signos forman la esencia de la opulencia, pero los Estados no pueden conseguir la opulencia, sino por medio de las cosas; esto es, de hombres empleados en *trabajos útiles*, que aumenten la suma de los productos y les den todo el valor, que puede añadirles la industria.[107]

Work is a crucial component to multiply a state's prosperity. Furthermore, work acquires a particular bourgeois connotation in Durán's comedy: Just like Maravall focuses on his outlined new bourgeois mentality, stating that the individual's happiness is metonymic with the common good,[108] Durán takes the same stand in this regard. This view propagates the enlightened model of society, conveyed by the neoclassical theater, and includes honesty, compliance with the law, abiding the obligations towards family and society, virtues that now serve as key values of the rising bourgeoisie.[109] In the face of a "gran mayoría de los dramas de esta época", in which Gies notes that "no trabaja nadie, [...] la defensa que hace Esteban del trabajo [...] parece casi radical."[110] Work as a bourgeois value is enacted in Durán's play as a charitable action for the sake of the community, to which the enlightened, socially responsible patriot voluntarily commits himself to. However, since the community as well as the individual benefits from work, it can be considered a worthwhile investment. The result thereof is a *win-win* situation, portrayed in the comedy of Durán by using the example of Esteban, the embodiment of the exemplary entrepreneur-paternalist.

With regard to the ideal of the merchant, it was already established that his economic activities are always guided by *sensibilidad* and *amistad*, and thereby he contributes to the nation's benefit. The same mindset is adapted by enlightened thinkers like Cabarrús and Foronda, and their view on work as a charitable activity is summarized as follows by Maravall:

> [...] si se trabaja, si se hacen esfuerzos que benefician a los demás, son también beneficios necesariamente para sí; y a la inversa es no menos cierto también: quien trabaja en su propio interés trabaja para los demás.[111]

---

[107] Ramos (1769, p. 79), quoted in Elorza (1970, p. 48), italics mine.

[108] See Maravall, José Antonio (1979, p. 318): "[...] fin individual y fin común se identifican".

[109] See Urzainquí (1992, p. 376), who speaks of "una sociedad asentada en los valores del trabajo, de la honradez, del acatamiento a las leyes, del decoro, y del cumplimiento de los propios deberes familiares y sociales".

[110] Gies (1996, p. 454).

[111] Maravall (1991, p. 257).

Bruno's financial aid is depicted as a gift in Comella's play, and in Durán's sentimental comedy the aspect of the 'fair reward' comes to the fore. Pursuant to Esteban's role as a manufacturer of textiles, it is a piece of clothing, not just any, but namely Esteban's best, which the entrepreneur awards to his apprentice because of the latter's zeal to weave the best clothes.[112] Blas' effort to not get off the weaving loom before his hands mastered the art of weaving, is remunerated graciously by his master. Already at a previous point in time, Esteban had rewarded him with a coin, since Blas was the only employee who was still in his weaving loom in contrast to all other workers who already left.[113]

Work is depicted as an honorable activity worth pursuing, and is even of greater value, if the worker gives up his pleasures and makes a sacrifice in order to be laborious. On stage, we can observe a constant *mise-en-scène* of how Blas' enthusiasm for work is instantly rewarded. The scene, in which the manufacturer awards his clothing as an end product of his efforts to his apprentice, is inversely reflected with Prudencio, the representative of the monarch,[114] awarding Esteban a *vestido de gala* and a Cross of Merit of the Spanish state. The action on a small scale in the constellation master – apprentice is repeated on a large scale between the monarch and his subject. The role allocation of teacher and learner is revisited, as the play reverts to the dialogue between Prudencio and Blas. Once again, the narrative 'from rags to riches' and the connected fair reward due to diligent work become a recurring theme.

8.5 Conclusion

With regard to the type of the merchant or entrepreneur drawn up in the plays, one can quite rightly say that Bruno the merchant as well as Esteban the entrepreneur portray enlightened and at the same time paternalistic characters, who act in an exemplary way due to their patriotic and, ipso facto, due to their philanthropic gestus. In the first place, they exhibit this kind of behavior on a small scale in the microcosm of their immediate social environment: As a prudent merchant, Bruno restores the insolvent household of his former benefactor's son, while Esteban, the socially responsible entrepreneur, is described as the benefactor and savior of his

[112] See Durán (n.d., p. 7): "*[Blas] [q]uítase la casaca y la chupa, y las arroja en el rincón en que está la estamena. D. Est.* Por que haces esa locura?/*Blas.* Porque quiero ropa nueva/mas honrada ya que tengo/con el doblón para ella; /y porque voy a aplicarme/día y noche cuanto pueda, /para que antes que se rompa/sepan texer mis muñecas/todo quanto necesito/*D. Est.* Mereces, Blas, que te ofrezca/mi mejor vestido: toma."

[113] Durán (n.d., p. 6): "[...] y toma *le da una moneda/*un doblon en recompensa/del honrado proceder/y la aplicacion que muestras, /pues del telar no te apartas/hoy que están todos de huelga."

[114] The play leaves no doubt that Prudencio assumes the role of a representative sent by the monarch. See Durán (n.d., p. 11): "[...] el mundo sepa/como nuestro rey distingue/los vasallos que fomentan/la industria ..."

workers, represented by the young apprentice Blas, who is in deep need of further guidance and instructions. Both plays place great emphasis on the fact that the actions of the merchant and entrepreneur on a small scale, which prove to be morally and economically profitable, result on a large scale in added value to the macrocosm of the nation. While the character of the honorable Bruno and the interdependence of rightful *action* and patriotic *trade*, is at the center of Comella's play, Durán gives weight to Esteban, an entrepreneur-paternalist who is able to motivate others to get down to work.[115] The latter illustrates that exemplary behavior leads to a fair reward in the form of the award of a Cross of Merit given Esteban by an envoy of the monarch as well as the necessary solemnization of marriage, which appertains to a rightful ending of a comedy. Esteban marries Cecilia, a weaver, whose craftsmanship ideally complements her husband's entrepreneurial *know-how*.[116] Correspondingly, the merchant's 'sabia economía' is perfectly matched by the modestly budgeting Antonia. In both comedies, the microcosms of the textile manufacturer's workshop and of Lorenzo's household and business, which is restored by the honorable merchant Bruno, symbolically represent the national macrocosm of Spain with the monarch being the chief patriarch. It is ultimately the monarch represented by his Minister who rewards the virtuous in Duráns play, a circumstance accounted for by the role of the neoclassical theater as a 'school for the people' serving as an instrument of propaganda of enlightened absolutism.[117]

The integration of investment, gift, and gift in return into the plot in the case of Comella's *Hombre agradecido* can be interpreted as the *mise en abyme* of Gervais' *trusted chain of correspondents*. Within the framework of the play, this chain gradually abandons the economical context and is rather turned into an allegory of social interactions, where the members of society can rely on each other, and the rightful or wrongful behavior of individuals can induce collective gain or loss. In *La industriosa madrileña*, the 'fair reward' has to be taken into account in connection to work as a social asset. In this case, too, a chain of morally and economically interacting members is construed, with the monarch being the initiator and benefactor at the very beginning as well as the end. It is the monarch, initially the epitome of the feudal order and now an enlightened reformer, who introduces in his role as one of the main protagonists a new symbolic asset, which the merchant and the manufacturer, apart from money, love, and success, receive as a reward for their performance: social esteem and reputation. These merits supersede the value of the aristocratic title and represent a 'new' value in a society where the bourgeoisie is on the rise.

---

[115] A similar point was stated by Angulo Egea, see (2006: 113).

[116] See the author's analysis in Schuchardt (2015).

[117] See Álvarez Barrientos (2005, p. 189).

References

Álvarez Barrientos, Joaquín. 2005. *Ilustración y Neoclasicismo en las letras españoles*. Madrid: Editorial Síntesis.

Angulo Egea, María. 2006. *Luciano Francisco Comella (1751–1812). Otra cara del teatro de la Ilustración*. San Vicente: Publicaciones de la Universidad de Alicante.

Artola, Miguel. 1969. América en el pensamiento español del siglo XVIII. *Revista de Indias* 29: 51–77.

Barber, Elinor G. 1975. *La burguesía en la Francia del siglo XVIII*. Madrid: Biblioteca de la Revista de Occidente.

Bourdieu, Pierre. 1998. *Praktische Vernunft. Zur Theorie des Handelns*. Frankfurt: Suhrkamp.

Comella, Luciano Francisco. 1795. *El hombre singular o Isabel Primera de Rusia*. Madrid: Librería de Cerro. .Source: http://www.cervantesvirtual.com/obra/el-hombre-singular-o-isabel-primerade-rusia-drama-en-dos-actos-que-ha-representado-la-compania-del-senor-francisco-ramosel-dia-4-de-noviembre-del-ano-1795-en-celebridad-de-los-dias-de-nuestro-augusto-soberano. Accessed 18 May 2015.

———. 1796. *El hombre agradecido*, ed. Ministerio de Cultura 2009. Source: http://bvpb.mcu.es/es/catalogo_imagenes/grupo.cmd?path=10800. Accessed 12 Mar 2016.

de Cabarrús, Conde. 1813 [1795]. *Cartas sobre los obstáculos que la naturaleza, la opinión y las leyes oponen a la felicidad pública*. Madrid: Imprenta de Collado.

de Jovellanos, Gaspar Melchor. 1952a [1781]. Discurso sobre los medios de promover la felicidad de Asturias dirigido a su Real Sociedad por Don Gaspar Melchor de Jovellanos. In *Obras publicadas e inéditas de D. Gaspar Melchor de Jovellanos. II. Biblioteca de Autores Españoles*, ed. Cándido Nocedal, vol. 50, 438–453. Madrid: Atlas.

———. 1952b [1785]. Informe dado a la Junta General de Comercio y moneda sobre el libre ejercicio de las Artes. In *Obras publicadas e inéditas de D. Gaspar Melchor de Jovellanos. II. Biblioteca de Autores Españoles*, vol. 50, ed. Cándido Nocedal, 33–43. Madrid: Atlas.

———. 1998. In *Espectáculos y diversiones públicas: Informe sobre la ley agraria*, ed. Guillermo Carnero. Madrid: Cátedra.

Cruz, Ramon de la. 1813. *La falsa devota*. Valencia: Jose Ferrer de Orga. Source: http://www.cervantesvirtual.com/obra-visor/la-falsa-devota-sainete-nuevo-para-once-personas-0/html/. Accessed 28 Feb 2016.

Durán, Francisco. n.d. *La industriosa madrileña, y el fabricante de Olot*. Source: Fondos digitalizados de la Biblioteca de la Universidad de Sevilla, en: http://fondosdigitales.us.es/fondos/libros/4687/1/la-industriosa-madrilena-y-el-fabricante-de-olot-o-los-efectos-de-la-aplicacion-comedia-en-tres-actos. Accessed 1 Mar 2016.

Derrida, Jacques. 1991. *Donner le temps. 1. La fausse monnaie*. Paris: Galilée.

Diderot, Denis. 2005a [1757]. Entretiens sur Le Fils naturel. In *Diderot et le théâtre: Le drame. Entretiens sur Les Fils naturel (Dorval et moi) suivi de Discours sur la poésie dramatique*, ed. Alain Menil, 59–148. Paris: Agora.

———. 2005b [1758]. Des genres dramatiques. In *Le père de famille*, ed. Gerhardt Stenger, 139–150. Paris: Editions Espaces.

Elorza, Antonio. 1970. *La ideología liberal en la Ilustración española*. Madrid: Tecnos.

Foronda, Valentín. 1984. Disertación sobre lo honrosa que es la profesión del comercio, leída en las Juntas Generales que celebró la Sociedad Bascongada en Vilbao el año de 1778. In *Valentín de Foronda. Los sueños de la razón*, ed. M. Benavides and C. Rollán, 587–602. Madrid: Editora nacional.

Fuentes, Yvonne. 1999. *El triángulo sentimental en el drama del Dieciocho (Inglaterra, Francia, España)*. Kassel: Edition Reichenberger.

Fulda, Daniel. 2005. *Schau-Spiele des Geldes. Die Komödie und die Entstehung der Marktgesellschaft von Shakespeare bis Lessing. Niemeyer, Tübingen*. Tübingen: Niemeyer.

García Garrosa, María Jesús. 1990. *La retórica de las lágrimas. La comedia sentimental española, 1751–1802*. Valladolid: Secretario de Publicaciones de la Universidad de Valladolid.
———. 1991. El comerciante inglés y El fabricante de paños: de la traducción a la adaptación. *Anales de Literatura Española* 7: 85–95.
Gervais, Pierre. 2008. Neither imperial, nor atlantic. A merchant perspective on international trade in the eighteenth century. *History of European Ideas* 34 (4): 465–473.
Gies, David T. 1996. Sentencias y buenas máximas: Francisco Durán, dramaturgo y poeta ilustrado. El siglo que llaman ilustrado. Homenaje a Francisco Aguilar Piñal, Álvarez Barrientos, Joaquín, 451–457. Madrid: Consejo Superior de Investigaciones Científicas.
———. 1998. Forner, la amistad y la patria: *La escuela de la amistad o El filósofo enamorado* (1769). In *Juan Pablo Forner*, ed. Jesús Cañas Murillo and Miguel Ángel Lama, 449–460. Mérida: Editora Regional de Extremadura.
Guinard, Paul. 1984. Sobre el mito de Inglaterra en el teatro español de fines del siglo XVIII: una adaptación de Valladares de Sotomayor. *Anales de Literatura Española* 3: 283–304.
Haidt, Rebecca. 1998. *Embodying enlightenment. Knowing the body in eighteenth-century Spanish literature and culture*. New York: Macmillan.
———. 1999. Luxury, consumption and desire: Theorizing the petimetra. *Arizona Journal of Hispanic Studies* 3: 33–50.
———. 2003. A well-dressed woman who will not work: Petimetras, economics, and eighteenth-century fashion-plates. *Revista Canadiense de Estudios Hispánicos* 28 (1): 137–157.
Hale, Jane A. 1988. Le drame bourgeois et ses espaces. *Studies on Voltaire and the Eighteenth Century* 256: 185–193.
Hontanilla, Ana. 2008. The airy and the irrational: Elaborating on the meanings of the Petimetra from a selection of Goyas Caprichos and the Spanish Periodical El Censor. *Decimónica* 5 (1): 48–64.
Huerta, Fernando. 1991. El comediógrafo mal tratado: Lucano Comella y la Ilustración. *Bulletin of Hispanic Studies* 68 (1): 183–189.
Isenmann, Mechtild. 2017. Das Bild des Kaufmann-Bankiers in oberdeutschen Familiengesellschaften der Frühmoderne. In *Der ehrbare Kaufmann zwischen Bescheidenheit und Risiko*, ed. Christoph Lütge and Christoph Strosetzki, 79–98. Heidelberg: Springer.
Lagarde, André Michel Michard. (eds.). 2003. *Les grands auteurs: XVIIIe siecle*, vol. 2. Paris: Bordas.
Lillo, George. 1965 [1731]. In *The London merchant*, ed. William H. McBurney. London: Arnold.
Llanos Mardones, Bernadita. 1989. Integración de la mujer al proyecto de la Ilustración en España. *Ideologies and Literature* 4 (1): 199–223.
Maravall, José Antonio. 1991. *Estudios de la historia del pensamiento español. Siglo XVIII*. Madrid: Mondadori.
Maravall, Antonio. 1979. Espíritu burgués y principio de interés personal en la Ilustración española. *Hispanic Review* 47 (3): 291–325.
Marti, Marc. 2010. Affectivité et sentiment en économie politique: Cartas sobre los obstáculos que la naturaleza, la opinión y las leyes oponen ala felicidad publica (1795) du comte de Cabarrús. *Littératures et sciences* 18: 1–11. Source: http://narratologie.revues.org/6124. Accessed 24 Feb 2016.
McCloskey, Deirdre. 2016. *Bourgeois equality. How ideas, not capital or institutions, enriched the world*. Chicago: University of Chicago Press.
Möller, Beate. 2018. Das Konzept der felicidad zwischen Affekt und Ökonomie in der spanischen Literatur des 18. Jahrhunderts. In *Affektökonomien im 18. und 19. Jahrhundert in Frankreich und Spanien*, ed. Susanne Schlünder and Andrea Stahl, 241–258. Munich: Fink.
Normante y Carcavilla, Lorenzo. 1784. *Discurso sobre la utilidad de los conocimientos económico-políticos y la necesidad de su estudio metódico*. Zaragoza: Blas Miedes.
Pappas, John. 1981. Diderot et le drame bourgeois. *Diderot Studies* 20: 225–244.
Pataky-Kosove, Joan L. 1979. The Influence of Lachrymose Comedy on Moratíns *El viejo y la niña*. *Hispanic Review* 47 (3): 379–391.

Rommel, Thomas. 2006. *Das Selbstinteresse von Mandeville bis Smith. Ökonomisches Denken in ausgewählten Schriften des 18. Jahrhunderts*. Heidelberg: Winter.

Schuchardt, Beatrice. 2014. Von *petimetres* und *petimetras*. Strukturen von Ökonomie und Verschwendung in Moratíns *La petimetra* (1762) und Iriartes *El señorito mimado* (1787). In *Handlung, Verhandlung. Theater und Ökonomie in der frühen Neuzeit in Spanien*, ed. Beatrice Schuchardt and Urs Urban, 269–282. Bielefeld: transcript.

———. 2015. Fe y prosperidad: Sobre la conexión entre lo religioso y lo económico en la comedia *La industriosa madrileña y el fabricante de Olot* (1789) de Francisco Duran. In *La religión, las letras y las luces: El factor religioso en la Ilustración espanola e hispanoamericana*, ed. Markus Ebeling and Veronika Österbaur, 109–122. Frankfurt/Main: Lang.

———. In print. Freundschaft und Reziprozität als Leitbilder ökonomischen Handelns in sentimentalen Komödien der Spanischen Aufklärung. In *Affektökonomien im 18. und 19. Jahrhundert in Frankreich und Spanien*, ed. Susanne Schlünder and Andrea Stahl. Munich: Fink.

Stamer, Gerhard. 2010. Die Philosophie der Gabe. Gabe ohne Gegengabe? In *REFLEX. Philosophie zur Zeit – Zeit zur Philosophie, Vortrag auf dem Symposium Konzepte der Gabe in der Gegenwartskunst, 10.-13. Juni 2010 im ZIF Bielefeld*. Source: http://stamer-reflex.com/files/Die%20Philosophie%20 der%20Gabe_0.pdf. Accessed 4 Feb 2015.

Tietz, Manfred. 2017. Der lange Weg vom 'Täuscher und Betrüger' zum 'ehrbaren Kaufmann'. Das Bild des Kaufmanns in der spanischen Literatur und ihren Kontexten vom 16. bis zum Ende des 18. Jahrhunderts. In *Der ehrbare Kaufmann zwischen Bescheidenheit und Risiko*, ed. Christoph Lütge and Christoph Strosetzki, 99–124. Heidelberg: Springer.

Urzainquí, Inmaculada. 1992. Crítica teatral y secularización: el Memorial literario (1784–1797). In La secularización de la cultural española en el Siglo de las Luces. Actas del congreso de Wolfenbüttel, ed. Mnfred Tietz and Dietrich Briesemeister, 247–286. Wiesbaden: Harrassowitz.

Valladares de Sotomayor, Antonio. n.d.. *El fabricante de paños o el comerciante inglés*. Madrid, Isidro López. Source: http://www.cervantesvirtual.com/nd/ark:/59851/bmcvx0b3. Accessed 3 Jan 2017.

von Stackelberg, Jürgen. 1992. *Das Theater der Aufklärung in Frankreich. Ein Abriss*. Munich: Fink.

Wegmann, Jürgen, Dieter Zeibig, and Hubertus Zilkens. 2009. Die Renaissance des ehrbaren Kaufmanns. In *Der ehrbare Kaufmann. Leistungsfaktor Vertrauen – Kostenfaktor Misstrauen*, ed. Jürgen Wegmann, Dieter Zeibig, and Hubertus Zilkens, 7–16. Cologne: Bank-Verlag.

Witthaus, Jan-Henrik. 2017. *Homo oeconomicus*, Kaufmannsethos und Liberalismus im Spanien des aufgeklärten Absolutismus. In *Der ehrbare Kaufmann zwischen Bescheidenheit und Risiko*, ed. Christoph Lütge and Christoph Strosetzki, 151–173. Heidelberg: Springer.

Chapter 9
The Homo Oeonomicus, Merchant Ethos, and Liberalism in Spain Under Enlightened Absolutism

Jan-Henrik Witthaus

Abstract The following article deals with the formation of economic discourse in eighteenth century Spain. It argues that concepts such as *common welfare* or *honorable businessman* supported the establishment of economic thinking in the context of Bourbon Reformism – the predominant political current throughout the eighteenth century. A particular instance of this development are the *Discursos mercuriales* de Juan Enrique Graef: While Graef ran into serious trouble with censorship, he was also the first economic journalist and founder of the genre of economic press in Spain. With the introduction of liberal thought by Gaspar Melchor de Jovellanos and others, the concepts mentioned lost their prevalence, whereas the opposing notion of individual economic interest became an important reference point of economic thinking at the end of Enlightenment Spain.

9.1 Introduction

In various studies, most recently in *Das Gespenst des Kapitals*, Joseph Vogl explored the advent of the homo oeconomicus in the eighteenth century. He characterizes it as a radical re-modelling of social existence under the banner of "liberal despotism."[1] From the eighteenth century, therefore, the economically calculating individual and his field of action, the market, generally became a paradigmatic constellation of social interaction. This could only happen, however, to the extent that the homo oeconomicus itself became an index of human nature. Insofar as human beings obey their nature, they adhere to their affects and desires, reflect on their own interests, and make demands. The process by which this individual action is generalized in relation to the actors of a society should also be *natural* and result in a balance of interests.

[1] Vogl (2012), p. 46. See also Vogl (2004), pp. 346–351.

J.-H. Witthaus (✉)
University of Kassel, Kassel, Germany
e-mail: witthaus@uni-kassel.de

C. Lütge, C. Strosetzki (eds.), *The Honorable Merchant – Between Modesty and Risk-Taking*, Ethical Economy 56, https://doi.org/10.1007/978-3-030-04351-3_9

> The expansion of local markets into a market society requires [...] readjusting the relationship between economy, politics, and society. The market executes, as it were, a natural law and all other good laws and institutions must be judged on how they can guarantee obedience to this natural law, i.e. to spontaneous economic mechanisms (Translated from German).[2]

While eye-opening in many respects, Vogl's depiction, which attributes liberalism its discursive power up to the present day, also seems to be an oversimplification. Certainly, the allegedly uncontested triumph of the *homo oeconomicus* and its anthropological premises has also given rise to opposition and differences. The spread of the economic image of the world and of man is often met with great skepticism, especially in the wake of the financial market crisis from 2007 onwards. Occasionally, as in the much-noticed opinion of Giorgio Agamben, a distinction is made between the economy and other forms of existence that should be saved. Referring to Alexandre Kojève, Agamben opposed the "Latin Empire" to the German claim to leadership.

> Une Europe qui prétend exister sur une base strictement économique, en abandonnant toutes les parentés réelles entre les formes de vie, de culture et de religion, n'a pas cessé de montrer toute sa fragilité, et avant tout sur le plan économique.[3]

It seems plausible that, at a purely lifeworld level, one faces the "economization" of various social sectors or the everyday consequences of European financial policy decisions. However, denouncing the power of the economy ("le plan économique") over existence in the wake of the euro crisis reflects only one possible interpretation. One would have to alternately ask if "life forms," "culture" and "religion" should actually be distinguished from *the* economy.[4] Or henceforth: Are there not perhaps different economies, variations or deviations that need to be embedded in divergent cultural contexts and traditions?[5]

Thus, the respective meanings of economy and homo oeconomicus should be clarified or adjusted historically. Instead of understanding the economy as the counterpart of culture, one should inquire about *cultures of the economy*. In another, slightly older, context of contemporary history, it is possible to pursue such a problematic juxtaposition of economy and culture – namely, at the time of the economic blossoming and tourism boom of the late Franco-Spain regime. In this context, Juan Goytisolo become skeptical. He criticizes the Spaniards' overly rapid adaptation to external forms of behavior and pleads for an identity-based evolution of European integration:

---

[2] Ibid.

[3] Agamben (2013a).

[4] It is revealing that Agamben (2013b) in his interview with the FAZ, which is frequently qualified, does not differentiate the conception of the economy, but rather allows it to exist as an antithesis of a culturally diverse and historically aware Europe: For more than two centuries, human energy has been focused on the economy. There are many indications that the moment has perhaps come for *homo sapiens* to reorganize human actions beyond this single dimension. It is precisely here that the Old Europe can make a decisive contribution to the future."

[5] On this point and the following, see Schoepp (2015).

> Toda una línea del pensamiento español, desde Quevedo hasta Unamuno y Menéndez Pidal, había decretado que los españoles, por el mero hecho de serlo, poseían un destino particular y privilegiado, ajeno a las leyes sociales y económicas del mundo moderno. Fundándose en una concepción metafísica del hombre, pretendían elaborar una imagen del español distinta de la de los demás seres humanos: la de un ser sediento de absoluto, preocupado ante todo por la muerte. El hecho de que, a lo largo del siglo XIX, las regiones más dinámicas de la periferia (Cataluña, Vascongadas, Asturias) se hubiesen plegado sucesivamente al modelo europeo no conmovía a estos escritores, contagiados del inmovilisimo fascinador de la meseta castellana y de su proverbial impermeabilidad histórica. Para ellos, y para muchos españoles y europeos, el *homo hispanicus* no era ni podría devenir nunca el *homo economicus*.[6]

According to this, such economically remote genealogies stem from the Middle Ages. Unsurprisingly, the central source for Goytisolo is the highly regarded Spanish mediaevist Américo Castro.[7] It is necessary, however, to review several chapters in the rapid historical process – and not only those decades of prosperous economies immediately after the discovery of America, preceding the unprecedented decline of the colonial empire.[8] In view of this quote, Enlightenment researchers are also forced to wonder whether the tradition Goytisolo's cites is so uninterrupted, and not only because of the economic dynamism of the northern Spanish regions in the nineteenth century. Beyond this, have there not also been stages of economic thought in the history of Spanish ideas and discourse? How can this economic thought be characterized? If we were to specifically look at the eighteenth century, it would be necessary to first ask to what extent trade was not only rehabilitated in the economic treatises of that time as an ethical way of life (under the aegis of the "will to reform" initiated by the Bourbons), but whether there was an – if you will – anthropologization of "economic thought." Vogl detects such a development during the eighteenth century period, even though it may in fact differ from the era's discursive montage. Culture, religion and economy therefore stop appearing as mutually exclusive spheres of life. To be sure, Max Weber seems to have provided us with a convincing answer to such issues[9] and, in his wake, the connection between economic thought and Protestantism seems to have prevailed. Indeed, this was quite evident over the course of the debate on the euro crisis. At the same time, some of the texts from the eighteenth century in Spain reveal that economic thought in the context of the Spanish Enlightenment experienced a

[6] Goytisolo (1979), p. 190.

[7] In Américo Castro's main work *España en su historia* (1938) the opening chapter contains a sketch of a tradition which can be described as non-economic. See specifically Castro (2001), p. 28, where a quote from Alonso Cartagena (1384–1456, Spanish humanist and Bishop of Burgos) is remarked on by Castro as follows: "El espíritu nobiliario unido al desdén por las actividades comerciales marcan ya el abismo que separará a España de la Europa capitalista: para este judío archiespañol, Cosme de Médicis no era sino un vil mercader."

[8] See Geisler (2013), p. 18f. Cf. the description of the economic development of Spain under Habsburg rule in Haebler (1888).

[9] Cf. also the historical model in Hirschman (1980), in which, however, references to the Spanish cultural area are in short supply (cf. e.g. ibid., p. 67). See Max Weber ibid., p. 138. See also Pocock (1993), pp. 60–96.

remarkable explosion. One at least comes away with this impression when reading – as one of the more famous sources of the eighteenth century – Gaspar Melchor de Jovellanos' eulogy on Charles III, which talks about a "renaissance" of economic thought in Spain:

> Renace entonces el estudio de esta ciencia [la economía pública], que ya por aquel tiempo se llevaba en Europa la principal atención de la filosofía. España lee sus más célebres escritores, examina sus principios, analiza sus obras; se habla, se disputa, se escribe, y la nación empieza a tener economistas.[10]

This passage is followed by a number of questions concerning the meaning of the concept ("la economía pública") and the political-historical context of the Bourbon reform, our focus here. What sort of economy was initiated in this period, and, above all, what are its anthropological foundations?

9.2 Economic Reforms Based on Christian Anthropology

Any connection between the economic writings of the Spanish eighteenth century and the economic policy measures of the Bourbons can only be detected selectively or asynchronously. Otherwise, Jaume Vicens Vives' thesis is indeed valid that the reforms and legal interventions of the crown were determined by foreign policy constraints and events: "[…] la actitud gubernamental está menos influida por los economistas (ninguno de los cuales alcanzaría talla para imponer su criterio personal) que por las contingencias de los tratados de comercio o de las guerras internacionales."[11]

According to the same source, economic policy can be seen as a fluctuation between protectionism and liberalization in the context of intra-Spanish or colonial trade.[12] In view of this liberalization, the study by Antonio Elorza, which can now be regarded as a classic study, may be read along the same lines: "La política comercial tendrá, pues, como criterio eliminar los obstáculos que se oponen a la *libertad de comercio interior*."[13] And further:

> En su inmensa mayoría, acordes con la política del gobierno de Carlos III, los ilustrados españoles serán proteccionistas en cuanto al comercio exterior […], acudiendo una y otra vez a la argumentación de la decadencia económica de España por la importación de productos manufacturados y la situación de la inferioridad vigente ante los países más avanzados.[14]

---

[10] Jovellanos (1987), p. 188. Predecessors here would not only be the Neo-Scholastics, but also the *arbitristas*, i.e. "project makers" of the seventeenth century, who have been wrongly forgotten, not least because of Quevedos satire in *Buscón*.

[11] Vicens Vives (^{2}1974), p. 165.

[12] See ibid., p. 164.

[13] Elorza (1970), p. 34 (italics in the original).

[14] Ibid.

Given this economic policy "realia," a review of the economic literature of this period almost seems secondary. Such a perspective, though, leaves the question of different economic cultures and the specific anthropological foundations completely unanswered. And it is conceivable (although this would be rather secondary *for us*) that the interventionism of the Bourbons may be derived from them, not just from the constraints of the overall historical conditions.

The treatise *Theorica, y practica de Comercio y de Marina* from 1724 from Basque scholar and politician Gerónimo de Uztáriz is among the central expert economic policy surveys of the eighteenth century. It was remarkable success, not only in Spain; a second, extended edition appeared in 1742, and translations were published in English, French and Italian, among other languages. As the treatise is closely tied to the Bourbon reform efforts, one could be tempted to selectively interpret the above-mentioned dictum from Vicens Vives. The Bourbons needed to rebuild and administratively centralize the country after the war of succession, which had been a triumph for them. At the same time, they had to strengthen the economic structures and increase the revenues of the crown.

In *Theorica y practica*, mercantilist theorems are dealt with *grosso modo*. They are viewed, however, in reference to the Spanish predicament and thus reformulated with a view to the deficient American trade. Uztáriz's analysis centers on the realization that the domestic production of goods, exports and a positive trade balance have been neglected, partly due to an abundant influx of American precious metals. In this context, the author first pursues the rehabilitation of trade. In light of the cultural genealogies given by Goytisolo and Castro, the reader is left feeling somewhat surprised. For Uztáriz, the promotion of commercial activities is deeply rooted in the tradition of the Spanish monarchy, going back to measures catalog of the Catholic kings. Charles I and Philip II also bore it in mind. Above all, there is a universal argument which the author makes in the first chapter that further elevates his discussion: Trade-oriented policy corresponds with human reason ("Comprehendiendo todo Hombre racional la importancia del Comercio [...].")[15] The argument here fundamentally concerns the tradition of natural law, in which man participates as a rational being in the divine order. For Uztáriz, however, economic thought is now an essential part of human reason. José Campillo y Cossío, to whom the *Nuevo sistema de gobierno económico para la América* (est. 1743) was attributed (and which will be discussed below), makes this point even more explicitly:

> Las máxîmas del buen Gobierno, como fundadas en la razon natural, son claras, y llevan consigo la recomendación necesaria para ser bien admitidas su establecimiento. [...] El comercio no es ningun misterio. La luz natural, que es comun á todos, nos descubre los principios en que se funda para establecerle y aumentarle.[16]

But just how is the natural law dimension of trade to be deduced? Initially, nothing more is said than trade, good governance and its rules are in conformity with human reason.

---

[15] Uztáriz (^{3}1757), p. 1.

[16] Campillo y Cossío (1789, p. 68f).

It is conceivable that there is a linkage between the direct evidence in Uztáriz of trade necessarily imposing itself, or the self-evident nature of "good governance" suggested in Campillo, to the significance of work in the society. In this respect, the following quotations should be read in the context of their underlying scholastic and neo-scholastic foundations. Uztáriz's argument regarding work that derives from human nature is twofold. First, with a view to salvation history, he refers to original sin:

> Carga precisa es al afán, pena heredad de nuestro primer Padre, y que, como impuesta por la Divina Justicia à la vida humana, comprehende tambien à todos los Individuos del Estado, aunque no exerzan Ministerio publico, obligando à cada uno, segun el talento, y aptitud, que la Naturaleza, y la suerte le huvieren repartido [...].[17]

Together with the divine condemnation of Adam, man is also imparted his various talents by way of nature. With the Fall of Man, the world is thus set up in such a way that the late descendants of the ancestor must make their respective abilities available to the common good as subjects of a state system. Apart from the argument drawn from salvific history, there is also one of natural law: The reciprocity of social cooperation is based on the contributions of individuals of different backgrounds, which creates a mutual commitment that is in the common good and also does not allow anyone to rest on the backs of their contemporaries:

> La noble Ley del agradecimiento nos prescribe también la assistencia reciproca, trabajando los unos para los otros. Con la respectiva tarèa de cada uno se ha de labrar la proporcionada convenencia de todos: iniquidad serìa, que se sustentassen ociosos los unos, usurpando à los otros el fruto de sus fatigas.[18]

Two key concepts refer back to the political ideas of Thomas Aquinas: first, the "tarèa de cada uno," and, second, the "convenencia de todos," i.e. division of labor and the common good. The principle of the division of labor is reflected in Thomas in *De regno ad regem Cypri*, on the one hand, analogously in the human body and its organic diversification,[19] and, on the other, it is based on the Aristotelian premise that the human being exists only as a social being and, because he is inadequately equipped, can only survive in a cooperative association.[20] With these correlations, wherein Thomas explains his idea of social justice, he essentially refers to the arguments of natural law that are found in his main work, *Summa Theologiae*. Here he "explains the relationship of human law to natural law, whose norm he, in turn, establishes in the divine *lex aeterna*." (Translated from German)[21]

---

[17] Uztáriz (^{3} 1757), from the prologue, not paginated. The reference to the Fall of Man is not uncommon in the tradition of Spanish economic treatises. It can be found in Tomás de Mercado, cf. Geisler (2013), p. 47.

[18] Uztáriz (^{3}1757, p. 1).

[19] See Thomas von Aquinas (1954): "sicut et corpus hominis et cuiuslibet animalis defluenet, nisi esset aliqua vis regitiva communis in corpore, quae ad bonum commune omnium membrorum intenderet." The Spanish tradition will come back to this, e.g. Pedro Fernández de Navarrete in his text *Conservación de monarquías y discursos políticos* (1626), see Geisler (2014), p. 61.

[20] See Once again Thomas (1954): "Nam unus homo per se sufficienter vitam transigere non posset. Est igitur homini naturale quod in societate multorum vivat."

[21] Mensching (2007), p. 83.

It seems necessary to take into account the political context in which Thomas's genuine economic considerations are situated. For although it is possible to interpret Thomas' condemnation of the independent trade and credit system as ideological and an attack on the early forms of capitalist economic models,[22] one may also refer his economic thought back to its Aristotelian foundations. Within this scope, the "political animal [...], in so far it is political, is to be interpreted as economic." Thus, with respect to *De regno ad regem Cypri*,[23] it is worth considering whether it is not the apologia of estate-based society, but the achievement of the common good that reflects the decisive premise to which all economic thought must also be subordinated.[24]

This tradition subordinates human aspirations to the achievement of the social common good. Trade at the beginning of Uztáriz's *Theorica, y practica* is ultimately exploited by the different distribution of talents and activities within a society. In retrospect, then, one may inquire at which historical point work is recognized as a value-creating power – i.e. as a productive force. This question, incidentally, not only coincides with Marx,[25] but, on another level, with the analysis in Max Weber's *Protestant Ethics.* Weber here distinguishes work and division of labor in Thomas from the later Protestant work ascetic insofar as "work is only a naturali ratione necessary to preserve the life of the individual and the collective. Where this purpose ceases to exist, so does the validity of the regulation; it concerns only the species, not every individual." (Translated from German)[26]

Under this premise, if we refer back to the "project designers" ("arbitristas") of the seventeenth century – who first emphasized the productive power of work – and thus follow Eberhard Geisler (who dealt with the economic theories of Spain in the early modern era at a very early stage), we lose sight of the extent to which economic knowledge is still shaped up through the eighteenth century by the Aristotelian concept of the common good. Certainly, one already finds before the turn of the seventeenth century in Tomás de Mercado, probably the best-known representative of the Salamanca School, text passages – above all his *Suma de tratos y contratos* (1569) – which show the importance of personal gain for the overall economic development of a social network: "Digo que en las mercadurías necesarias se ha de tener respeto principalmente al bien común y también, secundariamente, a la ganancia de los mercaderes, para que, con el cebo del interés y gusto, insistan y trabajen

[22] See Geisler (2013), p. 35.

[23] Vogl (^{6}2012), p. 117. Following Geisler (2013), p. 32, it is undoubtedly worth remembering that the Aristotelian subsistence economy within the *oikos* was largely based on slave labor, which, for its part, was not subject to any appreciation or value creation. On the other hand, this ideology-critical view leaves out the form in which the Aristotelian distinction between regular economy and crematism is shaped by a cultural viewpoint, in which the anthropological primacy of the political community is inescapable and, moreover, is embedded in a specific form of the ancient cyclical conception of time (see Vogl, p. 122f.).

[24] See Geisler (2013), p. 37.

[25] See Geisler (2014), p. 62ff.

[26] Weber (^{3}2010), p. 185.

mejor en proveer la ciudad."[27] The phrase "lure of interest" is especially striking with regard to the future, as this concept would only be taken up later. The quote, however, also reveals the priority that Mercado gives to the "common good" – at least as concerned the pricing of goods for one's livelihood.

Returning now to the quotations found in Uztáriz and Campillo, they read like a recitation of the anthropological foundations which representatives of scholasticism (above all Thomas) had adopted from Aristotle and placed in the context of Christian natural law. Uztáriz hence speaks of divine justice and laws. His rehabilitation of the dealing and trading human being seems to be ultimately indebted to the Christian foundations of natural law. The goal of the common good, the flagellation of inertia (laziness), and the postulate of the division of labor are the starting point for each subsequent reflection.

9.3 The Honorable Merchant in Juan Enrique Graef

The mercantilism that we still find to a large extent in Uztáriz is regarded by the classic works of economic history as part of the raison d'état. The main aim of the promotion of trade is to increase revenues into the royal coffers, and thereby the monarch's capacity to take, but also defend and represent, political action. The basis for this, however, is the prosperity of the nation. The foreword to *Teorica, y práctica de comercio* alone impressively illustrates this interrelationship between the state's motivation and mercantilism. The specificity of the Spanish point of view here lies in the problem of American trade and the related mystery of how the discovery of rich precious metal deposits in America did not contribute to Spain's prosperity, but rather to its downfall. It should be emphasized that Uztáriz is able to support his views by invoking economic authors of the seventeenth century, not only Diego Saavedra Fajardo, but also on the above-mentioned "project makers" ("arbitristas"), whose advice (e.g. to stop exporting raw materials, to promote national manufacturing) preceded the heyday of mercantilism under Colbert.[28]

In the course of the eighteenth century, however, knowledge of commerce is increasingly being presented as an sphere that has its own laws, thus liberating it from its subordination to statesmanship. The *Discursos mercuriales* (1752–1756) of the electoral Madrilene of Dutch origin Juan Enrique Graef is a milestone in the self-declared differentiation of a science from commerce. For some years now, this

[27] Mercado (1977), not paginated [chapter VII]. See Geisler (2013), p. 45. According to this, Mercado's significance lies in the renunciation of the scholastic doctrine of "fair price," but above all in the knowledge that wealth is created by investing in goods. Mercado thus goes beyond the idea of a mere subsistence economy (cf. ibid.). In all this, it cannot be overlooked that Mercado's entire treatise is permeated by the maxims of Christian natural law, which play a central role in his arguments.

[28] See Geisler (2013), p. 53–70.

magazine project of the middle of the century has been increasingly become a focus of Spanish enlightenment research.[29]

Graef also pleads for the strengthening of domestic production of goods, making the rehabilitation of the mechanical arts in Spain – contemporaneous with the French *Encyclopédie* – his most urgent concern. Above all, however, he voted in favor of including experts in trade matters in the reform policy, pointing out that a genuine culture of experts had developed in this area. "Es el comercio una ciencia, que como las demás, tiene principios, reglas, axiomas y postulados."[30] Nevertheless, as the trade of a nation is so complex, a proper casuistry of the corresponding doctrines must come into effect in view of the range of possible cases: "Hay casos en que una regla o precepto será acomodado y verdadero y con la mutación de la más leve circunstancia se hará en su observancia dudoso y quizás dañoso."[31]

On the other hand, Graef is far from demanding the independence of trade from the regulatory grip of the crown. Rather, the government turns out to be the "father" with his hand on the rudder, while trade is the "mother," who financially supports the nation.[32] Therefore, trade is always to be subject to the sovereign power of the state – although this should not keep it from vociferously asserting its importance in the discussion of the common good.

Graef's plea in favor of trade rests on Christian anthropology. He not only argues historically that trade has always cleared the way for the proselytizing of foreign peoples. In addition, the world has been set up by God in such a way that the natural goods were unequally distributed among territories and regions, which were differently formed by climate and geography. The necessity of trade was therefore, in essence, primordial.[33] This argument is ultimately teleological or physico-theological[34]: Man gleans from the nature of creation a divine order and his own standing within it. Accordingly, every nation is always in need of the goods of its neighbor – undoubtedly an economic interpretation of altruism.

More central, however, is the argument that man only attains the human state of freedom if he knows how to escape from poverty, for otherwise he is a kind of machine man. Graef put it this way, perhaps with a view to La Mettrie's *L'homme machine* (1748): "La probreza convierte a los hombres en máquinas que sólo se mueven a voluntad e impulso ajeno. Los pueblos, esclavos de su miseria, no conocen la libertad que les dio la naturaleza."[35] Thus only trade puts men in their natural state of freedom, making it possible for them to make decisions, shape their own destiny, but also to be guilty. Such thinking, which is influenced by natural law and

---

[29] See Sánchez-Blanco (1990), Witthaus (2014), pp. 265–316.

[30] Graef (1996), p. 191.

[31] Ibid., p. 213.

[32] See ibid., p. 206.

[33] For a similar conception in Jacques Savary, see the contribution of Christoph Strosetzki in this volume.

[34] For similar conceptions in France, see the work of Gipper (2002), especially with regard to Abbé Pluche: pp. 244–258.

[35] Graef (1996), p. 191.

ultimately by Christianity,[36] still differs to a great extent from the later developmental stages of economic discourse in the eighteenth century. For, as we saw, Graef considers trade to be subject to its own laws, but by no means *autonomous*. It is thus subordinated to government of the crown and its ministers. Moreover, the interplay of individual interests is not yet a pre-established harmony, but rather a matter of coordinating the interests of the crown, trade, and the common good: "El gobierno que sabe unir constante e inseparablemente los intereses del pueblo con los de la Corona obliga a que éste le sea favorable en cualquier suceso y se ofrezca para ejecutar las cosas más arduas en beneficio de todos."[37] This implies a form of selflessness in the trader, who is committed to the common good in every one of his schemes. There is always the risk that the individual's pursuit of wealth and his particular interests will turn into egoism, which Graef eloquently denounces as Machiavellianism:

> Bien sé que tal vez me dirán que [...] la comodidad y bien particular es el único objeto que debe desvelar a los hombres. ¡Bella moral! Los *maquiavelistas* teóricos la enseñan; los *maquiavelistas* prácticos la demuestran en su modo de vivir y de acumular riquezas.[38]

These passages in the text clearly show the cultural-historical legacy of the concept of the common good in the traditional value system, which, as we have seen, derives from Scholasticism. This term stands in opposition to commercial self-interest and the accumulation of wealth – endeavors that both clearly contradict the "Protestant economy" and the theorems of the emerging liberalism. However, while Graef, on the one hand, puts individual economic advantage into the line of fire of Spanish anti-Machiavellianism, some rhetorical statements, on the other hand, are made *argumentum e contrario* to place the social common good at the heart of the economic enlightenment.

The construction of the honorable merchant found in Juan Enrique Graef proves to be a byproduct of the cited requirements. At a critical juncture in his economic articles, the author combines the activities of commerce with a long catalogue of requirements, but also with a series of moral imperatives. On the one hand, Graef's merchant seems to possess almost encyclopedic knowledge, but all the listed fields of knowledge are tailored to his economic activities. For example, he must be a geographer, historian, lawyer, natural scientist, mathematician, yet only insofar as this knowledge relates to his own commercial activities. "Sensibles a la gloria, los verdaderos comerciantes son héroes que a costa de sus bienes y vidas procuran la felicidad al país donde habitan [...]."[39] In other words, there is a threshold in which the merchant relegates his self-interest to the common good of the country in which he lives.

---

[36] See Isidore of Seville (1911), not paginated: V, 4: "ut viri et feminae coniunctio, liberorum sucessio et educatio, communis omnium possessio, et omnium una libertas, adquisitio eorum quae caelo, terra, marique capiuntur."

[37] Graef (1996, p. 207). The skeptical use of the term "los intereses" may also be attributed to the traditional meaning of *interés* as monetary interest.

[38] Ibid., P. 203f. (in italics in the text).

[39] Ibid.

> Ya toda esta ciencia no la debe tener el comerciante para hacer únicamente su propia fortuna, sino para repartirla con todos por medio de las ganancias que hace en socorrer las públicas necesidades, previendo la falta de cosechas y ocupando una multitud de personas en las fábricas y maniobras.[40]

Ultimately, heroic self-sacrifice outweighs the pursuit of one's own monetary interests. The striving for profit proceeds with a handbrake: The protagonists of trade are construed as moral-patriotic subjects, where the dynamism of their interests only unfolds within constraints that are attuned to the monarch's guidance of the nation. What is anti-Machiavellian here is the attribute of honorableness, which is implicitly, but nevertheless unambiguously, directed against that solemn passage in the *Principe* suggesting that the prince may break his word to maintain power[41]:

> Nunca debe el comerciante firmar, ni prometer aquello que sabe no poder o no querer cumplir. Su palabra debe tener fuerza y exactitud de ley, y así la falta de cumplirla causa siempre perjuicios y desorden en los negocios de los que creyeron y se arreglaban por ella.[42]

In this way, the trader becomes the guarantor of the honor of an entire society, and honor, conversely, becomes the social glue of human coexistence. The merchant is thus paradigmatic:

> Aquel dicho memorable, de que si se perdiera la fe en el mundo, debiera encontrarse en la boca de los reyes, se puede aplicar a los comerciantes con igual justicia, pues en ellos debe residir esta estimable virtud y carácter. Su verdad debe ser tan grande y decisiva que en todos los tribunales haga probanza su palabra.[43]

9.4 Regulation of Emotions and Interests Under the Banner of "Policey": Campillo y Cossío

Graef demonstrates that the ideal of the honorable merchant and his duty toward the common good and even the moral state of a society are closely linked to the guiding will of the crown. In the scholastic tradition, if the monarch wants to avoid the fatal terminology of tyranny or succumbing to Machiavelli's teachings after the dawn of early modernity, he is, to a certain extent, subordinated to the general interest under natural law. Graef separates economic learning from political knowledge theoretically. In practice, however, every economic individual remains committed to the model of the honorable merchant and thus – analogously to the king – to the common good of the social network. If the *Discursos Mercuriales* is to be located in the mercantilist paradigm, then it also can be ascribed to the Spanish variant of a "good

---

[40] Ibid., p. 202.

[41] See Machiavelli (1986), p. 136: "Non può, pertanto, uno signore prudente, né debbe, osservare la fede, quando tale osservianza li tornio contro e che sono spente le cagioni che la feciono promettere."

[42] Graef (1996), p. 205.

[43] Ibid.

raison d'etat"[44] – indeed, raison d'etat can be regarded as the conceptual framework of mercantilism as a whole.[45]

Against the backdrop of these demands, an idea gained momentum over the course of the eighteenth century that can be described as an improvement and economic exploitation of what we might call today the quality of life of the population. The concern here was with increasing the population's consumption and productive forces, but also their numerical observation for creating feedback loops. The concept of "policey," which is taken up by José Campillo y Cossío quoted above, plays a central role in this context.[46] This politician is remembered in the history of eighteenth century Spanish literature, because his name can be found above the *Nuevo sistema moderno de gobierno para la América*,[47] which was published posthumously in 1789. In hindsight, this text concerning the liberalization of American trade[48] is one of the most important economic texts of the period:

> En Indias, como en otras partes, se debe considerar en punto de Gobierno, el Político, y el Económico. Por Gobierno Económico se entiende la buena policía, el arreglo del comercio, el modo de emplear civilmente los hombres, el de cultivar las tierras, mejorar sus frutos, y en fin, todo aquello que conduce à sacar el mayor beneficio y utilidad de un pais.[49]

In this description of economic government, the Spanish possessions in America are particularly in need of reform. The "civic employment" of people becomes the main goal of the project, namely to activate the indigenous people's labor force, but also their purchasing power. Their demand should flourish in the metropolis. This project is accompanied by a general view on indigenous cultures,[50] which is central to the question of the anthropological implications of the economic intelligence of the eighteenth century. For the author, it is to be shown that land ownership and the yield of one's own agriculture significantly increases the productivity of the individuals working in agriculture. It is demonstrated before this, however, that the indigenous are rational beings, a fact that some of the conquistadors and chroniclers of the early times had disputed. Although the author later qualifies the extent of the indigenous intelligence, pointing out that the subjects' limitations might also be a great advantage for the rulers. However, the underlying considerations regarding the

---

[44] Recourse to the Jesuit Father Pedro de Ribadeneira. See Maravall (2001), p. 58.

[45] See Heckscher (1932), Vol. 2, pp. 3–20.

[46] On "policey in Spain, see Witthaus (2011), pp. 213–219.

[47] The discussion concerning the true author of *Nuevo sistema* (see also Navarro García 1983), to which is linked a further discussion about the supposed plagiarism of the text by Bernado Ward in his *Proyecto económico* (the American part of Ward is largely identical to the *Nuevo sistema*) is rather enigmatic for our purposes. Incidentally, in my view the topic of the "policey" in *Nuevo sistema* suggests a later transcript, presumably at a time when Campillo was no longer alive. Therefore, there should be a lot of skepticism about whether Campillo is the real author of the *Nuevo sistema*.

[48] See Bernecker (2002), p. 88f.

[49] Campillo y Cossío (1789), S. 3.

[50] See Campillo y Cossío (1789), p. 89–93. In Ward (1779), p. 257, this section – again, whose wording is almost identical – is entitled "Sobre los Indios."

rationality and culture of the indigenous ethnic groups are quite central, for only by virtue of these preconditions can they be regarded as economic entities and thus governmental objects of the "policey."

At the heart of the economic considerations lies another thought: Henceforth, there should be a proper "investiture of the indigenous people." Specifically, they should be permitted to wear Spanish clothing. This would give them de facto equality with the Creoles and Spaniards as subjects of the crown. With this collective ascent, however, the natives and mestizos are primarily taken as economic agents whose needs and affects are being addressed. One therefore first accounts for the alleged innate human desire for jewelry, comfort, and luxury.

> La ambición que en todos es casi natural de tener conveniencias y lucir, es la madre de la industria; y no habiendo otro medio de logralo que trabajando, será el atractivo mas poderoso para inclinarlos al trabajo el de la permision en el uso de todas clases de telas para sus adornos y compusturas [...].[51]

On the other hand, the author recognizes the supposedly peculiar tendency of indigenous peoples toward vanity. Governing human beings thus becomes regulation, an exercise in addressing their aptitudes and needs by means of the measures and offerings of those who rule.

> El verdadero político no se dexará llevar de impresiones tan vulgares, ni de la cruel máxîma de aniquilar las Naciones. Para tenerlas sujetas hallaria otros medios mas nobles, mas christianos y mas humanos, que nunca faltan à quien sabe pensar, y entiende el grande arte de gobernar à los hombres, pues en sus mismo genios y afectos descubren ellos mismo el modo de manejarlos y de corregirlos.[52]

In light of all the efforts toward a new American policy, the observations on the indigenous population and its economic potential (which is compared to the economic problems in European countries) proves unmistakably to be speculation about the anthropological foundations of economic activity. Hirschman has prominently linked this to the then virulent search for man "as he really is."[53] Contrary to classical liberalism, the affects are not left to their own devices, but rather proclaimed as sites of economic regulation: "manejarlos" and "corregirlos."[54] It is remarkable to what extent the reader can also comprehend the re-coding of affect into interest described by Hirschman on the basis of the *Nuevo Sistema*. Consider, for example, the passage just quoted in connection with the following passage:

> Y como ningun estímulo es mas poderoso que el interes y el honor, se podrá proponer algun premio ó distincion al que cultive la mayor cantidad y de mejor calidad de los principales des estos frutos, particularmente de aquellos que estan mas abrazados en el comercio.[55]

---

[51] Ibid., p. 131.

[52] Ibid., p. 134f.

[53] Hirschman (1980), p. 20 and passim.

[54] It thus seems apparent that an investigation of the discourses on affects and interests within the framework of the policey is still missing.

[55] Campillo y Cossío (1789), p. 150.

9.5 Exponents of Early Liberalism in Spain: Valentín de Foronda, Jovellanos and the "Holy Interest"

There have been numerous descriptions of the practical and sometimes technocratic course of the Spanish reform movement, which in the eighteenth century[56] was of course neither uninterrupted nor continuous. Although there has been some disagreement about the use of the term "High Enlightenment" with regard to the reign of Charles III from 1759 to 1788, a number of historical phenomena deserve to be mentioned which speak for a dynamic of enlightenment thinking during this period. Among other things, there was the expansion of the press and the foundation of economic societies.

Although the above-mentioned *Discursos Mercuriales* by Juan Enrique Graef was censored in 1756, Graef nevertheless caused the medium of the periodical to be an important point of departure and reference for economic thought. The commercial press thus counted further projects such as the *Semanario económico* (1765–1767) or the *Memorias instructivas y curiosas* (1778–1791), and articles on economic issues also piled up in so-called encyclopedic journals. One of the best-known examples of these encyclopedic periodicals is undoubtedly the *Espíritu de los mejores diarios literarios*, published by Cristóbal Cladera between 1787 and 1791. Cladera designed this journal in such a way that both contributions from the international press are compiled and translated and articles and letters are also included from local authors. In such a compilation, for example, there are numerous documents that emphatically support, in one way or another, liberalistic thinking or the idea of free trade. One example here would be a treatise translated from French, which responds to the question raised by Abbé Raynal at the Academy of Dijon as to whether the discovery of America was in fact useful for Europe.[57] The author answers this question positively with regard to the economic effects. Then, in an article taken from the *Spectator*, one finds a paean to the worldwide exchange of goods, whose putative hub is London:

> La naturaleza parece puso especial cuidado en sembrar sus dones sobre las diferentes regiones del mundo, con la mira de este mutuo tráfico, y comercio de los hombres, para que los naturales de ciertas partes del Globo dependieran de los de otras, y para que estuvieran todos unidos por su comun interes.[58]

We addressed this ultimately teleological argument earlier. In view of these and other passages from the cited article, one is reminded of Voltaire's description of the London Stock Exchange from his *Letters on the English*. The brokers here are said to resolve their religious differences in order to do business with each other,

[56] In reference to the scientific-political domain of the Bourbons, see Lafuente and Peset (1988), pp. 29–79.

[57] See Cladera (1787), pp. 458–461, 475–479. For a comparison to the French original, see Lüsebrink and Mussard (1994), pp. 71–95.

[58] Cladera (1788), p. 865.

precisely because, contrary to all affects, they are united by the "common interest" expressed in *Espíritu*.

The best-known contribution of liberalism, however, is contained in the letters written by Valentín de Foronda.[59] The natural law sections of these letters could be associated with Foronda's reading of the Physiocrats. Nonetheless, as we saw, arguments based on natural law or physico-theological arguments were part of the common repertoire which had envisaged the rehabilitation of trade since Gerónimo de Uztáriz.

Foronda identifies the three pillars of his political thinking – slightly modified from John Locke's natural law – in the principles of freedom, property, and security.[60] These principles are mutually dependent, but they are, as it were, dowries that the Creator has given to His creatures qua nature.

> En estos principios está cifrado el acierto de los gobiernos, ellos son los elementos de las leyes, el Monarca de la naturaleza los ha escrito sobre el hombre, sobre sus organos, y sobre su entendimiento, y no sobre debiles pergaminos que pueden ser depedazados por el furor de la superstición o de la tiranía.[61]

Man becomes a storage medium of his law and his rights. Both are inviolable. No positive law, law books, authorities, or shysters may threaten them, because these laws and rights are written upon the human body. Thus, Foronda later refers even more precisely to the corresponding topos of natural law reflection, which originates in Paul's Second Epistle to the Corinthians. The maxims of liberalist thought are accordingly engraved in the hearts of people: "¿No están [estas verdades] gravadas en los corazones de todos los hombres?"[62]

Substantively, however, we already find ourselves in a different world from that of Graef: While he found individual interest to still be susceptible to anti-Machiavellist condemnation, for Foronda it is inalienable. As a monarch, one must not set any limits to wealth and self-interest. The happiness of the community depends on the happiness and fundamental rights of its individuals – following the motto, for instance, that if you pay your taxes, do not steal, or kill anyone, or inflict another with injustice in your environment, you owe nothing to the crown and society.[63] Nevertheless, this view is informed by the Thomistic criticism of tyrants ("el furor[...] de la tiranía"). The crucial point is that the "common good," which Thomas took as a given, was itself becoming vulnerable to such critique:

> De ningun modo exîja Vm. de sus vasallos que empleen sus caudales de este ó de aquel modo, baxo el especioso pretexto del bien público, pues en este caso ya no son dueños absolutus de sus haveres sino unos administradores espuestos al arbitrio de otro.[64]

---

[59] See Elorza (1970), p. 131f.

[60] Locke, however, derives these rights from the Decalogue, which in turn has a natural relationship to human reason. See Waldron (2002), p. 97.

[61] Foronda is cited from the original source in *Espíritu*: Cladera (1788), p. 593.

[62] Ibid. See 2. Corinthians 3:3.

[63] See ibid., p. 565.

[64] Ibid., p. 593f.

This observation has serious consequences. For with it, Foronda turns against the axiomatic value of the common good. Often it must serve as an excuse for tyrannical or arbitrary decision-making processes, which in turn vindicates individual economic interest.

The bases upon which Foronda criticizes the deficient economic development of his epoch are as follows: a widespread regulatory frenzy; the determination of prices, when there is a true impartial judge, namely, competition; finally, the granting of privileges for the production of goods by the crown and guilds, such as the creation of monopolies and the restriction of the freedom of movement of the nation's subjects. Individual interest is protected against all these forms of paternalism and, last but not least, shielded from the common good, since the latter emerges from the former.

In his famous *Informe de la ley agraria,* Gaspar Melchor de Jovellanos (1795), quoted at the outset, expresses the benefits of private interest with even greater clarity than Valentín de Foronda. The text is an expansive document on bringing about agricultural reform that was read out in Madrid's economic society. The author already freely quotes Adam Smith's *Wealth of Nations.*[65] It is telling, however, how Jovellanos derives and justifies the interplay of private interests.[66] At a central point in the introduction, he closely cites passages of the Bible to argue that, after the Fall of Man, the world was divinely transferred into man's possession. From this, Jovellanos concludes that it is imperative that man secure his own livelihood. The author, however, demonstrates this using the phrase "holy interest," which may allude to Graef's flagellated individual interest. Jovellanos, however, also finds that it was the self-preservation instinct that became the starting point and condition for the future possibility of civilization:

> A este sagrado interés debe el hombre su conservación, y el mundo su cultura. Él solo limpió y rompió los campos, descuajó los montes, secó los lagos, sujetó los ríos, mitigó los climas, domesticó los brutos, escogió y perfeccionó las semillas y aseguró en su cultivo y reproducción una portentosa multiplicación a la especie humana.[67]

Here we find a different narrative that deviates from the scholastic tradition and attributes the social development of humanity to the freedom of the individual to pursue his or her own interests. Cultural history and economic history thus take a parallel, even interdependent course. The fact that this is to be understood in this way becomes clear at the point where the common good is brought into play as a nemesis:

---

[65] See Jovellanos (^{2}1998), p. 235.

[66] Particularly if one compares this with a detailed examination of economic historical events from the third book of Wealth of Nations.

[67] Ibid., p. 243. It is possible that Jovellanos is responding here to Rousseau, where in the second discourse the self-preservation instinct qua *amour de soi* plays a central role in the state of nature, even though the civilizational process is viewed critically and as existing under the banner of self-love, *amour-propre*.

> En esta dirección no se propusieron por objeto la utilidad particular sino el bien común, y desde entonces las leyes empezaron a pugnar con el interés personal, y la acción de ese interés fue tanto menos viva, diligente e ingeniosa cuanto menos libre en la elección de sus fines y en la ejecución de los medios que conducían a ello.[68]

Like Foronda, Jovellanos also criticizes the excessive number of laws that plague the individual and his private interests. Of course, as with Adam Smith, Jovellanos incorporates discursive safety measures. Naturally, the excess of self-interest must be preceded by a statutory bar. "Concluye solamente que protegiendo la libre acción del interés privado mientras se contenga en los límites señalados por la justicia, sólo debe salirle al paso cuando empiece a traspasarlos."[69] Furthermore, it becomes equally clear that linking economy to the instinct of self-preservation gives it – at least in preliminaries of the agricultural report – a subsistence-economic dimension.

9.6 Conclusion and Outlook

After reviewing the possible mergers of *homo hispanicus* and *homo oeconomicus* in the eighteenth century, findings can be collected for the still-outstanding reconstruction of an economic discourse and its development in Spain. The following keywords should guide the future analysis[70]:

9.6.1 Common Good

First of all, the central importance of the common good in the overall discourse of Bourbon reform policy, but also in the tradition of scholastic natural law, should be emphasized. There are clearly different views on how this common good can be achieved. There is agreement among all those authors who write economic treatises that state or social prosperity can only be achieved through trade, craftsmanship, and prosperous agriculture. One need only read Juan Enrique Graef to know that the traditional *homo hispanicus* was already the subject of critique in the eighteenth century, specifically in the *Discursos mercuriales*. It is also a myth that he exercised his authority without interruption in the time of the Habsburgs. On the other hand, the role of private interests in this context is viewed differently by all the referenced authors. Graef condemns them as an expression of selfishness, which cannot be

[68] Ibid., p. 244f.

[69] Ibid., p. 245.

[70] Even if the architecture of this article – raison d'etat, policey, liberalism – is owed to the sequence of government models in Foucault (2004), in the last section the peculiarity of the Spanish development should nevertheless be more strongly outlined.

tolerated. For him, the first advisers to the crown were the economic wise men. Campillo y Cossío ties the economic government to the passions of human beings, which should provide the necessary impetus for the economic flourishing of a community. It is not until Foronda and Jovellanos, who of course have already read Smith, that it becomes clear that private interests require the greatest possible latitude for creative freedom and decision-making in order to be able to act as a motor for the economic conditions of a country. It is revealing that the common good, on the other hand, becomes a target as a nemesis, which must often be used as an excuse to regulate the flow of trade and profit through taxes. In a negative sense, both still labored on this term whose significance in the context of the Spanish Enlightenment can hardly be overestimated.

9.6.2 Natural Law

From Uztáriz to Jovellanos, economic thought asserts its universality – and always against the background of Christian anthropology. Economic knowledge is nothing less than an expertise with autonomy, as Graef claimed at the latest. Nevertheless, his calculus is a manifestation of God-given reason. Social networks are described in this way whose individuals are conceived anthropologically less as economic subjects than as legal subjects, mostly in terms of natural law or, in some cases, via physico-theological arguments. The problem of the common good and the individual's obligation to provide are naturally anchored in the socialization of man. The fact that such a common good, i.e. civil society and its achievements, emerge from the interplay of private interests is not expressed until the Late Enlightenment – combined, though, with a considerable "Pauline pathos," by means of which natural law thought is now brought to the fore: In contrast to the pleadings and the legal deluge of the administration and judicature, legislative austerity should be limited only to the protection and maintenance of inherent liberties, needs, and activities. As Foronda expresses it, no laws are actually needed for they are inscribed in everyone's heart or on their body. A comparative analysis of the natural law foundations of eighteenth century economic reflection which takes into account the literature of the different European countries is still missing.

9.6.3 Merchant's Honor

For Graef, the merchant's honor is be viewed as a social obligation, which is nonetheless paradigmatic for the contractual and verbal loyalty of a society. As freely circulating trust, this is the glue that holds society together more than trade itself. As Bourdieu would put it, the belief in symbolic capital still outweighs confidence in financial capital – an attitude that is found in an author who otherwise exhaustively criticizes the indolence and pride of the aristocracy. Consequently, Graef does not define freedom in terms of the individual, as it was later defined by Foronda or Jovellanos, but rather as the extensive participation in trade for the benefit of the common good, thereby limiting poverty. Virtue and honesty, on the one hand, and private interest, on the other, are difficult to reconcile with each other. In Spain, the anti-Machiavellian way of thinking certainly played a significant role here. Yet what remains largely unexplored in terms of a critique of the private interest, may be found in another, divergent tradition, which has recently been taken up in this context: picaresque literature.[71]

Bibliography

Agamben, Giorgio. 2013a. Que l'Empire latin contre-attaque! *Libération*. http://www.liberation.fr/monde/2013/03/24/que-l-empire-latin-contre-attaque_890916. Accessed: 18 Sept 2015.

———. 2013b. Die endlose Krise ist ein Machtinstrument. http://www.faz.net/aktuell/feuilleton/bilder-und-zeiten/giorgio-agamben-im-gespraech-die-endlose-krise-ist-ein-machtinstrument-12193816.html. Zugegriffen: 18 Sept 2015.

Bernecker, Walther. 2002. *Spanische Geschichte. Von der Reconquista bis heute*. Darmstadt: Primus.

Castro, Américo. 2001. *España en su historia: christianos, moros y judios*. Barcelona: Crítica.

Cladera, Cristóbal. 1787. *Espíritu de los mejores diarios literarios que se publican en Europa*, Nr. 47, 48. Madrid: Espinosa.

———. 1788. *Espíritu de los mejores diarios literarios que se publican en Europa*, Nr. 96, 155. Madrid: Espinosa.

de Campillo y Cossío, José. 1789. *Nuevo sistema moderno de gobierno para la América*. Madrid: Benito Cano.

de Jovellanos, Gaspar Melchor. ^{4}1987. Obras en prosa, ed. José Caso González. Madrid: Castalia.

———. ^{2}1998. Espectáculos y diversiones públicas; Informe sobre la Ley Agraria. Guillermo Carnero. Madrid: Cátedra.

de Mercado, Tomás. 1977. *Suma de tratos y contratos*, ed. Nicolás Sánchez-Albornoz. http://www.cervantesvirtual.com/obra-visor-din/suma-de-tratos-y-contratos%2D%2D0/html/. Zugegriffen: 07 Oct 2015.

de Uztáriz, Gerónimo. ^{3}1757. Theorica, y practica de comercio y de marina. Madrid: Antonio Sanz.

Elorza, Antonio. 1970. *La ideología liberal en la Ilustración española*. Madrid: Tecnos.

Foucault, Michel. 2004. *Sécurité, Territoire, Population. Cours au Collège de France. 1977–1978*. Paris: Gallimard.

Geisler, Eberhard. 2013. *El dinero en la obra de Quevedo. La crisis de identidad en la sociedad feudal española a principios del siglo XVII*. Kassel: Edition Reichenberger.

———. 2014. Reziprozität und Gabe im spanischen Theater des Siglo de Oro. In *Handel, Handlung, Verhandlung. Theater und Ökonomie in der Frühen Neuzeit in Spanien*, ed. Beatrice Schuchardt und Urs Urban, 59–93. Bielefeld: Transcript.

Gipper, Andreas. 2002. Wunderbare Wissenschaft. In *Literarische Strategien naturwissenschaftlicher Vulgarisierung in Frankreich*. München: Fink.

Goytisolo, Juan. 1979. *España y los españoles*. Barcelona: Lumen.

Graef, Juan Enrique. 1996. Discursos mercuriales, ed. Francisco Sánchez-Blanco. Sevilla: Fundación el Monte.

Haebler, Konrad. 1888. *Die wirtschaftliche Blüte Spaniens im 16. Jahrhundert und ihr Verfall*. Berlin: Gaertners.

[71] See Urban (2014).

Heckscher, Eli. 1932: Der Merkantilismus, 2 Vols. Jena: Gustav Fischer.
Hirschman, Albert O. 1980. *Leidenschaften und Interessen. Politische Begründungen des Kapitalismus vor seinem Sieg*, Autorisierte Übersetzung von Sabine Offe. Frankfurt a. Main: Suhrkamp.
Lafuente, Antonio, und José Luis Peset, eds. 1988. Carlos III y la ciencia de la Ilustración. Madrid: Alianza.
Lüsebrink, Hans-Jürgen, and Alexandre Mussard, eds. 1994. *Avantages et désavantages de la découverte de l'Amérique: Chastellux, Raynal et le concours de l'Académie de Lyon*. Saint Étienne: Université de Saint-Étienne.
Machiavelli, Niccolò. 1986. In *Il Principe. Der Fürst*, ed. Philipp Rippel. Stuttgart: Reclam.
Maravall, José Antonio. ^{3}2001. Maquiavelo y maquiavelismo en España. Estudios de historia del pensamiento español. José Antonio Maravall, 41–66. 3. Madrid: Ediciones Cultura Hispánica.
Mensching, Günther. 2007. Thomas von Aquin. Über die Herrschaft des Fürsten. In *Geschichte des politischen Denkens. Ein Handbuch*, ed. Manfred Brocker, 78–92. Frankfurt a. Main: Suhrkamp.
Navarro García, Luis. 1983. Campillo y el Nuevo Sistema: Una atribución dudosa. *Temas Americanistas* 2: 67–84.
Pocock, John G.A. 1993. *Die andere Bürgergesellschaft. Zur Dialektik von Tugend und Korruption*. Frankfurt a. Main/New York: Campus.
Sánchez-Blanco, Francisco. 1990. Los *Discursos Mercuriales* (1752–1756) de Juan Enrique Graef: Opinión y poder en el movimiento ilustrado español. *Estudios de Historia Social* 52 (53): 477–489.
Schoepp, Sebastian. 2015. *Mediterraner Kapitalismus*. http://sebastian-schoepp.blogspot.de/. Zugegriffen: 18 Sept 2015.
Urban, Urs. 2014. Tausch und Täuschung. Performative Kompetenz als Grundlage ökonomisch erfolgreichen Handelns im spanischen Pikaro-Roman. In Handel, Handlung, Verhandlung. Theater und Ökonomie in der Frühen Neuzeit in Spanien, ed. Beatrice Schuchardt, und Urs Urban, 161–177. Bielefeld: Transcript.
Vicens Vives, Jaume. ^{2}1974. *Historia de España y América social y económica. Vicens-bolsillo*. Vol. 4. Barcelona. (Los Borbones. El siglo XVIII en España y América).
Vogl, Joseph. 2004. *Kalkül und Leidenschaft. Poetik des ökonomischen Menschen*. Zürich: Diaphanes.
———. ^{6}2012. Das Gespenst des Kapitals. Zürich: Diaphanes.
von Aquin, Thomas. 1954. *De regno ad regem Cypri* [*Textum Taurini 1954 editum*]. http://www.corpusthomisticum.org/orp.html. Accessed 5 Oct 2015.
von Sevilla, Isidor. 1911. Etymologiarvm sive originvm, ed. Wallace M. Lindsay, Vol. 1. Oxford: Univsersity Press.
von Tschilschke, Christian. 2013. Der spanische Patient. Krisendiagnose, Reformdiskurse und Projektemacherei im spanischen 18. century. In Die Krise als Erzählung. Transdisziplinäre Perspektiven auf ein Narrativ der Moderne, ed. Uta Fenske, Walburga Hülk, und Gregor Schuhen, 169–187. Bielefeld: Transcript.
Waldron, Jeremy. 2002. *God, locke, and equality: Christian foundations in Locke's political thought*. Cambridge: Cambridge University Press.
Ward, Bernardo. ^{2}1779. Proyecto económico. Madrid: Ibarra.
Weber, Max. ^{3}2010. Die protestantische Ethik und der Geist des Kapitalismus. Vollständige Ausgabe Dirk Kaesler. München: Beck.
Witthaus, Jan-Henrik. 2011. Reform der Moral im Zeichen sozialer Mimesis. Überlegungen zu Politik und Policey in der Moralischen Wochenschrift *El Censor*. In *Die Spectators in der Romania – eine transkulturelle Gattung?* ed. Klaus-Dieter Ertler, 195–216. Frankfurt a. Main: Peter Lang.
———. 2014. *Sozialisation der Kritik im Spanien des aufgeklärten Absolutismus. Von Feijoo bis Jovellanos*. Frankfurt a. Main: Klostermann.

Chapter 10
"A Traveling Salesman from Hades". On the Critique of the Acquisitive Mindset in Nikolai V. Gogol's Novel *Dead Souls* (1842)

Christian von Tschilschke

Abstract In Nikolai Vasilievich Gogol's (1809–1852) *Dead Souls* (1842), a novel belonging to the global literary canon, the middleclass, economic concept of the honourable businessman is evoked *ex negativo*: by the foil Pavel Ivanovich Chichikov, a dubious profiteer and fraudulent speculator. Chichikov plans large-scale credit fraud in provincial Russia based on the illegal idea of taking out a loan against so-called "dead souls", i.e. dead serfs. Referring to more recent contributions on the relationship between literary and economic discourses and taking into account the social-historical situation in nineteenth century Russia as well as the literary context, this contribution investigates the legal, moral, economic, metaphysical and anthropological implications of this fictive planned deception. From the perspective of 'economic literature', Gogol's novel can be read as a result of dealing with disconcertment through fiction, but also as a product of the fascination sparked by the spirit of modern capitalism that was perceived as new and predominantly 'un-Russian', by the eldritch and uncanny way in which money works, and by the credit economy, still unusual in Russia. Furthermore, this contribution also shows that Gogol's satirical novel reveals striking structural parallels to current literary and filmic portrayals of today's financial crises.

10.1 The Honorable Merchant in Russian Literature

This article focuses on the topic of the "honorable merchant" in literature from a rather marginal perspective in two respects. First, the following deals with Russian literature, albeit Nikolai Vasilievich Gogol's (1809–1852) novel *Dead Souls* (1842) is considered an undisputed classic. Secondly, because the honorable merchant

C. von Tschilschke (✉)
University of Siegen, Siegen, Germany
e-mail: tschilschke@romanistik.uni-siegen.de

C. Lütge, C. Strosetzki (eds.), *The Honorable Merchant – Between Modesty and Risk-Taking*, Ethical Economy 56, https://doi.org/10.1007/978-3-030-04351-3_10

appears above all *ex negative* in his manifestation as a dubious profiteer and fraudulent speculator. He is, as Vladimir Nabokov characterized the protagonist of the novel Pavel Ivanovich Chichikov in his brilliant lectures on Russian literature, "the ill-paid representative of the devil, a traveling salesman from Hades, 'our Mr. Chichikov' as the Satan & Co firm may be imagined calling their easy-going, healthy-looking but inwardly shivering and rotting agent."[1]

Merchants are certainly not unfamiliar to Russian literature, and the acquisitive type of person found an early first chronicler in the Königsberg post-doctoral thesis by the Slavicist Eugen Häusler, *Der Kaufmann in der russischen Literatur* (*The Merchant in Russian Literature*) (1935). The German reader and theatergoer will perhaps first think of the honest and well-meaning merchant Lopachin from Anton Chekhov's tragic comedy *The Cherry Orchard* (1903). With a heavy heart, he decides to cut down the flowering cherry orchard to build holiday homes for summer guests. The British historian Orlando Figes calls him the "first merchant hero on the Russian stage."[2] One may also call to mind the figure of the exemplary German-born businessman Andrei Stoltz from Ivan Goncharov's novel *Oblomov* (1859), who is active in the import-export business.[3] On his behalf, the Russian reader and theatergoer may well also think about the memorable portrayal of the merchant milieu in Maxim Gorky's first novel *Foma Gordeev* (1899), and, above all, the numerous plays by Alexander Ostrovsky, the most important Russian playwright of the second half of the nineteenth century. Here, the bourgeois merchant and the Moscow merchant environment are central.[4]

What all these texts have in common is that the merchant – through his behavior and the evaluation of his actions – becomes the emblematic figure of social change in nineteenth century Russia. This change takes place in the area of tension between religious tradition and secular modernity, which has characterized Russian literature and culture since the eighteenth century; between resistance to progress and an orientation towards the future; between the aristocratic-feudal social order and the bourgeois world. This tension, in turn, coincides with a deeply rooted thinking of alterity, which quite clearly distinguishes Russia from Europe or rather the "West."[5]

With regard to the representation of economic reality, Gogol's novel *Dead Souls* plays a pioneering role in nineteenth century Russian literature. The ambivalence of the novel's above-mentioned protagonist, Pavel Ivanovich Chichikov, who is characterized by a well-developed business sense and an aggressive acquisitive mindset – above all in Chichikov's bizarre and macabre business idea – is a general

---

[1] Nabokov (1983), p. 17. The cited edition of Nabokov's lectures by Fredson Bowers is not entirely reliable in that they include texts from Nabokov's Gogol book *Nikolai Gogol* (1944). Cf. summary of the Nabokov-Gogol relationship in Fanger (1995).

[2] Figes (2011), p. 239. Chekhov's father was a businessman himself, if a rather unsuccessful one. See Ginzburg (1990), p. 7.

[3] See also the economic aspects in Günther (2001).

[4] See Russian literature and cultural history in general from an economic perspective in Weitlaner (2001).

[5] Cf. inter alia Nohejl (2009).

reflection of the epochal dissolution identified by Jochen Hörisch, in which the "defining medium" ("Leitmedium") of religion is supplanted by that of money. Hörisch highlights in particular the especially stubborn resistance of German Letters to the "conversion from God to money" ("Umstellung von Gott auf Geld").[6] At the same time, however, Chichikov's plans also manifest the replacement of different economic forms in a more specific sense, or, as Hans Günther emphasized, the "penetration of profit-seeking and money into an agricultural domestic economy oriented towards subsistence."[7]

What makes Gogol's novel interesting beyond the confines of nineteenth century Russian literature, however, is not only that it concisely characterizes the "spirit of capitalism" in the context of the opposing moods of malaise and euphoria. It also evokes in a highly suggestive way the "specter of capital", recently analyzed by Joseph Vogl, and thus achieves a kind of anticipatory power regarding the way we still react in the immediate present to the crises of global finance capitalism.[8]

I would like to follow these two theses in four steps. First of all, it is necessary to briefly introduce the peculiar business scheme to which the novel owes the oxymoron in its title "Dead Souls" – *Dead Souls* is the story of a carefully planned credit fraud. Then, the legal, moral, economic, and metaphysical implications of this scheme will be revealed with reference to the historical context. I will next reconstruct the anthropology of the new economic man and the utopian orientation that Gogol takes as the basis for the conception of his interim businessman Chichikov. Finally, I will look with *Dead Souls* at the artistic portrayal of contemporary financial crises.

10.2 Gogol's *Dead Souls*: The Planned Credit Fraud

Considering the basic plotline, *Dead Souls* is designed as a story about an ingenious business idea and a long-planned credit fraud. The novel's story takes place at some point between 1812 and 1821, during the time of Czar Alexander I. The setting is "not far from the two capitals",[9] that is, between Moscow and St. Petersburg and thus ultimately in the middle of the Russian provinces. Initially as nondescript is the protagonist, Pawel Ivanovich Chichikov, a "man without qualities" – "not a handsome man, but not too bad to look at, neither too fat nor too thin; it could not have been said that he was old, but he was not too young either."[10] Nevertheless, he seems to be pursuing a certain plan, what exactly this plan is, or who Chichikov is, is not communicated to the curious reader until the eleventh and final chapter of the novel. After a few professional failures, including in the customs service, Chichikov

[6] Hörisch (1998), p. 32.

[7] Günther (2003), p. 235.

[8] Cf. Vogl (2010/2011).

[9] Gogol (2013), p. 309.

[10] Ibid., p. 9.

arrives on his own at "the most stunning idea ever entertained by a human brain."[11] When pledging a run-down estate, he notices that the bonded slave peasants had also been pledged. No consideration was thus given to the recently deceased as long as they only appeared in the corresponding revision list. Chichikov decides to take advantage of this oversight to obtain wealth fast.

It is important to realize that the Russian landowners were obliged to inform the authorities every 5 years of how many peasants – also referred to as "souls" – they officially owned. On the basis of these revision lists, the landowner's taxes were calculated for the next 5 years – regardless of whether the number of peasants had increased or decreased in the meantime. As Adolf Stender-Petersen explains: "Under certain circumstances, in the event of an epidemic or war, it was extremely detrimental to the landowner to pay taxes on *souls* who had recently died, but still existed on paper."[12] Chichikov's "ingenious idea" is to buy up from the landowners free of charge or at the lowest possible price the officially still living, but actually dead souls – who no longer bring in any earnings, but only cause costs – before the new revision lists are submitted and to have the purchases officially confirmed. On the basis of this fictitious fortune, he would apply for a loan from a state-owned bank and then make off with the money. In anticipation of executing his plan, Chichikov is already enthused by this prospective revenue: "If I, let's say, acquire a thousand and the guardianship authority gives, let's say, 200 rubles per soul, I'll have 200,000 in capital in one fell swoop!"[13]

With this ill-gotten capital, Chichikov wants to realize the dream of a sedentary bourgeois life. But he only wants to possess what others already have had for a long time: his own estate, which could be called "Chichikovo" or "Pavlovskoye"[14]; "a blonde bride with red cheeks and a dimple in her right cheek"[15]; and an offspring who worships him. Chichikov is therefore not a businessman for professional reasons and, as Horst-Jürgen Gerigk calls him, he is merely "a temporary cheat."[16] Among the basic types of capitalist entrepreneurship Werner Sombart identifies in his *Der Bourgeois. Zur Geistesgeschichte des modernen Wirtschaftsmenschen* (1913), Chichikov therefore probably most closely corresponds (as Hans Günther notes[17]) to the type of speculator who distinguishes himself through "the suggestive power with which he alone realizes his plans,"[18] and whose prevailing mood is "an enthusiastic lyricism."[19]

---

[11] Ibid., p. 361.

[12] Stender-Petersen (1986), p. 179.

[13] Gogol (2013), p. 362.

[14] Ibid., p. 362.

[15] Ibid., p. 225.

[16] Gerigk (2007), p. 127.

[17] Günther (2003), p. 227. For this reference to the historical background, see also the aforementioned Tschilschke (1996), p. 95.

[18] Sombart (1920), p. 121.

[19] Ibid., p. 121.

It is fitting here that the narrator of the *Dead Souls* himself expressly points out the difficulty of positively assessing this new type of man: "It is most apt if we call him an owner and acquirer."[20] The two terms "owner" and "acquirer" well reflect the different economic forms to which the figure of Chichikov is related. As Hans Günther explains, the Russian word for "owner" – "choziain" – contains the Greek "oikodomos," meaning "master of household management."[21] This points to Chichikov's pre-modern, old European landowner's ideal. On the other hand, "acquirer" – "priobretatel"– evokes the spirit of capitalism, which is expressed in Chichikov's well-developed business sense and his tireless pursuit of profit.

The extremely simple, episodic and picaresque plot development of the *Dead Souls* is now completely geared toward showing Chichikov in the gradual implementation of his plan and in his capacity as "acquirer." After arriving in the small Russian town "N." Chichikov visits five different landowners from the area to do business with them. The author dedicates a detailed portrait to each of these landowners. This not only raises the profile of Chichikov's own commercial behavior, but also assigns each individual landowner to a different type of economic behavior, depending on his or her reaction to Chichikov's offer.[22]

The first landowner, Manilov, turns out to be completely out of touch when it comes to economic matters. He cedes his dead souls to Chichikov free of charge and even assumes the expenses for the purchase contract. The second landowner, the enterprising widow Korobochka, leaves Chichikov with 18 men for 15 rubles. She then travels, however, to the city to inquire about the market price at which dead souls are traded. The third landowner, Nozdryov, is a quarrelsome gambler who surpasses himself in making excessive exchange offers without any specific intention of winning a profit. He is the only one that Chichikov has to leave without closing a deal. The fourth landowner, Sobakevich, sells his dead souls after tough negotiations for two and a half rubles a piece and insists on a down payment of 25 rubles. Sobakevich's behavior is especially peculiar because he has lost any sense of the fictitious character of the traded goods, praising in detail the human and professional qualities of his peasants as if they were still alive. According to Hans Günther, who takes up a formulation from Georg Simmel's *Philosophie des Geldes* (1900), he thus represents, in an incorrigible way, "a kind of disposition that is widespread in the rural milieu 'directed at the substantiality of things'."[23] The fifth and final landowner, Plyushkin, resembles the monomaniacal protagonist in Honoré de Balzac's eponymous short story *Gobseck* (1830). He suffers from pathological greed and a senseless compulsion to collect, whereby all economic activity has come to a halt. He takes 32 kopecks per soul.

It is important to stress that none of these landowners – who have often been described as the actual dead souls of the novel – have even the slightest suspicion of what Chichikov is actually up to and what exchange value the dead souls really possess. By the same token, the landowners Korobochka, Sobakevich and Plyushkin

[20] Gogol (2013), p. 364.

[21] Günther (2003), p. 227.

[22] Cf. In detail Valentino (1998).

[23] Günther (2003), p. 231, as well as Simmel (1989), p. 302.

at least reveal commercial thinking to the extent that they instinctively react to a demand. While its meaning remains a mystery, they recognize that the offer is advantageous to them. Chichikov concludes his shopping spree with a visit to Plyushkin. In the end, he has acquired 400 souls, whose purchase he has officially confirmed in the seventh chapter.

In the remaining chapters, we read how Chichikov first becomes the idolized figure in small-town society for his legendary commercial success. Rumors, however, then start to circulate about the dubious character of his purchases, making him the target of the most ludicrous speculations: Chichikov is allegedly the disguised Napoleon, who escaped from St. Helena, or even the resurrected Antichrist. He then leaves the city in a hurry and heads off, as the narrator announces, into a promising future. Its presentation was reserved for the two volumes of *Dead Souls*, but only a few fragments of the second part have survived.

10.3 *Dead Souls* in Historical Context

Now that we have taken a brief excursion through the novel's plot, three objects have crystallized of an economic reading of *Dead Souls*: the character of Chichikov, the essence of his business idea, and the behavior of his trading partners. In the following, they will be questioned more precisely on their legal, moral, economic and metaphysical-religious implications and classified in terms of the time period of the novel's genesis.

From a legal standpoint, Chichikov's behavior is unlawful. Nonetheless, the degree of culpability of his actions at the time of the novel is limited to the fact that he conceals in the purchase contracts – which he concludes with the landowners and has duly authenticated in the *guberniya* town – that there are in reality no serfs. The matter would only become a real credit fraud if Chichikov, as planned, actually pledged the audited souls that only existed on paper to a state bank. But it does not come to this. The socio-critical point of Gogol's construct lies in the circumstance that the state itself enables Chichikov to carry out his deception in the first place by clinging to the institution of serfdom. If it were not possible to sell serfs like goods, it would also not be possible to use them as collateral for loans. Even though Gogol was not himself an opponent of serfdom, this critical reading nonetheless lies within the realm of historical possibility. For instance, after the uprising of the Western-minded Decembrists of 1825, the abolition of serfdom was demanded, among other things. The narrator explicitly emphasizes that the instrument of pledging was not yet taken for granted at the time of the novel's action, and that it encountered a certain amount of distaste: "Pledging to the state treasury was then still a new practice, and it was not undertaken without fear."[24]

Morally speaking, Chichikov distances himself in many respects from the ideal of an honorable merchant – and not only because his actual or planned violations of the law are morally objectionable. Thus he fleeces his business partners, the land-

[24] Gogol (2013), p. 361. On the historical background, see Valentino (1998), pp. 545f.

owners, by leaving them in the dark about the true exchange value of the dead souls. Above all, however, he tries in an repugnant manner to capitalize on the misery and death of others. The indecent, misanthropic side of Chichikov's acquisitiveness reveals itself, for example, when he considers shortly before departing: "The timing is just right: recently there was an epidemic, and the people died in droves, thank God."[25]

From an economic point of view, Gogol's keen sense of the irrational elements of capitalism and the ghostly-uncanny aspects of the inner workings of money and the banking industry is particularly remarkable. The complete blindness of the landowners, officials and city dwellers to the true nature of Chichikov's undertaking therefore reflects the surrender of common understanding to a seemingly unfathomable economic event. In the grotesque exaggeration of the expression "dead souls", the astonishment and concern about the possibility of making money out of fictions and creating value from nothing are crystallized. It is informed by a fundamental suspicion that the (money) signs in circulation can no longer be covered by an equivalent secured value.[26] In the specific case, the dead souls, quite bewilderingly, attain a degree of presence through their exchange value, which they probably never had during their lifetime. According to Hans Günther, Chichikov's "soul buying" "illustrates the revitalizing effect of money in a provocative and outlandish way – on the basis of the human soul as a money equivalent."[27] And, last but not least, a moment of the imaginary is also revealed in the process of price determination, which dominates the dialogue with the trade-willing landowners: The total arbitrariness in fixing prices makes "any exchange value appear in an almost fantastic light,"[28] and even more so given the context that the goods do not even exist and therefore have no practical value. To paraphrase Karl Marx, "the expression of price here becomes imaginary like certain magnitudes of mathematics."[29]

From a metaphysical-religious point of view, *Dead Souls* is ultimately a first-rate provocation. The title of the Russian first edition ordered by the Tsarist censors therefore also had to be "Chichikov's Adventure". This is because in the understanding of contemporary authorities, souls were immortal and therefore could not be described as dead. But even those, like Chichikov, who regard souls as pure trading goods deny their immaterial character. In addition, the reference loss of a financial asset based on dead souls threateningly suggests the loss of a transcendental signifier, i.e. the death of God. Chichikov, finally, also has some traditional attributes of the devil, insofar as he acts as a travelling soul buyer and evidently understands himself as the miraculous transformation of the something worthless into something valuable. He thus in fact appears as Vladimir Nabokov's aptly put it, as a "traveling salesman from Hades".

---

[25] Gogol (2013), p. 362.

[26] For more information about the concerns due to the upcoming credit business and its causes in the eighteenth century see Vogl (2010/2011), pp. 53-82.

[27] Günther (2003), p. 235.

[28] Gerigk (2007), p. 125.

[29] Marx/Engels (1975), p. 117, cited after Günther (2003), p. 236 (here slightly corrected).

But it almost goes without saying that the contamination also happens the other way around. Not only is religion undermined in one's contact with money, but the money and credit economy is also religiously charged. It can therefore be stated that Chichikov's appearance and his business practices are shifted systematically into an aura of the unlawful, immoral, uncanny, and unchristian. Undoubtedly, this articulates a fundamental feeling of disconcertment towards the spirit of modern capitalism – perceived as new and "un-Russian" and embodied in the merchant, speculator, or entrepreneur. On the other hand, a positive light is also thrown on this spirit, for it contrasts favorably with the state of Russian society, which – as the unsparing portraits of the landowners show – is urgently in need of reform. This spirit, moreover, flows into the ideal of the new human being, which, according to the author's designs, Chichikov is to develop into in the subsequent volumes. This raises the question of the anthropological basis and the utopian character of *Dead Souls*.

10.4 Anthropology and Utopia of *Dead Souls*

In the biography of Chichikov, which is presented to the reader in the last chapter of *Dead Souls*, Gogol draws up a veritable anthropology of the economic man. Numerous parallels may be found to Benjamin Franklin's later wisdom teachings and the descriptions of this character type in Max Weber.[30] Iron discipline, diligence, cleanliness, frugality, practical intelligence, a willingness to deny oneself, skillful opportunism and, above all, "an almost extraordinary business acumen"[31] are hallmarks already of the pupil Chichikov and also hint at the shrewd businessman and speculator, whom the reader gets to know at the beginning of *Dead Souls*.

Chichikov has obviously thoroughly internalized the motto of his father: "But above all, save money and hold on to every kopek: this is the most reliable thing in the world."[32] Gogol consistently portrays Chichikov's coolly calculating rationality and his reckless fixation on material advantages in a negative light. In contrast to Chekhov's and Goncharov's works quoted at the beginning, these qualities are completely in keeping with the traditional prejudice against the merchant in Russian literature.[33] On the other hand, Chichikov's energetic entrepreneurial spirit, which sets him apart from all the other figures, has positive traits that already point to the

[30] Cf. Tschilschke (1996), pp. 97f.

[31] Gogol (2013), p. 341.

[32] Ibid., p. 340.

[33] See economic historian Klaus Heller (2006), p. 1: "If, in the post-Soviet period, the historical role of the traditional Russian merchant on his way to becoming a modern entrepreneur and bourgeois is viewed rather positively, it indicates a decided departure from a picture of the Russian merchant, often distorted in public and especially in literature (*kupec*) with mostly repulsive features, whose origins extend beyond the Soviet era to the nineteenth century and earlier. Thus, even in Tsarist Russia, it was socially acceptable for anyone who believed himself to be superior by social status or education, looked down upon the merchant, and indeed regarded him as a social non-person who had always only been identified by 'dishonor'."

conclusion of the novel and the fragments of the second part of *Dead Souls*. At the end of the first part, the intention to reconcile money and religion with one another – to bring together the “economy of money and the soul in the medium of literature” – is already signaled.[34] Thus, in the long lyrical passage, which concludes the only completed first part of *Dead Souls*, the narrator contemplates whether the “incomprehensible passion”[35] that drives Chichikov might be subordinated to “higher plans”[36] and destined for a “good”[37] unknown to himself.

It cannot be ascertained with certainty what spiritual historical sources inform “the providential interpretation of the acquisitive instinct.”[38] In any case, according to Dmitry Chizhevsky, the “pathos of religiously sanctified and morally sanctioned economic management,”[39] which is peculiar to the existing fragments of the second part, reveals a certain proximity to both Protestant-Puritanian predestination ethics and Russian economic thinking. Gogol’s ambitious follow-up project was oriented – as near as we can tell – in terms of a national-religious plan of salvation, which envisaged a Christian purification of Chichikov and his transformation into a patriarchal landowner. Western concepts were to coalesce with Russian Orthodox ideas, and the acquisitive drive aimed at earthly gain, mistrusted by the Slavophile defenders of the Russian tradition, was to be integrated into a moral-religious ideal as a welcome stimulus. This can be recognized in any event in the fragments of the second part of Chichikov’s visit to the exemplary landowner Kostanshoglo and the encounter with the multi-millionaire tax collector Murazov, who serves as Chichikov’s new conscience of business ethics. It should be noted, however, that Gogol’s utopia of a “synthesis of agrarian household management and a profit and monetary economy tamed in the sense of orthodox business ethics[40]” was no longer artistically implemented.

10.5 Gogol’s *Dead Souls* and the Financial Crises of the Present

So far, we have depicted the new capitalist economic mentality in *Dead Souls* as manifested in Chichikov’s character, his commercial activities and his adventurous business idea. This was done within the historical context of the overlapping of modern and pre-modern economic forms and – at least in the broader outlines – in the area of tension between the ideological conflict between “Westerners” and

[34] Günther (2003), p. 237.

[35] Gogol (2013), p. 359.

[36] Ibid., p. 365.

[37] Ibid., p. 366.

[38] Günther (2003), p. 227. There you will also find further expositions on the economic discourse in Russia after 1800 (pp. 228-230). See also Zweynert (2002).

[39] Chizhevsky (1966), p. 76.

[40] Günther (2003), p. 236.

"Slavophiles."[41] Now, by way of conclusion, a connection will be established between *Dead Souls* and the financial crises of the present. Indeed, this kind of connection readily presents itself and has therefore already been discussed on many occasions.

For example, the cultural journalist Fritz Göttler is on the right track when he speaks of the "drive of a serfdom bubble" and describes Chichikov's business "as bold as that of today's high-stakes gamblers in our bankers' crisis system." Göttler's remarks appeared in the *Süddeutsche Zeitung* on the occasion of the 2013 paperback edition of the new translation of *Dead Souls* into German by Vera Bischitzky, the novel's seventeenth German translation, which is also cited here.[42] And the Russian cultural scholar Vladimir Elistratov already stated in 2009 in the Russian magazine *Snamja* that from today's perspective, *Dead Souls* reads like a prefiguration of the global financial crises from the beginning of the twenty-first century.[43]

In fact, the parallels to phenomena in the present are unmistakable. The general contours of the following can all be found in *Dead Souls*: Complaints about the insatiable greed and fraudulent practices of financial and stock market speculators; the unmanageable risks of a dematerialised capital economy; the media-generated cult of personality surrounding some particularly spectacularly failed protagonists of the banking system; as well as the incomprehension and helplessness with which the public and politicians react to the events in the financial world. What is more: Parallels to *Dead Souls* – formal and structural – are also striking in the current literary and cinematic portrayals of the financial crisis. They bear witness to the fact that there is evidently not only a timeless artistic fascination for certain phenomena of capitalism, but also a constant endeavor to "tell the story."[44]

For instance, Don DeLillo's novel *Cosmopolis* (2003), filmed by David Cronenberg in 2012, is based on a very similar compositional scheme as that underlying *Dead Souls.* The young fund manager and stock exchange speculator Eric Packer rides through New York in a white stretch limousine one day in April 2000, recalling the allegorical journeys of the *Odyssey* and Dante's *Divina commedia.*[45] Martin Scorsese's 3-h feature film *The Wolf of Wall Street* (2013), based on the best-seller of the same name by stockbroker Jordan Belfort, very much resembles *Dead Souls* for it appears to be affected precisely by what it describes: The delirious opulence and rapid dynamics, which sweeps away all morality. And, finally, there is the German documentary film *Der Banker – Master of the Universe* (2013) by Marc Bauder. The former high-ranking investment banker Rainer Voss offers a privileged inside view of the financial system, which he has left behind. Here, the same secular conversion scheme comes into play that was intended for the incomplete second part of *Dead Souls,* in which the "acquirer" Chichikov looks back regretfully on his former self.

---

[41] See inter alia Conrad (2013), pp. 623f.

[42] Göttler (2013), p. 14.

[43] See Elistratov (2009), p. 169.

[44] See Vogl (2010/2011), p. 10.

[45] Don DeLillo's novel is also the point of departure in Vogl (2010/2011). The reference to Homer and Dante can also be found here (see pp. 11 and 15). Cf. Homer and Dante as role models for Gogol Tschilschke (1996).

Bibliography

Chizhevsky, Dmitry [Tschiżewskij, Dmitrij]. 1966. Der unbekannte Gogol'. In *Gogol', Turgenev, Dostoevskij, Tolstoj. Zur russischen Literatur des 19. Jahrhunderts*, ed. Dmitrij Tschiżewskij, 57–87. München: Fink.

Conrad, Barbara. 2013. Nachwort. In *Tote Seelen*, ed. Nikolai Gogol, 614–635. Trans. V. Bischitzky. München: Deutscher Taschenbuch Verlag.

Elistratov, Vladimir. 2009. Chichikov i ipotechnoye kreditovanye: k metafisikye finansovogo krisisa. *Znamya. Literaturny i Obshestwenno-Politichesky Shurnal* 7: 169–173. http://magazines.russ.ru/znamia/2009/7/el18.html. Accessed: 22 Dec 2015.

Fanger, Donald. 1995. Nabokov and Gogol. In *The Garland companion to Vladimir Nabokov*, ed. Vladimir E. Alexandrov, 420–428. New York: Garland.

Figes, Orlando. 2011. *Nataschas Tanz. Eine Kulturgeschichte Russlands*. Trans. S. Baumann, B. Rullkötter. Bonn: Bundeszentrale für politische Bildung.

Gerigk, Horst-Jürgen. 2007. Nikolaj Gogol': *Mertvye duši (Die toten Seelen)*. In *Der russische Roman*, ed. Bodo Zelinsky and Jens Herlth, 117–138, 501–503. Köln: Böhlau.

Ginzburg, Natalia. 1990. *Anton Čechov. Ein Leben*. Trans. M. Pflug. Berlin: Wagenbach.

Gogol, Nikolai. 2013. *Tote Seelen. Ein Poem*. Trans. V. Bischitzky. München: Deutscher Taschenbuch Verlag.

Göttler, Fritz. 2013. Drive einer Leibeigenen-Blase – Gogols "Tote Seelen", neu übersetzt. *Süddeutsche Zeitung*, 14. 6.12.2013.

Günther, Hans. 2001. Homo oeconomicus und russische Kultur. Zu Gončarovs Roman *Oblomov*. In *Kultur, Sprache, Ökonomie. Beiträge zur gleichnamigen Tagung an der Wirtschaftsuniversität Wien 3.-5. Dezember 1999*, ed. Wolfgang Weitlaner, 101–113. Wien: Gesellschaft zur Förderung slawistischer Studien.

———. 2003. Ökonomie und Religion in Gogol's "Mertvye duši". *Die Welt der Slaven. Halbjahresschrift für Slavistik* XLVIII (2): 227–238.

Häusler, Eugen. 1935. *Der Kaufmann in der russischen Literatur*. Königsberg: Gräfe und Unzer.

Heller, Klaus. 2006. *Geschichte des modernen Unternehmertums in Russland bis 1917. Digitales Handbuch zur Geschichte und Kultur Russlands und Osteuropas*. Vol. 17. https://epub.ub.uni-muenchen.de/760/1/Heller_Unternehmertum.pdf. Accessed 15 Dec 2015.

Hörisch, Jochen. 1998. *Kopf oder Zahl. Die Poesie des Geldes*. Frankfurt am Main: Suhrkamp.

Marx, Karl, und Friedrich Engels. 1975. Das Kapital. Vol. 1. Berlin: Dietz.

Nabokov, Vladimir. 1983. Nikolay Gogol (1809–1852). In *Lectures on Russian literature*, ed. Fredson Bowers, 15–61. London: Picador.

Nohejl, Regine. 2009. *"Das Andere des Westens" und die "Arche Noah der Weltkultur". Zur Spezifik von Identität und Alterität in russischen kulturgeschichtlichen Diskursen*. München/Berlin: Otto Sagner.

Simmel, Georg. 1989. *Philosophie des Geldes*. Frankfurt am Main: Suhrkamp.

Sombart, Werner. 1920. *Der Bourgeois. Zur Geistesgeschichte des modernen Wirtschaftsmenschen. 5. und 6. Tausend*. München/Leipzig: Duncker & Humblot.

Stender-Petersen, Adolf. 1986. *Geschichte der russischen Literatur*. Trans. W. Krämer. 4th ed. München: Beck.

von Tschilschke, Christian. 1996. *Epen des Trivialen. N.V. Gogols "Die toten Seelen" und G. Flauberts "Bouvard und Pécuchet". Ein struktureller und thematischer Vergleich*. Heidelberg: Winter.

Valentino, Russell Scott. 1998. A catalogue of commercialism in Nikolai Gogol's "Dead Souls". *Slavic Review* 57 (3): 543–562.

Vogl, Joseph. 2010/2011. *Das Gespenst des Kapitals*. 3rd ed. Zürich: Diaphanes.

Weitlaner, Wolfgang, ed. 2001. *Kultur, Sprache, Ökonomie. Beiträge zur gleichnamigen Tagung an der Wirtschaftsuniversität Wien 3.-5. Dezember 1999*. Wien: Gesellschaft zur Förderung slawistischer Studien.

Zweynert, Joachim. 2002. *Eine Geschichte des ökonomischen Denkens in Rußland 1805–1905*. Marburg: Metropolis.

Part IV
The Image of the Merchant in Non-European Contexts

Chapter 11
The Ethics of the Merchant in the Islamic Faith: From Ibn Khaldoun to Islamic Finance

Dominique de Courcelles

Abstract As monotheism has broken with the idea of an eternal, unchanging world outside of history, the historicization of religious faith also implies an ethics of acting in the world, and, in particular, an ethics of economic and commercial activity. The three monotheistic world religions have accordingly developed their own economic practices. In Islam, the prophet was himself a merchant and keenly aware of various economic and commercial pursuits. Later, the thinker Ibn Khaldoun became interested in regulating these practices. This article will deal with the question what Islam can teach us today in the contemporary globalized market economy.

11.1 Introduction

Monotheism broke with the idea of an eternal, unchanging world outside of history. In the beginning there is one God, creator of the earth and mankind. The uniqueness of God points to the universality of morality – which, in turn, is expressed by the universality of the commandment of charity and the conception of a historical humanity, internalized in a community heading toward the realization of its ideal. The historicization of religious faith implies an ethics of acting in the world, and, in particular, an ethics of economic and commercial activity. The three monotheistic world religions have accordingly developed their own economic practices, each in their own way. To the extent that the prophet of Islam was himself a merchant, he was keenly aware of various economic and commercial pursuits. Later, it was the thinker Ibn Khaldoun who became interested in regulating them. What can Islam teach us today in the contemporary market economy of our globalized world? This question is the point of departure for the discussion that follows.

D. de Courcelles (✉)
Centre Jean Pépin -Théorie et Histoire de l'Esthétique, de la Technique et des Arts,
Paris Sciences Lettres Université de la Recherche-Ecole normale supérieure Paris/CNRS,
Paris, France

C. Lütge, C. Strosetzki (eds.), *The Honorable Merchant – Between Modesty and Risk-Taking*, Ethical Economy 56, https://doi.org/10.1007/978-3-030-04351-3_11

11.2 The Three Monotheistic World Religions, Wealth, and Money

The three monotheistic world religions agree that God alone created something out of nothing. It is an assertion with profound consequences. After all, how can human beings presume to create something out of nothing and dare to compete with the divine power? The primary ban on lending was imposed in human history, because the creditor who extends credit effectively creates value out of nothing. Every interest is a yardstick of man's arrogant self-regard. What's more, it resembles negative wear and tear. The prohibition on interest is part of a principle of economic recommendations, which yields new responsibilities and expectations.

Regarding wealth and money, the three monotheistic world religions have developed very similar stances which mainly deal with the equitable distribution of goods. According to biblical wisdom, money, vanity, and wealth are transient pleasures and their accumulation is proscribed. *Deuteronomy*, traditionally attributed to Moses, the founder and judge of Judaism, contains a series of very precise economic and ritual guidelines. A well-codified system of solidarity makes it possible to achieve greater social justice. The sacred texts of Christianity are much less explicit in economic and financial terms, even if they allow the first texts of the Hebrew Bible into their canon. The founder of Christianity, Jesus Christ – rejected by Judaism but recognized by Islam as a prophet – is a craftsman in an agrarian village and a master of wisdom. The *Gospels* that transmit his teachings contain few recommendations on the economic order and even fewer financial recommendations. His teachings, in fact, mention field work and stress the importance of alms. It therefore makes sense that the first powerful economic and cultural infrastructures of the Christian Occident are monasteries with large territorial properties. Money is a source of sin, an object of suspicion. By the same token, this did not prevent the authorities of the Christian Church, in particular the Pope as head of the Church, from having great financial and economic power.

In the thirteenth century, the famous Dominican theologian Thomas Aquinas held the view that if work is needed for the livelihood of individuals and communities, this necessity disappears once the goal has been attained. The absolute value is that of the individual's relationship with his or her God – which, in turn, implies the correct regulation of relations between people and also the notion of an individual's responsibility towards others and the world. From the sixteenth century onwards, Protestantism, which does not recognize the authority of the Pope, liked to refer to the parable of Jesus Christ (under Calvinism in connection to the Geneva marketplace and later under Methodism, established in the United States by John Wesley): "Lord, you have given me five cents; behold, I have thus gained another five cents" (Matthew 25:20). Through work, man spiritualizes the material, including money. Therefore, work is indispensable. Enrichment, especially through commerce, is the hallmark of divine blessing. Accumulation, however, is forbidden. Profit is legitimate and the concept of putting capital at risk is allowed. Protestant societies, which are founded on trust, quickly become more powerful than Catholic societies, in which the centralized powers tend to appropriate resources for themselves. There is thus a different relationship to authority. In accordance with the social doctrine of the Catholic Church, trade and free competition were long condemned. Indeed, it was not until 1991 that Pope John Paul II finally accepted the "free market." In some cases, Calvinist Puritanism led to conformism and blockades.

The society in which the Prophet lives, and Islam develops, is a market society in a country of nomads. Field work is not remunerated. According to the Koran, whose canonical text was written in the seventh century, money in the Islamic faith is a gift from God, as everything belongs to God. Money, therefore, cannot be exchanged for itself. Man is the lineage holder of God and he is responsible before God for the riches he possesses. Individual property is desirable, and profit is legitimate. The second surah of the Quran, entitled "The Cow – Al-Baqara" – with 286 verses it is the Quran's longest – contains numerous verses dealing with economic questions, often in a very technical manner. It should be borne in mind that commercial society was already very well organized in the seventh century. Moreover, the Prophet himself married a rich female merchant and was personally active in trade. The traditions of the Prophet such as the *Sunnah* and the *hadiths*, which contributed to the consolidation of the Sharia (the "Holy Law"), privilege the life and problems of the city's inhabitants, praise commerce, specify the taxes of peasants, etc. Enrichment is permissible – it is a sign of mercy or God's blessing. One *hadith* articulates this conviction particularly well: "God, give mercy to those who are generous in their buying, generous in their selling, and generous in their business dealings." Waste and excess are forbidden, and it is important to manage wealth properly. Accumulation is prohibited because it takes money out of the economic cycle and thus reduces the growth of community resources. Surah 104 "The Slanderer – Al-Humazah" warns: "Woe to every jiber and slanderer who amasses a fortune and returns it counted. He thinks that his wealth will make him immortal. Let him be wary! Allah's fire shall strike him" (Koran 104: 1–6). Money should always be used to create real value.

The social logic rests on participatory reasoning. The concept of risk capital thus quickly became accepted, as has the concept of the effective distribution of risks and profits for the legitimacy of an income. Like the other two monotheistic world religions, Islam attaches great importance to solidarity and social justice. Sincerity and trust are a central part of the business relationship and Muslim law is contractually oriented. The Koran, for example, lays out the jurisdiction of both contracting parties and specifies that the application of the contract by means of signing it is indispensable for safeguarding the rights of the individual, along with – if necessary – the issuance of a pledge: "Believers, if you take out a loan, it must be recorded in writing … If you are traveling and have not found a notary, the issuance of a pledge must be demanded" (Koran 2:282–283). One hadith further remarks: "God is the third party of the two business partners, as long as they do not betray each other. If one betrays the other, God will forsake them."

The Islamic economy can thus be classified as a global economy, with a morality that is an application of the rules expressed in divine law and therefore covers the totality of daily actions. Revelation is directed at the true essence of man, who unites good and evil in himself. Moreover, man's fear of sanctions can and should result in the imposition of certain fixed forms of action. The divine law regulates the sociability of human beings by appealing to their intelligence and reason. It is significant that the Arabic equivalent of the word "economy" is *iqtiçâd*, which is formed from the root *qasd* and refers to the aspiration, intention, and goal, but also the correct measure, the mean, and moderation. The doctrine of the Islamic economy cannot in fact be reduced to a purely social dimension, even if Islam structures society at its foundations through an emphasis on equality and thus aims to eradicate poverty. What needs to be examined is whether "self-complacency" – *al-kifâya* – is the right middle ground concerning wealth when it comes to meeting the basic needs of the individual's daily life. With this in mind, legal alms are meant to rehabilitate the poor and the impoverished. In this way, the believer can discover his or her integration and commitment in the perfect world order: Good is harmony, evil is disharmony. In this intimate union of the spiritual and the temporal, faith appears as the cornerstone of economic life. Every "economic" act has religious significance.[1] The activity involved in all commercial transactions thus appears to be fundamental. From an etymological point of view, even the notion of justice *adl* means "equal" and "just." Several concrete examples are given: in arbitration, in custodial accounts, in the judiciary, in commercial transactions, or in testimonies. In each case, the concern is to not harm others. In this context, there is a fundamental "economic" dimension: justice in the Aristotelian sense, which is the ethical virtue par excellence.

Ethics is the science of correct behavior and, by implication, the equitable distribution of material and immaterial goods. It comprises three levels – the universal, the particular, and the individual – which standardize human behavior. The universal is the ideal, never attained level – the horizon of truth that is always sought. The particular is the level of belonging to groups or communities in which laws, guidelines, rites, and customs have been established. Finally, the level of the individual is the personal level, in which freedom and responsibility towards oneself, others, and the world are obligatory. The three levels of ethics must not be confused with each other, and every decision or human act expresses the three levels in a very different and specific way.[2] Islam now affirms the solidarity of horizontal order among all forms of creation, and this solidarity is attributed to the spiritual connection between God, everything else, and the human being. The biased disparity between rich and poor is unacceptable and the equitable sharing of risks, that is to say of gains and losses, seems entirely reasonable. In this way, Islam expresses the three levels of ethics – the universal, the particular, and the individual.

11.3 Ibn Khaldoun (1331/732–1406/808), Theorist of Commercial Activities

Ibn Khaldoun, who was born in an Andalusian family in 1332 in Tunis and died in 1406 in Cairo, is the brilliant precursor in the fourteenth century of many modern scientific disciplines such as history, economics, sociology, and geopolitics.[3] As dis-

[1] See Boisard (1979), p. 65 f.

[2] See Courcelles (2009), pp. 19–98.

[3] As the hand-made copies of Ibn Khaldoun's works were scattered throughout the Muslim world, from Fez to Istanbul, it was not until the eighteenth century that they were translated into Turkish.

ciple of the philosopher Abû Nasr al-Fârâbî (ca. 870–950), he was interested in economics. The term originates from the Greek *oikonomia*, which, when translated literally, means the "rules" – *nomoi* – of good administration of a "house" – *oikos*. Here, the latter connotes the new political-religious order and, in line with the Greek tradition, the "city." Al-Fârâbî developed a "philosophical" idea of religion by defining economic tasks of philosophical reflection in relation to theology and jurisprudence and by associating economic tasks with morality. Later, Averroes became the first Muslim philosopher, followed by Thomas Aquinas, to grasp the need to come to terms with Aristotle's *Politics*. The distinction he makes between the supernatural and the natural is roughly the same as the distinction Aristotle established between practical and theoretical wisdom.

With history as the point of departure, and focusing on the concept of civilization, Ibn Khaldoun aims to understand the laws that govern the birth, life, and death of human societies. In addition to the Koran and the Sunnah, he draws on all available sources, including Greek, Byzantine, Muslim, and Arab ones. He defines two different but complementary ways of thinking: in the humanities, the perspective of reason, since man is intelligent and rational; in religious studies, the perspective of faith, which is based on the revealed texts. This distinction is all the more remarkable because Ibn Khaldoun – to the extent that he functioned as a Malikite judge – is a recognized authority in the field of theology. In this way, he made discoveries and contributions to the epoch – which is described as modern and contemporary – with a coherence that made it possible to overcome all the limitations of time, space, and ideologies.[4]

Ibn Khaldoun emphasizes:

> The aim of history is to deal with the human population, i.e. universal civilization. It deals with the essence of this civilization, namely, the immoral life and social life – the particularisms caused by the spirit of the clans and the modalities by which one human group dominates another. This last point leads to an investigation into the emergence of power, dynasties, and social classes. Secondly, history is also interested in the lucrative professions and the different ways of earning a living – which are part of human activities and efforts – as well as in the sciences and the arts. Ultimately, it aims to understand everything that characterizes a civilization.[5]

If the lifetime of the Prophet is a privileged moment because it signifies the gift of truth, especially through the *hadiths*, it nevertheless cannot claim to have directly controlled the later epochs that function differently. There is indeed a relationship of radical difference between God and creation, which leaves room for the registers of understanding and interpretation and allows for reflection on the possibilities and impossibilities of action. Ibn Khaldoun is aware of the difficulty of his deliberation.

They were then published in the nineteenth century in Arabic, before being translated into French and Portuguese. The first Arabic edition of *Al Muqaddima*, his famous introduction to the *Reflections on World History*, was printed in Bulaq near Cairo. Ibn Khaldoun's last manuscript, which he authenticated himself and is dated 1402 – 4 years before his death – is preserved in the Atif Efendi Library in Istanbul under the reference number 1936 AE.

[4] Two works deserve to be mentioned here: Smaïl Goumeziane (2000/2006) and Salem Mekki (2006).

[5] All quotations are from the translation and edition of Monteil (1967), here: p. 69.

Al Muqaddima reproduces life in Maghreb with extraordinary detail, whether it is the working conditions in the countryside and cities, or the different professions and the regulation of markets, or the relationships between social groups, social inequities, and injustices. Ibn Khaldoun developed categories and an economic theory that make him a pioneer of political economy. Experiencing deadly battles in both Muslim and Christian kingdoms, he outlined the following definition of politics, which recalls to some degree the Aristotelian definition of economy: "Politics is the art of administering a family or city according to the demands of morality and wisdom to inspire the masses by means of a behavior conducive to the preservation of time and space."[6] Ibn Khaldoun is thus very close to the definition of sustainable growth put forward in the 1987 Bruntland Report of the United Nations. The ruler must ensure the integrity and security of persons and goods by regulating conflicts of interest; he must ensure that expenditures and revenues are being managed; he must ensure that economic and social activities are regulated by rules governing production, trade, coinage, and the circulation of funds, and that natural resources and income are distributed fairly.

In recommending the state's intervention in the organization and equitable functioning of the commercial sector, Ibn Khaldoun aligns himself with what is today called the "regulation school" (in the twentieth century, stemming from the works of Karl Marx and even more so from John Maynard Keynes than the current liberal movement inherited from Adam Smith). He states: "Power touched on absolutism and served the vanities of the century, the application of strength and the arbitrary satisfaction of desires and passions."[7]

As a prudent Malikite judge, Ibn Khaldoun emphatically condemned accumulation, as well as a destructive force like speculation, which prevents the just circulation and distribution of riches in the sense of the following well-known verse: "Announce a painful punishment to those who hoard gold and money and do not spend it in the way of God" (Koran, 9:34). Trade thus has great relevance in the life of human societies. The expansion of the commercial economy is linked to the development of laws and institutions for the purpose of political regulation. It is required, for example, to safeguard the legal value of currency and to combat all forms of fraud, particularly with regard to money, food, and medicine. "It will become necessary to determine gold pieces, monetary values, and specific weights in accordance with religious law."[8] It is also necessary to control the markets and the organization of points of sale and professions: "The regulation of markets (*hisba*) is also a religious duty. It is a religious duty belonging to the guidelines of the good and the prohibition of evil."[9] The administrator of the markets appointed by the ruler, the *muhtasib*, must be both someone who ensures that the ethical principles of the Quran are observed and a competent expert on economic processes. According to Ibn Khaldoun, it is also desirable to fix prices. However, the Prophet and the

[6] Ibid., p.75.

[7] Ibid., p. 411.

[8] Ibid., p. 411.

[9] Ibid., p. 350.

jurists spoke out against such price fixing. Islam assigns it to the responsibility of the traders, who must know that their deeds are rewarded or punished in the hereafter, and it also preaches freedom.[10] Due to the interest in rates of return, the jurists restrict freedom by exploiting the weak. The ruler, who sets the prices of grain in times of need, hinders any speculation and preserves social peace. Ibn Khaldoun observes that without any kind of general regulation, everyone would try to exploit the weak.

The deregulation of the commercial economy generates an ever-increasing demand for luxury, waste, and the accumulation of wealth. It further entails the domination of minorities who have enriched themselves at the expense of the impoverished majority – at the risk, though, of disrupting society as a whole and destroying the very foundations of human civilization.

> You can see the increase in immorality, viciousness, lies, and deceit ... You start thinking of nothing more than making money and no longer look at the choice of means to do it. You see many people lying, deceiving, swindling, defrauding cheating, stealing, perjuring, practicing usury ... If there are many instances of such behavior, God then decides to destroy the nation or the city.[11]

Concerned with market regulation, Ibn Khaldoun continues:

> If blatant harms are inflicted to the home life, women, lives, people, and the dignity of individuals, this will lead to sudden disintegration, to ruin, to the rapid destruction of the dynasty due to the unavoidable unrest caused by injustice.[12]

By criticizing the private appropriation of wealth, Ibn Khaldoun is very much opposed to the trafficking activities of the rulers and their clans, as well as to the politicians who cannot help but cause the suffering of the people and the downfall of the economy. Ibn Khaldoun's clairvoyance already foretold the analyses of Amy Chua's work *World in Fire* or Hervé Kempf's *Comment les riches détruisent la planète* six centuries in advance.[13]

Ibn Khaldoun is convinced of the predominant role of cities in economic prosperity and, more generally speaking, in the flourishing of human civilization. When a city is being built, it must be ensured that it has water, arable land and pastures for livestock, forests, communication channels such as the sea or a river and, above all, clean air. It is indeed favorable conditions at the outset that are responsible for making certain that human beings can develop a fair and balanced exchange of ideas, and one that is based on solidarity and sustainability. Ibn Khaldoun laments that there are no major cities in Maghreb.

However, Ibn Khaldoun hardly addressed the question of usury regarding loan interest rates, not least because he repeatedly appealed to the prohibition in the Koran and criticized the accumulation of money by the powerful. An *ijtihad*, as

---

[10] See Souissi (1976).

[11] Monteil (1967), p. 765.

[12] Ibn Khaldoun, ibid (1967), p. 591.

[13] Amy Chua is a professor of law at Yale University: Chua (2007): Hervé Kempf is a journalist who specializes in environmental issues: Kempf (2007).

implemented by the Protestants in Geneva in the sixteenth century, would have made it possible in this area to define a legal limit on interest rates. This, consequently, would have allowed for the financing of productive risk activities by Muslim traders and investment in production and its improvement, thereby ultimately reducing the usurious activities of non-Muslims in the Muslim countries. The absence of an autonomous religious power in the Maghreb of his time – that of the jurists in line with the Malikite tradition – made it impossible to pursue the *ijtihad.* Specifically, it undermined the effort to understand and adapt some of the principles of Islam to his time, as the Prophet himself did in his own time. But as a Malikite judge who juxtaposes his observations with the legal texts and scientific rationality, this is exactly what Ibn Khaldoun would have liked to do.

The human being is at the center of Ibn Khaldoun's economic deliberations. Because man primarily strives to nourish himself, solidarity and cooperation are indispensable for him. Work is the basic economic category, the value par excellence, the source of real wealth. It leaves no room for speculation or chance. He writes: "The work of man, the aspect of profit and unfounded advantage."[14] A large population, with the diversification and the cooperation of its activities, is a factor for wealth and social peace. This theory of Ibn Khaldoun again pronounces the *division of social work*[15] later developed by sociologist Emile Durkheim (1858–1917): "Civilization, its welfare and public prosperity depend on the productivity and commitment of the people; in every direction, in their own interest, and for their own profit."[16] Work is only productive if it is based on private property. The individual interest that drives one's own motivation is linked to the collective efforts that serve the general interest. Ibn Khaldoun views have parallels to Adam Smith: "Initially, work served to satisfy needs; now it serves luxury and wealth."[17] "The human spirit does not stop perfecting all the arts, from the simple to the complex, from theory to practice, via the successive discovery of one thing after another, all the way to perfection. It takes time and several generations, especially in the technical field.[18] The education system that produces the intelligence is an important, highly productive component of the economy. Ibn Khaldoun stresses the importance of libraries and bookshops.

Politics, the economy, and ethics are interwoven. Ibn Khaldoun is particularly attentive to injustices affecting the productive social categories, which are now considered human rights. For example, while he closely considers the tax system, whose origins lie in the Quran, he also deplores the multiplication and increase of

---

[14] Monteil (1967), p. 799.

[15] This is the title of Emile Durkheim's dissertation, which he defended in 1893 during his thesis defense.

[16] Monteil (1967), p. 584.

[17] Ibid., p. 572.

[18] Ibid., p. 630.

taxes, which primarily affect the urban population and merchants, rather than the nomads. The application of such a system ultimately frustrates the people and causes "a general drop in national income."[19] "The lesson from history is that injustice ruins the population and thus also the dynasties ..."[20] The ethical and regulatory role of those who govern and set an example is therefore fundamental. Ibn Khaldoun enthusiastically quotes the letter from Tahir Ben Al Hussain, general of the Caliph Al Mamun, to his son Abdallah, who was appointed governor of a province of Egypt. One reads, for example:

> Be frugal in every respect ... Do not waste ... Regularly seek out jurists and people with life experience and wisdom ... Just decisions, justice before the courts and in any other matter, the right management of markets, generosity – all this contributes to the well-being of the citizens ... Stay away from any kind of corruption ... You should apportion the taxes fairly ...[21]

The ethics of merchants are crucial in a market economy. It is the merchants who, through their intelligence, integrity and generosity, can contribute to a balance of prices and the sharing of losses and profits in such a way that the rich and poor can nourish themselves[22]: "It is in the general interest to maintain low prices, especially for grains – even if this is to the detriment of trade. This is thc merchants' responsibility.

And that is why Ibn Khaldun, in the series with Al-Fârâbî, recommends the autonomy of the human mind and testing philosophy for the structuring of an economy in which goods are divided fairly. At issue here is not a virtuous, ideal city in the sense of the Platonic doctrine, but a real city, a human and Muslim city with the southern rivers of the Mediterranean – his Maghreb, which is at the same time a city that opens itself up to difference in an ideal way and is a commercial city. It is precisely on the basis of this real city that he wants to synthesize his reflections and criticism.

Is *Al Muqaddima* not, in a manner of speaking, the adumbration of the Enlightenment's *Encyclopédie*, which was published between 1751 and 1772 and whose exact title is *Dictionnaire raisonné des sciences des arts et des métiers*? Philosophers or scientists must be open to the world and it is sensitivity that can lead to the generally intelligible. Human laws are indispensable for regulating society in terms of a higher justice. It is thus also the case for Ibn Khaldoun that history and economic life are only conceivable in the form of a radical break with the divine origin of mankind, even if ethics remains informed by the principles of religion.

[19] Ibid., p. 436.

[20] Ibid., p. 448.

[21] Ibid., p. 617–631.

[22] Ibid., p. 627.

11.4 The Islamic Economy: Some Effects of the Ban on Credit for Commercial Activities

It is instructive to consider the ban of the three monotheistic world religions at their founding on lending in the context of the severe economic crisis of 2008. This prohibition, which today only Islam adheres to, is part of the theological logic of monotheism. It also entails a collection of important implications that are both spiritual and technical in nature. New financial forms inspired by the ethical principles of Islam can in fact help to regulate commercial activities, especially the fundamental issue of risk, loss, and profit sharing.

The Islamic approach of secondary negative effects of the market does not consist in rejecting the whole market mechanism as communism does. And unlike the proponents of traditional capitalism, it does not expect the market to somehow solve its own problems. The *Sharia,*[23] Islamic law based on the Quran and the Sunnah, refers to a highly dynamic image: that of a "wave" which leads to a source and from which one will be able to drink. One's understanding of this must be renewed and its actual meanings must be rediscovered. The Muslim exegetes define it as the "way of salvation," a "source or reservoir of meaning and values."[24] Eric Geoffroy notes: "The Sharia contains more than just a catalog of rules and prohibitions, but also intellectual principles that determine the adequate knowledge and practical modalities for achieving man's "noble traits."[25] The term *sharia* not only applies to Muslims; it refers to all "religious paths" of humanity. For this reason, the Islamic "economy" is closely tied to the cosmic order. *Sharia*, even in the legislative sense, is fully adaptable. By aiming to secure and preserve the faith, life, intelligence, offspring, and goods, *Sharia* cares for the free public interest or, indeterminately, *al-maslaha al-moursala.* In relation to the latter, there is no explicit text in the Quran or the Sunnah, but it nonetheless implies ethical creativity.[26] The *Sharia*'s recommendations proscribe the obtaining or charging of interest, since the application of interest transfers all the risks associated with a project to a single debtor. They also prohibit transactions that are separate from the real economy or serve purely speculative purposes, which in turn implies that any kind of financial transaction is to be based on tangible capital. They further prohibit investment in immoral activities such as those involving tobacco, alcohol, pornography, gambling, or weapons. Thus, the Islamic "economy" is a real economy centered on the well-being of persons, society, and the world itself.[27]

---

[23] With reference to the spelling *charia* or *chari'a*, which is often used in the French-speaking world, I have decided here to adopt the spelling *sharia*, which is also used e.g. by Mohammed Arkoun or Eric Geoffroy.

[24] Ferjani (2005), p. 73.

[25] Eric Geoffroy (2009), p. 148.

[26] Wahhâb (Al-) Khallâf (1997), pp. 119–122.

[27] I would like to take this opportunity to refer to the concluding statement of my article "L' entreprise et la quête de sens, au risque du monde: comment faire monde comun" (2012), pp. 9–14.

Under these conditions, the so-called Islamic financial economy is particularly well suited to accompany commercial activities. It not only allows economic entities to satisfy their financial needs in accordance with the Muslim religion,[28] but it also regulates their risks and protects the individual parties involved. While Islamic banks must control the process of saving and risk investment, they must at the same time remain faithful to certain principles[29] such as the prohibition on interest or *riba*, the supreme principle of the Islamic economy.[30] According to the Muslim religion, no one may use a method that yields profit without being exposed themselves to certain risks of loss. It is necessary to take a risk in order to make a profit; this is the point of departure for the principle of sharing losses and profits. Loan interest rates or usury have been subject to various forms of regulation throughout history. The interest rate, or *riba*, is a mechanism for the exponential growth of debt and represents an unrealistic self-replication of wealth. People cannot live on the interest of their mutual debt. Even if everyone decides to hoard something, the economy will collapse. An economy thrives on trade, but it cannot live on the interest of mutual debt. The system of interest rates is therefore unsustainable. Bankruptcy, recessions, and currency devaluation are natural reactions to regulate the imbalance of the system. That said, they constitute considerable risks for human beings. The capitalist economic systems thus have a natural tendency toward "financial fragility" – toward crises and collapses caused by increased debt levels. Debt increases are a cause of concern for all industrialized countries. An economy which invokes Islam necessarily sees a loan as a non-lucrative means: It is intended to help the beneficiary generate commerce, without however any income for the donor. In this way, loans allocated to the poorest will improve their welfare, without unduly reducing productivity. Through prohibiting interest on loans and limiting the time value of trade, the debt in an Islamic financial economy is automatically curtailed by the creation of wealth. Debt is the means to build up wealth rather than to destroy it. The prohibition of *riba* and *zakat* as a measure against accumulation follows the same logic:

- The prohibition of *israf*, excessive and unproductive waste, is a moral yardstick. This regulation directs the surplus of wealth towards the non-lucrative philanthropic sector, where wealth is redistributed to the poorest people.
- Money cannot be assigned its own value. It is a powerful asset, which needs to be linked to another source to produce a productive effect. This is where the principle of "asset-backing" comes from. Financial transactions must have a direct connection to the real economy (e.g. the prohibition on opening a line of credit). The money is thus channeled for the benefit of the real economy and not for that of pure finance. Speculation is forbidden.

---

[28] For further details, I refer here to an informative study by Sami Al-Suwailem, "Tenets of the Islamic Economic System" (2009).

[29] According to estimates by the ISFL based on "The Banker, Ernst & Young" at the end of 2008, Islamic commercial banks dominate the Islamic finance market at 73%.

[30] Even in ancient Greece, Aristotle wrote that "money doesn't create more money" and thus dismissed the role of interest. The occidental approach distinguishes "wear and tear" from "interest."

- The prohibition on investing in certain areas that are well defined by religion such as alcohol, pork, pornography, etc.
- The prohibition on excessive uncertainty or *gharar*, accompanied by the manipulation of information and corruption. This is the guarantee of transparency and justness and fairness in financial transactions. Hedging and gambling activities are therefore not permitted. Originally, *gharar* was a zero-sum game with an uncertain profit. It is commonly known that a zero-sum game does not create wealth – it merely transfers the riches from one side (the loser) to the other (the winner). Since the zero-sum game is a game where two parties are in direct conflict with each other, *gharar* violates the principle of fraternity described in the Koran (4:91), as well as *maysir* and as *riba*. *Gharar* can be seen as a commercial risk, detached from real wealth; *riba* can be seen as a trade of time, detached from the creation of wealth. But now risk and time are interwoven. *Gharar* and *riba* are thus joined together and consequently forbidden.

The financing offered by Islamic banks for economic activities is thus especially secure. There should be no risks. A distinction is made as follows:

- *murabaha* (mark-up financing): This is the most frequently practiced form of financing. The term refers to commercial operations. It is a purchase agreement on a cost-plus price by means of a previously agreed-to profit margin, which cannot be verified with respect to gains in the event of a late payment or misconduct. Now, however, the purchase and resale of goods by the bank must be real and not fictitious. In fact, the bank's profit margin is justified by the commercial part of the transaction, not by the financial part.
- *musharaka* (joint-venture profit sharing): This is a participatory technique in the capital of an existing company or a company that is yet to be founded. It involves a merger between the bank and its client. It is an active partnership. The bank and the client jointly contribute to the financing of the project. As a result, the profits and losses are allocated according to the respective capital contributions.
- *mudaraba* (trust profit sharing): This is a type of financing in which an Islamic bank contributes the entirety of funds in the form of monies or capital investments and the partner-client ensures the management of these funds. This union of capital and labor is a passive partnership. The proceeds are distributed according to the percentage agreed to in advance. The bank supports any losses and the client only loses the value of the work brought in. In case of misconduct or negligence on the part of the entrepreneur, the loss must be borne by both parties.
- *quard hassan* (interest free loan): This is a completely "free" loan, as the bank only covers the borrowed capital. In general, only reliable customers are designated, such as smaller producers.
- *ijara* (leasing) or *ijara wa iktina*: According to this process, the bank acquires land, equipment, residential buildings, and means of transport and rents them out to its customers on the basis of a fixed sum agreed to in advance and determined for a certain period of time. In the case of *ijara wa iktina*, the amounts paid for renting are paid into an investment account, which in turn contributes to the purchase of new borrowed goods.

- *istisn'a*: This technique allows the bank to serve its clients with the help of a specialized subcontractor. For example, the bank may participate in the construction of housing and award the contract for the construction to a specialized firm.
- *bai salam* (post-delivery sale): This is a purchase contract for goods with delayed delivery. It is mainly used in the area of financing agriculture. Its advantage is that it enables the customer to dispose of cash.
- Investments and equipment: They are used in the real estate markets, trade in goods and services, and the financial market, especially in the sukuk market, whether for the bank's own account or for the account of clients.
- Social financing is linked to the allocation of *zakat* funds, which are applied to the bank's own funds or to custodial accounts by means of instructions from the customer. They are allocated to people as required.

The various types of financing offered by banks to contemporary traders can be classified as co-sharing finance thanks to *mudaraba* and *musharaka*, which account for about 11% and 12% of the capital of Islamic banks. They can also be subdivided into sales financing such as *murabaha, bai salam, istisn'a* and lease financing thanks to *ijara* and *ijara wa iktina*. In addition, other forms of financing are based on the social and human principle, such as those linked to the *waqf*[31] or those associated with the allocation of *zakat*[32] funds.

In this vein, Islam can make a fundamental contribution to the regulation of trade activities, the intellectual and ethical education of merchants, and thus to their responsibility in a globalized world where the trading economy dominates. With the founding texts of Islamic finance, starting with such a profound and contemporary thinker as Ibn Khaldoun, Islam shows that the sharing of risks in the field of commercial activities by fundamentally prohibiting interest is a precondition of respect for human dignity and access to a shared physical, moral, and social well-being.

---

[31] *Waqf*, a good made of velvet gloves or religious foundations, could play an important role in projects of sustainable development, e. g. for hospitals, schools, or various infrastructures; this immobilization of a good allows for the continuous reproduction of a donation. This example could also be generalized for all cultures and religions.

[32] *Zakat* is a system of moral transmission that helps eliminate the concentration of wealth; it is the third pillar of Islam. The *Koran* contains over 80 verses dealing with *zakat*. This charity is regarded as the right of the poor to remove the surplus from the wealthiest. The duty of *zakat* strengthens social relations and economic efficiency. Currently, the regulation of *zakat* is being developed and is not comparable in all Muslim countries. There are two types of *zakat*: *zakat al-Fitr* is distributed after Lent by Aid al-Fitr, the feast at the end of Ramadan; and *zakat al-mâl* is the legal alms-giving of goods, corresponding each year to the sum that has not moved on an account; it is a minimum taxable amount. *Zakat* is obligatory for Muslims, but there are two problems: On the one hand, there are people, often the richest, who try to evade this responsibility; on the other hand, the ultimate aim of the collected funds is far from transparent. Islamic banks can thus be persuaded to play a regulatory role. See http://www.sajidine.com/les-piliers-de-lislam/zakat_questions/seuil_zakat.htm, last accessed: January 29, 2016.

Literature

Boisard, Marcel. 1979. *L'humanisme de l'islam*. Paris: Albin Michel.

Chua, Amy. 2007. *Le monde en feu – Violences sociales et mondialisation*. Paris: Seuil.

de Courcelles, Dominique. 2009. *Globale diversité: pour une approche multiculturelle du management*. Paris: Presses de l'École Polytechnique. Translation from Arabic, Riyad: King Saud University Press, 2011.

———. 2012. L'entreprise et la quête de sens, au risque du monde: comment faire monde comun. *Les Cahiers de Friedland: Redonner du sens dans l'Entreprise pour Sortir de la Crise* 9: 9–14.

Ferjani, Mohamed-Chérif. 2005. *Le Politique et le religieux dans le champ islamique*. Paris: Fayard.

Geoffroy, Eric. 2009. *L'islam sera spirituel ou ne sera plus*. Paris: Seuil.

Goumeziane, Smaïl. 2000. *Ibn Khaldoun (1332–1406). Un génie maghrébien*. Alger: EDIF. (Paris, 2006).

Kempf, Hervé. 2007. *Comment les riches détruisent la planète*. Paris: Seuil.

Mekki, Salem. 2006. *Faits et pensées économiques dans la Muqaddima d'Ibn Khaldoun*. Tunis: Union des écrivains tunisiens.

Monteil, Vincent, hrsg. 1967. Ibn Khaldoun. Discours sur l'histoire universelle Al-Muqaddima. Übers. Vincent Monteil. Beirut: Commission internationale pour la traduction des chefs d'œuvre.

Souissi, Najet Bacha. 1976. Le commerce au Maghreb du 4ème au 8ème siècle de l'hégire, Tunis: Publications de l'Université Tunisienne. http://www.sajidine.com/les-piliers-de-lislam/zakat_questions/seuil_zakat.htm. Accessed: 29 Jan 2016.

Suwailem (Al-), Sami. 2010. Tenets of the Islamic economic system. *Encyclopedia of Islamic Economics* 2: 235–245. French translation: 2011. Principes du système économique islamique. *Etudes en Economie Islamique* 5/1.

Wahhâb (Al-) Khallâf, Abd. 1997. *Les fondements du droit musulman*. Paris: Ed. Al-Qalam.

Chapter 12
The Most Successful and Moralistic Merchant at the Dawn of Japanese Capitalism. Shibusawa and His Confucianism

Itaru Shimazu

Abstract Ei-ichi Shibusawa contributed greatly to modernizing Japan, mainly as the president of the First Bank of Japan. But he was also a zealous preacher of Confucian ethics. The main question which my essay tries to answer is whether Shibusawa's Confucianism explains his success as a businessman. My answer is rather negative. His success was more due to his unique career started as a son of a rich farmer, the influence of Saint-Simon school which he was exposed to while sent to Paris International Exposition and his experience and connections he acquired in working as a leading bureaucrat in early days of Japan's nation-building. It is often the case that the reason of one's success given by oneself is not always for others to trust.

Ei-ich Shibusawa, 1840–1931, might be the most interesting man among Japanese leaders who contributed in shaping Modern Japan in late nineteenth century. He was unique in being business minded, tendency rarely found in his contemporary leaders who were, in a sense, politico-military maniacs. He believed that Confucian morality and business can go along well with each other and his favorite catchword in later years was '*Ron-go* (Since I do not know how Westerners pronounce Chinese names and books, let me put them in Japanese pronunciation or in my translation into English hereafter.) (Confucian Bible) and abacus!'

12.1 Brief Career

In the 2nd year after the Meiji Restoration he, at the age of 30, was hired by newly established Japanese government and remained there only for 5 years. But during these years, 1869–1873, he blueprinted modern money, finance and tax systems and

I. Shimazu (✉)
Dokkyo University, Soka, Japan
e-mail: hag00235@nifty.com

C. Lütge, C. Strosetzki (eds.), *The Honorable Merchant – Between Modesty and Risk-Taking*, Ethical Economy 56, https://doi.org/10.1007/978-3-030-04351-3_12

prepared complete reformation of feudalism to abolish *Daimyo*, or feudal lords,[1] once and for all. His position was not ranked at the top to give direct political decisions, but he chaired the cross ministry idea-exchanging committee with all leaders and high bureaucrats leading decisions at each ministry, and back in the Ministry of Finance, worked out detailed plans to implement them. He was a superbly efficient bureaucrat.

It is amazing that the revolutionary change during and after the Meiji Restoration was completed with minimal bloodshed. As the result, warriors, the ruling class, were gone as a whole. Small wars were fought within warriors while inter-class clashes were seldom. But warriors, including the winners, could not survive as a distinguished class, since the class distinction of warriors, farmers, artisans and tradesmen could not sustain itself through the great social change, though egalitarian motives were not among the dominant causes for the political instability which resulted in the extinction of classes. The biggest concern of the time was rather the pressure from Western colonialism. The greatest contributor to the comparatively peaceful revolution, I believe, was Yoshinobu Tokugawa, the last *Shogun*, who voluntarily 'returned' his reign to the Emperor even before local wars were fought. It would have been a civil war if he had used all power he had and resisted the Restoration, i.e. that of power by the Emperor.

During the years of 1864–1869, Shibusawa was hired by Yoshinobu who became *Shogun* in 1866. In 1867 Japanese delegates were sent to Paris International Exposition, accepting the invitation by Napoleon III, who was trying to rival British colonialism in Far East. Fourteen-year-old Akitake Tokugawa, Yoshinobu's brother, was officially leading the delegates and Shibusawa was among them as a low ranked clerk who was in charge of finance, something which proud warriors should care less. Although it was planned that Akitake would stay long enough to get meaningful education in France, outbreak of the Restoration made the plan impossible and Akitake Tokugawa and Shibusawa had no choice but to trip back to Japan in 1868 right after the Restoration, to see a new world there.

All biographers agree that Shibusawa's experience of Europe made his later great achievements possible. But one of them who is knowledgeable in French literature, Shigeru Kashima, proposes an interesting hypothesis that indirect influence of Saint-Simon school was decisive.[2] We might say that considerable portion of Napoleon III's socio-economic policy including the very idea of international exposition was Saint-Simonian. Considering the fact that at the center of Shibusawa's economic successes were stock companies, banks and transportation industry, i.e. railways and shipping, this hypothesis is very plausible.

Even when he was a governmental official working hard in shaping modernized Japan, he was more interested in doing business than bureaucracy or politics. His motive seems to have been to contribute to the radical social change through business, or to bring about Capitalism in Japan, rather than to make money of his own.

---

[1] Former feudal lords received nominal status as new aristocrats but lost all power.

[2] *Shibusawa Ei-ichi*, vol. 1 and 2, 2013(in Japanese), esp. vol. 1, Chap 2: Grasping the Essence of Western Civilization in Paris.

In the era when people respected public officials while tradesmen were placed at the bottom of class scale and despised, Shibusawa's occupational preference was very exceptional especially if it had little to do with his pecuniary concern.

In 1873 he resigned from the governmental position, which could have led to Minister of Finance, and entered the world of business. By 1916 when he announced his retirement from business scene, hundreds of companies were established by him or with his help. Another biographer says that the number of companies for which Shibusawa officially became an executive or audit etc. was 178.[3] And many of them are still Japanese leading companies at present.

During the time when Shibusawa was busy in economic activities several *zaibatsu*, or combines, grew to be main actors of Japanese economy; Mitsui, Mitsubishi, Yasuda, etc. They were usually owned by and inherited within each family. But Shibusawa was generally free from such desire for private wealth. He tried to make the companies financially open to the public or wide range of investors. Utilizing systems of stock company and bank, he let hoarded money stream to make new economic potentials real.

As a result he had become rich enough. But that was not his first motive. He thought that such activity was both necessary for Japanese modernization and difficult to be achieved by government. And considering his career and experiences, he thought, he was in a good position to lead the future growth in business field. Because he was very confident of himself in contributing in business to enrich the society, he resigned governmental position. But his move was difficult for his colleagues to understand. Since they were not yet free from older value standard in which government work is more respectable than farming and farming than artisanship or trade.

Shibusawa's retirement from business did not mean end of his social activities. In his long remaining years, he concentrated in education, social welfare, labor problem etc. until he died at 92 in 1931. Toward last days of his life, Japan-U.S. relation deteriorated. Both countries strengthened influence in Pacific Ocean and Far East. Anti-Japanese immigration acts were made in the U.S. which culminated in 1924 Federal Immigration Act banning any immigrant from Japan. It is still unsolved question of history if the Pacific War between Japan and U. S. could have been avoided. Anyway he tried his best in mitigating the hatred between the two nations through nongovernmental route by organizing visits and invitations of business leaders of both sides of the ocean.

12.2 Confucian Background

Shibusawa was born in a family of rich farmer. His father was successful in trading indigo while his uncle was even richer by dealing with indigo and silk. Rice was money in Edo Period, with which warriors were paid and farmers were taxed. So the more rice you grow the heavier the tax will be. But commodities like indigo and silk

[3] Masakazu Shimada, *Shibusawa Ei-ichi; a Pioneer Social Entrepreneur*, 2011 (in Japanese), 57.

was not efficiently taxed, although there were sporadic requests upon very rich farmers for virtually inescapable 'contributions' to the feudal lord. His father was not only wealthy but also well learned and initiated Ei-ich in *Ron-go*-reading. When Ei-ich had mastered elementary course, he started to learn further course of Confucianism under his cousin Atsutada (pen name: Aiko) Odaka, a locally famous Confucian. Ei-ich was brilliant and for all of his life he kept reading Confucian books.

Shibusawa published considerable number of books concerning practical ethics. In Edo Period learned man meant, especially among warriors, man of Confucian education. Ability to read Chinese language was at the core and *Ron-go* was one of the first books to start Chinese with. For Shibusawa, similarly, ethics meant that of Confucianism. He firmly stuck to it for his life. When he wrote or spoke about it, his attitude, we can say, was not 'detached' but filled with pragmatic concern. In the book, *Ron-go and Abacus*, his speeches are collected which were given mainly to the young, sometimes in colleges and high schools he had established. In speeches he talked about many contemporary issues quoting freely from Confucian literature. His message there was that men and women must be more ethical and then many problems, political, economic and social, can be solved and Japan will be a better place for people.

Probably the most interesting book he wrote, other than the fascinating autobiography, was *Lectures on Ron-go* which originally came in five volumes.[4] There he shows his wide and precise knowledge of Confucian literature and, while interpreting each teaching in his way, he talks about many relevant experiences from his long life. At the beginning of this book he is criticizing famous Confucian thinkers of Tokugawa era as being too theoretical and remote from daily life problems. Time to time he gives sharp critique to Confucius, for example about Confucius's negative attitude towards women.[5]

Reading these works I am almost tempted to say that Shibusawa was more a Confucian than a businessman. His main concern was always politics in a wider sense or welfare of the people as was the case with ancient Confucians and Confucius himself. And since Shibusawa believed that he could contribute most effectively to that goal by working in business, he chose to be a businessman. Confucian ethics was, saying at the least, deep at his heart and was not superficial decoration of a successful and wealthy businessman.

[4]As an extract from it put in present Japanese style, see Atsushi Moriya ed., *Shibusawa Ei-ichi's Lectures on Ron-go,* 2010.

[5]Shibusawa contributed in establishing Japan Women's University in 1901 and a half year before his death he became its president. Although Confucius's teaching shown in *Ron-go* is "Women and virtue-less men are difficult to rear" and Shibusawa supported separate education for women, he insisted that women's universities must give top level education equal to men's universities. See Kashima (note 3), 228–241.

12.3 Some Theoretical Considerations

12.3.1 Consequentialism?

Confucianism is a morality of human relation. Four different virtues (loyalty, filial piety, brother-love and trust) apply to four different types of human relation. In each case both parties of the relation are to act in good manner to respect each other accordingly. An ideal of harmonious society is described here in which people behave in good manners specified by their social positions. Different position requires different manner. This ethics, I can say, is not very egalitarian but mutual or reciprocal.

The vision of harmonious society Confucian ethics describes can work in one way as the goal of politics in general, or a monarch and it, in the other way, gives each individual moral ideal in daily life. When people believe in this, it is natural that people think those who abide by it are better than those who do not; the former are respected and the latter despised.

It, I believe, is human nature to love respect and to hate contempt though what is respected or despised change from culture to culture, from religion to religion. Once the moral circumstance has been set by a dominant belief, say Confucianism, people, while internalizing it, will become enthusiastic about behaving in a manner endorsed by it. The good consequences which were pointed out in rationally recommending Confucianism could become of secondary importance. People embrace it because of honor, external or internalized, or just because it is 'right' and not because that gives them some material benefit. As we know well, one could exchange even one's life for honor. In case of Confucianism, moral perfection of one's personality is the goal. It sometimes does not make sense here to ask what is that for, because that goal is of intrinsic value to be pursued for its own sake.

Shibusawa is pointing out repeatedly that Confucian ethics will bring about peaceful and harmonious society answering the question why it is good. He was active in the effort to mitigate labor relations too on such logic. If we understand his word to mean that peaceful society is the only reason for following Confucian ethics, Confucianism will be nothing but a means to achieve some goal. But I do not think he meant it.[6] If something is 'right' ('just' or 'true' as well) there must be many ways to prove it. And it is only a part of those ways that we can expect from it good social consequences, without mentioning good personal consequences. So believers of Confucianism can maintain their belief when Confucian behavior seemed to have brought them bad personal consequence. Martyrdom must be possible not only in Judaism, Christianity or Islam though that is of course a matter of degrees. Accordingly there must be a variation within Confucianism; a spectrum spreading from rationalistic consequentialism to religious fanaticism. My impression is that Shibusawa's version was, in spite of his apparent rationality, more to the latter.

---

[6] In one of the lectures in *Ron-go and Abacus* he is showing his deep antipathy against what he understood as utilitarianism. It seems that he took utilitarianism as open recognition of the pursuit of private interest with no consideration of its public cost. See Nobuyuki Kaji ed. 2008 (originally 1927), 264–267 'Extirpate Evil Science of Utility' (in Japanese).

12.3.2 Profit and Social Contribution

In Shibusawa's biography Kashima is also commenting on an industrialist's praise on Shibusawa's personality that can be taken as a criticism.[7] Souichiro Asano, founder of Asano Cement Corporation, made his fortune from scratch by Shibusawa's support. While expressing his admiration for the greedless manner of Shibusawa's decisions, he complained that with Shibusawa's cooperation both could have gained much more profit than they really did. The cases he pointed out were all concerned with disposal of governmental assets. But let me discuss in abstract terms without getting into the details.

Textbooks of Law and Economics tell us that when we talk about social wealth, say in Richard Posner's sense, we could ignore who gains by the transaction. If either side of the transaction gains more than what the other side loses, there will be, *ex hypothesi*, social gain, or 'bigger pie'. But in reality, as a businessman one should care how to profit oneself, not others. Otherwise you will lose in competition. But if the game is zero-sum, effort to profit oneself does not produce social gain but only cause others' loss, without mentioning that the effort itself will add to sheer loss, individual and social. In negative sum game, like exchange of vengeances, all participants may lose.

So in the case in which desire to profit oneself leads to social loss, some morality like Confucianism may work. Since consideration to others and social harmony are required as ethical norms, unmitigated pursuit for individualistic interest will be controlled.

But how about the cases where innovative activity of one actor causes loss of others while bringing about net gain to society? Any innovation in the market will betray some expectation of others expelling older ways of production or consumption. As economists tell us, such results are realized usually by strong desire for personal profit. For Asano, who complained about Shibusawa's indifference for personal profit potential, who to win the profit is most important. He even admits that it is his greed that makes him complain. But since Bernard Mandeville, 'private vice is public good' is in our arsenal of social science. Saying the least, one's motivation to do some economic activity and what results from it are two different things. Imagine how the world would be if greed is banned totally. Maybe we need some rules that prohibit destructive display of greed while condoning productive exhibit of it. Shibusawa, as a Confucian, was more a good public agent than a clever merchant, who belonged to a different kind to the eyes of competing actor of the market game like Asano.

As was described above, Shibusawa's career was very extraordinary. Starting from anti-Tokugawa radical, he spent one and a half year in Europe with his keen eyes open, acquired Saint-Simonian view of financing big enterprises, designed and implemented new systems of money, finance and banking to feudalistic Japan in a few years, and left the government. It is no wonder that Mitsui group, the biggest

---

[7] Kashima (note 3) vol.2, 330–341.

capital then and on in Japan, tried in vain to acquire him as their leader. They were afraid to have too strong an enemy. Possibly he was the best potential manager for any big company at the time. That, but not his Confucianism, made him most qualified as the president of the First National Bank of Japan. So, his success in business, I believe, had little to do with his Confucianism. But his Confucian detachment from personal interest gave him a unique position in business world, where a person free from greed is hard to find. He became the president of First National Bank of Japan and worked for many years as the leader of Japanese businessmen. His Confucianism made him a good leader; honest, trustable, humble, well-meaning, faithful to friends, etc. But it is rather his extraordinary talent and experience combined which were really rare or almost unique in Japan at his time than his Confucianism that made him such a successful merchant. By the way his wide web of personal connections with major politicians and businessmen, acquired as a super public servant and later, was also an important source of his influence. And Confucianism, as an ethics of good personal relation, might have worked to this extent positively for his success.

12.3.3 Confucian Twist

Can Confucianism and modernity go along well, as Shibusawa expected? There are apparent differences between Confucian aspiration and what is understood as principles of modern society. The most conspicuous is that while the former tends to be personal the latter is required to be impersonal. The former is predominantly ethics of intimate relation but the latter is mainly rules of 'Great Society' in Adam Smith's sense. As was emphasized by F. A. Hayek repeatedly quoting Smith, standard human relations in modern society are those of strangers.[8] In train terminals of a big city hundreds of thousand people pass by every day, and in department stores great variety of commodities are sold at any moment to anonymous customers. And main virtue there is justice, the goddess of which usually comes with blinder over her eyes, symbolizing the feature that irrelevant differences must be ignored in justice; equality and fairness are the priority and special treatments are to prevent as favoritism.

Reflecting the society in which Confucius lived, his ethics is focusing on intimate relations in a hierarchical society. In such a society where only ruling class can learn from books, as was the case until sometime in premodern Japan or Korea, the teaching of following content can be self-intoxication; people who have upper hand are not only learned but also 'ethical' because they have learned Confucianism. And the fact that only they are ethical gives them the source of their pride and status of ruling class.

[8] *Law, Legislation and Liberty vol.2 The Mirage of Social Justice*, 112–113, 'Though not a single economy, the Great Society is still held together mainly by what vulgarly called economic relations'.

Ei-ichi Shibusawa started as a farmer's son, but his family was exceptionally rich. And Ei-ich was a diligent learned youth. A turning point came when he was humiliated by a low rank worrier-bureaucrat coercing his father to voluntarily contribute some big money to the feudal lord. It was obvious that Shibusawa was much more learned than the worrier but because of class system he could not resist the unethical coercion by an unlearned worrier. As Shibusawa explained tens of years later, that was the experience that led him to be a radical revolutionary. Though his group's plan of violent revolution was fortunately miscarried, in my analysis, he tried to counter the class society by making the lower classes learned enough. Not only worriers but farmers, artisans and merchants also must learn Confucianism. After Shibusawa experienced Europe his view of modern Japan changed extensively and he had become a bit Saint-Simonian, but his focus on Confucianism remained for his life.

But I am suspicious if the teaching of Confucianism could go till the end with modernization. It might be the case that Confucianism could at best produce 'crony capitalism'.

At the same time societies, premodern or modern, cannot be run without intimate human relations. Caring is as important feature as 'justice' for a good society. And in the context of the limited sphere of intimacy, something like Confucian ethics should make sense because it tells us how to be nice to each other while considering the different position each of us is put on. But in a modern society we should learn to apply different ethics to the public and the private. Originally Confucianism meant to be the ethical or religious framework for whole society. But I believe it is suited for a static and hierarchical society and cannot be one for modernity where innovations are immanent. In the era when Shibusawa was active there were many Confucian teachers and theorists. But none of them could make another Shibusawa.

MIX
Papier aus verantwortungsvollen Quellen
Paper from responsible sources
FSC® C105338

If you have any concerns about our products,
you can contact us on
ProductSafety@springernature.com

In case Publisher is established outside the EU,
the EU authorized representative is:
Springer Nature Customer Service Center GmbH
Europaplatz 3, 69115 Heidelberg, Germany

Printed by Libri Plureos GmbH
in Hamburg, Germany